# Metric Conversion Table

| Inches (in.) | 1/64 | 1/32 | 1/25 | 1/16 | 1/8 | 1/4 | 3/8 | 2/5 | 1/2 | 5/8 | 3/4 | 7/8 | 1 | 2 | 3 | 4 | 5 | 6 | 7 | 8 | 9 | 10 | 11 | 12 | 36 | 39.4 |
|---|---|---|---|---|---|---|---|---|---|---|---|---|---|---|---|---|---|---|---|---|---|---|---|---|---|---|
| Feet (ft.) | | | | | | | | | | | | | | | | | | | | | | | | 1 | 3 | 3¼† |
| Yards (yd.) | | | | | | | | | | | | | | | | | | | | | | | | | 1 | 1½† |
| Millimeters* (mm.) | 0.40 | 0.79 | 1 | 1.59 | 3.18 | 6.35 | 9.53 | 10 | 12.7 | 15.9 | 19.1 | 22.2 | 25.4 | 50.8 | 76.2 | 101.6 | 127 | 152 | 178 | 203 | 229 | 254 | 279 | 305 | 914 | 1,000 |
| Centimeters* (cm.) | | | | | | | 0.95 | 1 | 1.27 | 1.59 | 1.91 | 2.22 | 2.54 | 5.08 | 7.62 | 10.16 | 12.7 | 15.2 | 17.8 | 20.3 | 22.9 | 25.4 | 27.9 | 30.5 | 91.4 | 100 |
| Meters* (m.) | | | | | | | | | | | | | | | | | | | | | | | | .30 | .91 | 1.00 |

To find the metric equivalent of quantities not in this table, add together the appropriate entries. For example, to convert 2⅝ inches to centimeters, add the figure given for the centimeter equivalent of 2 inches, 5.08, and the equivalent of ⅝ inch, 1.59, to obtain 6.67 centimeters.

\* Metric values are rounded off.
† Approximate fractions.

## Conversion factors

| To change: | Into: | Multiply by: |
|---|---|---|
| Inches | Millimeters | 25.4 |
| Inches | Centimeters | 2.54 |
| Feet | Meters | 0.305 |
| Yards | Meters | 0.914 |
| Miles | Kilometers | 1.609 |
| Square inches | Square centimeters | 6.45 |
| Square feet | Square meters | 0.093 |
| Square yards | Square meters | 0.836 |
| Cubic inches | Cubic centimeters | 16.4 |
| Cubic feet | Cubic meters | 0.0283 |
| Cubic yards | Cubic meters | 0.765 |
| Pints (U.S.) | Liters | 0.473 (Imp. 0.568) |
| Quarts (U.S.) | Liters | 0.946 (Imp. 1.136) |
| Gallons (U.S.) | Liters | 3.785 (Imp. 4.546) |
| Ounces | Grams | 28.4 |
| Pounds | Kilograms | 0.454 |
| Tons | Metric tons | 0.907 |

| To change: | Into: | Multiply by: |
|---|---|---|
| Millimeters | Inches | 0.039 |
| Centimeters | Inches | 0.394 |
| Meters | Feet | 3.28 |
| Meters | Yards | 1.09 |
| Kilometers | Miles | 0.621 |
| Square centimeters | Square inches | 0.155 |
| Square meters | Square feet | 10.8 |
| Square meters | Square yards | 1.2 |
| Cubic centimeters | Cubic inches | 0.061 |
| Cubic meters | Cubic feet | 35.3 |
| Cubic meters | Cubic yards | 1.31 |
| Liters | Pints (U.S.) | 2.114 (Imp. 1.76) |
| Liters | Quarts (U.S.) | 1.057 (Imp. 0.88) |
| Liters | Gallons (U.S.) | 0.264 (Imp. 0.22) |
| Grams | Ounces | 0.035 |
| Kilograms | Pounds | 2.2 |
| Metric tons | Tons | 1.1 |

# THE FAMILY
# *Handyman*®
# OUTDOOR
# PROJECTS

# THE FAMILY Handyman®
# OUTDOOR PROJECTS

**OVER 20 PROJECTS FOR IMPROVING YOUR OUTDOOR LIVING SPACE**

Reader's Digest

THE READER'S DIGEST ASSOCIATION, INC.
Pleasantville, New York/Montreal

Produced by Redefinition, Inc.

Library of Congress Cataloging in Publication Data

The Family handyman outdoor projects.
      p.    cm.
   Includes index.
   ISBN 0-89577-623-5
    1. Garden structures—Design and construction—Amateurs' manuals.
  I.   Reader's Digest Association.   II.   Family handyman.   III.   Title:
Outdoor projects.
TH4961.F36   1994
717—dc20                              94-14897

Printed in the United States of America
Second Printing, May 1995

# *Foreword*

If you like the outdoors, you'll love the projects in this book — all items that will enhance your enjoyment of the space around your home. And they carry a bonus benefit: Most of the building can be done outdoors, too. That means you're not cooped up in a dingy shop, breathing paint thinner, or traipsing drywall dust through the house.

Outdoor projects usually have a quick payoff, too: They're straightforward and direct, without a lot of tedious finish work. The result: You receive lots of satisfaction in return for relatively little time and labor. What's more, you'll get some good exercise, too.

In this book you'll find 22 of the most popular outdoor projects from *The Family Handyman,* the leading magazine for do-it-yourself homeowners. We designed these projects to be as close to goof-proof as possible. All have been built and tested by our staff and readers. To make it easier for you, we've included step-by-step instructions, complete parts lists and hundreds of photos, so everything you need to know is explained and illustrated. So roll up your sleeves, put on some sunscreen, and have fun building.

Ken Collier, Senior Editor
The Family Handyman

# Contents

See page 60

See page 76

See page 126

See page 178

# *Introduction*

There's something for everyone in THE FAMILY HANDYMAN OUTDOOR PROJECTS — a simple sandbox that's perfect for the beginning builder and a spectacular gazebo that will test even an experienced do-it-yourselfer; a practical retaining wall and a romantic garden arbor and swing. There are enough projects here to provide you with years of building and pleasure. As your experience, ambition, and tool kit grow, you'll find new and challenging projects. The simplest items require only common household tools. They are straighforward enough for a novice. But even those projects that seem difficult may surprise you with their ease of construction, because everything here was designed with the backyard builder in mind. Tools and techniques are low tech. For example, a table saw is never specified if a circular saw will do the job. All the procedures were streamlined so that, whether you're a beginner or a pro, you'll spend more time enjoying the results of your work. Step-by-step instructions will speed up construction. The how-to photos, exploded-view drawings, and complete shopping and cutting lists mean that you can get right to work with a minimum of head-scratching and wasted motion.

When you start any project, work safely. Always wear your safety glasses. And when you're building with pressure-treated wood, follow the guidelines for handling it on page 186.

# *Outdoor Furniture*

Whether your taste runs toward the sophisticated or the utilitarian, here are eight outdoor classics sure to make your leisure hours more pleasant. Their construction ranges from simple to challenging.

# Introduction

There's something for everyone in THE FAMILY HANDYMAN OUTDOOR PROJECTS — a simple sandbox that's perfect for the beginning builder and a spectacular gazebo that will test even an experienced do-it-yourselfer; a practical retaining wall and a romantic garden arbor and swing. There are enough projects here to provide you with years of building and pleasure. As your experience, ambition, and tool kit grow, you'll find new and challenging projects. The simplest items require only common household tools. They are straighforward enough for a novice. But even those projects that seem difficult may surprise you with their ease of construction, because everything here was designed with the backyard builder in mind. Tools and techniques are low tech. For example, a table saw is never specified if a circular saw will do the job. All the procedures were streamlined so that, whether you're a beginner or a pro, you'll spend more time enjoying the results of your work. Step-by-step instructions will speed up construction. The how-to photos, exploded-view drawings, and complete shopping and cutting lists mean that you can get right to work with a minimum of head-scratching and wasted motion.

When you start any project, work safely. Always wear your safety glasses. And when you're building with pressure-treated wood, follow the guidelines for handling it on page 186.

# Folding Sawhorses

## What You Need

**To build two folding sawhorses:**

**27 linear feet of 2" x 2" pine**

**30 linear feet of 1" x 2" pine**

**7 linear feet of 1" x 4" pine**

**4 1½" steel corner braces**

**4 ³⁄₁₆" x 2" machine screws and wing nuts**

**12 ⁵⁄₁₆" x 2½" carriage bolts and nuts**

**64 1⅝" drywall screws**

**8 1¼" drywall screws**

Every project is made easier by a couple of sawhorses. When you're not using this folding sawhorse, just loosen two wing nuts, pivot two braces, and fold in the legs so you can hang the horse from hooks or tuck it in a corner.

## Assembling

- Cut three top piece 1x2s to length.
- Cut the pivoting leg braces to size, drill the ⁵⁄₁₆-inch hole, cut a 45-degree angle on one end, and round the other end of each. Attach the L-bracket.
- Line up the three top piece 1x2s and the pivoting leg braces.

Then cut the 1x2 end piece to size and attach to the three top pieces with drywall screws.
- Cut and attach the 1x4 top with drywall screws.
- Cut and attach the 2x2 legs with carriage bolts.
- Drill the holes for the carriage bolts and bolt the two 1x2 pivoting leg braces in place.
- Hold the 2x2 leg brace in position against the legs, mark and cut the angles, lapping the ends halfway.
- Hold the 2x2 horizontal leg brace in position again and rotate each pivoting leg brace into position. Mark and drill the vertical ³⁄₁₆-inch holes.
- Attach the leg braces.

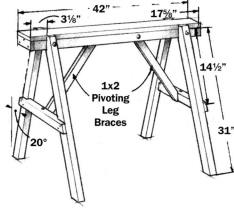

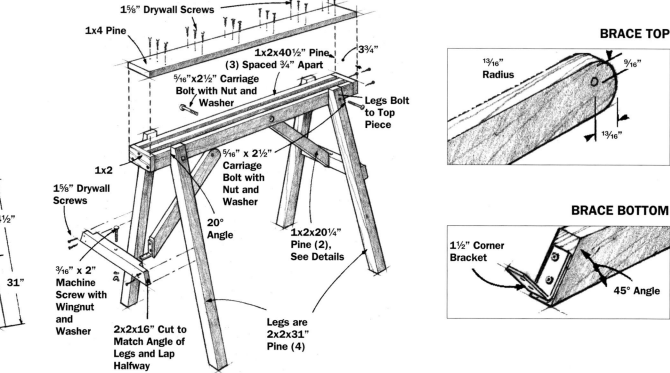

# Adjustable Sawhorses

## What You Need

**To make two adjustable sawhorses:**

**21 linear feet of 2" x 4" pine**

**28 linear feet of 2" x 2" pine**

**34 linear feet of 1" x 4" pine**

**1 x 2-foot piece of ½" exterior-grade plywood**

**4 ¾" x 5" carriage bolts with wing nuts**

**92 1¼" drywall screws**

**22 2½" drywall screws**

The support on this adjustable sawhorse can be raised as much as 20 inches to give you a more comfortable working height (just don't raise the adjustable top above the lower 2x2 guides). You can also create a scaffold by laying 2x10 planks 12 feet or less across the tops of two sawhorses. This horse is light because of the built-up 2x2 construction used.

## Assembling

- Cut and assemble the 2x4 lumber for the adjustable support. The notch is ¾ inch deep (see Detail 1). Cut out the notch by making repeat passes with your circular saw and chiseling out the waste.
- Tack nail the top 2x2 to the edge of a work table, then nail a 2x4 alongside it to hold it in place. Measure ½ inch in from the edge of the 2x2 and cut the 20-degree angle.
- Rip a 2x4 in half to get the 1⅝-inch center portion. Cut that center piece into two 6-inch-long pieces and one 18-inch-long piece.
- Lay the parts from the previous two steps on a flat surface, position the adjustable support to align them, then assemble the top portion with 2½-inch drywall screws. Note that the 2x2s with the 20-degree cut are oriented wide side down.
- Cut the 1x4 legs and attach.
- Cut the 1x4 leg braces and attach.
- Cut the ½-inch plywood to match each end and attach.
- Cut the lower 2x2s to length and attach to the plywood to add rigidity and serve as guides for the adjustable support.
- Slide the adjustable support into place. Add short 1x2 or scrap lumber guides to both sides of the support's two legs.
- Finally, mark and drill a series of centered ½-inch holes through the support's two legs for the ⅜-inch bolt.

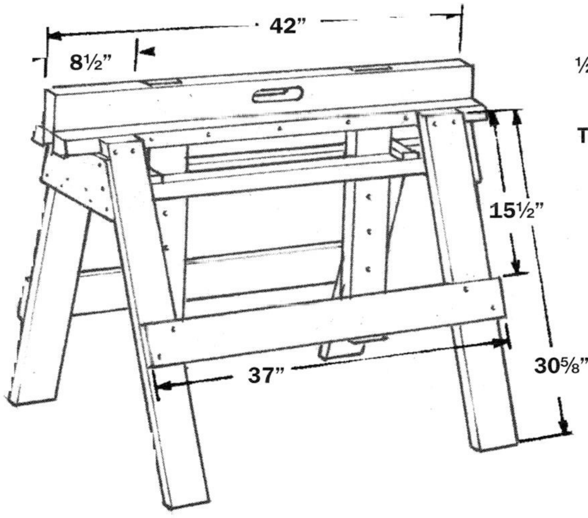

42"
8½"
15½"
37"
30⅝"


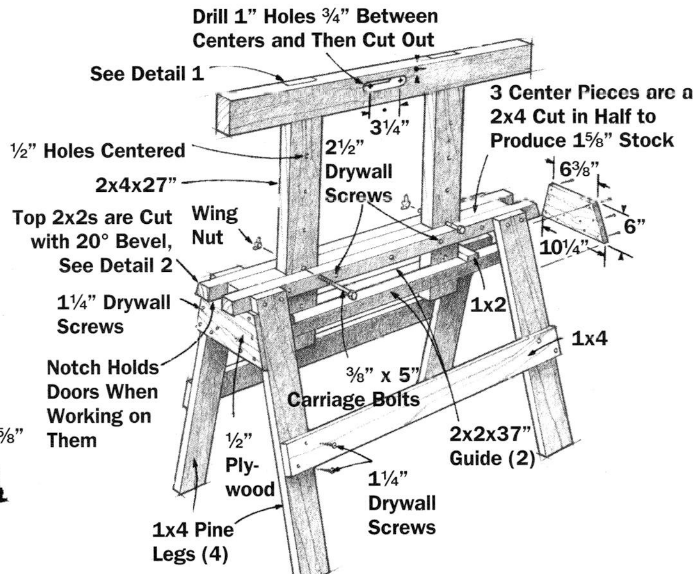

Drill 1" Holes ¾" Between Centers and Then Cut Out
See Detail 1
3¼"
3 Center Pieces are a 2x4 Cut in Half to Produce 1⅝" Stock
½" Holes Centered
2½" Drywall Screws
2x4x27"
6⅜"
6"
10¼"
Top 2x2s are Cut with 20° Bevel, See Detail 2
Wing Nut
1¼" Drywall Screws
1x2
1x4
Notch Holds Doors When Working on Them
⅜" x 5" Carriage Bolts
½" Ply-wood
2x2x37" Guide (2)
1¼" Drywall Screws
1x4 Pine Legs (4)


DETAIL 1

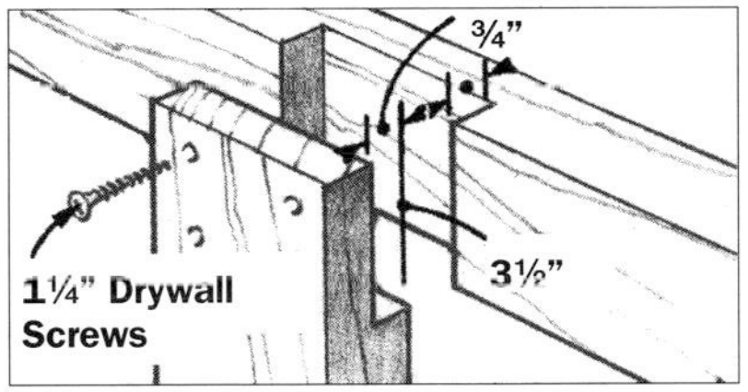

¾"
1¼" Drywall Screws
3½"


DETAIL 2

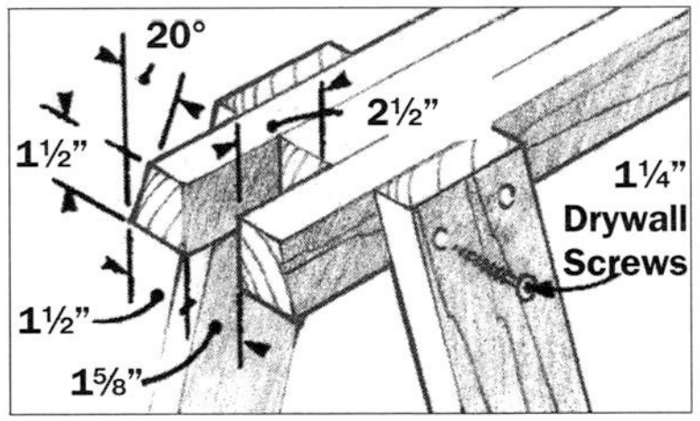

20°
2½"
1½"
1¼" Drywall Screws
1½"
1⅝"

# *Outdoor Furniture*

W hether your taste runs toward the sophisticated or the utilitarian, here are eight outdoor classics sure to make your leisure hours more pleasant. Their construction ranges from simple to challenging.

## Cutting List: Chair

| Key | Pieces & Description | Size |
|---|---|---|
| A | 4 seat box members | ¾" x 5½" x 22" |
| B | 2 back legs | 1 1/16" x 3½" x 21½" |
| C | 2 front legs | 1 1/16" x 4" x 21½" |
| D | 2 arms | 1 1/16" x 5½" x 30" |
| E | 1 lower back brace | 1½" x 1½" x 22" |
| F | 1 middle back brace | 1½" x 1½" x 25" |
| G | 1 back stiffener | ¾" x 3" x 20½" |
| H | 1 rear seat brace | 1½" x 2¾" x 22" |
| J | 1 front seat brace | ¾" x 1½" x 22" |
| K | 1 upper back brace | ¾" x 1½" x 22" |
| L | 2 seat slats | ¾" x 3½" x 19¼" |
| M | 2 seat slats | ¾" x 3" x 19¼" |
| N | 1 seat slat | ¾" x 5½" x 19¼" |
| P | 4 back slats | ¾" x 3" x 31 7/8" |
| Q | 1 back slat | ¾" x 5½" x 31 7/8" |
| R | 14 side slats | ¾" x 1½" x 16" |
| S | 2 lower side slat rails | ¾" x 1½" x 22" |
| T | 2 under arm cleats | ¾" x 1" x 22" |

## Shopping List: Chair

| Quantity | Item |
|---|---|
| 2 | 1" x 6" x 8 feet cedar |
| 3 | 1" x 4" x 8 feet cedar |
| 5 | 1" x 2" x 8 feet cedar |
| 2 | 5/4" x 6" x 8 feet cedar decking |
| 1 | 2" x 4" x 8 feet cedar |
| 22 | 1¼" galvanized deck screws |
| 64 | 1 5/8" galvanized deck screws |
| 22 | 2" galvanized deck screws |
| 4 | 2½" galvanized deck screws |
| ½ lb. | 4d galvanized finish nails |
| ¼ lb. | 6d galvanized finish nails |
| 1 tube | Construction adhesive |

### LEG AND BOX DETAIL

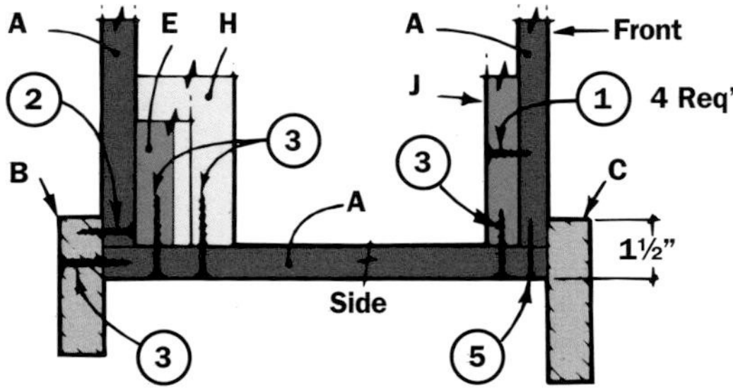
A
E
H
A
Front
J
4 Req'd
B
C
A
1½"
Side

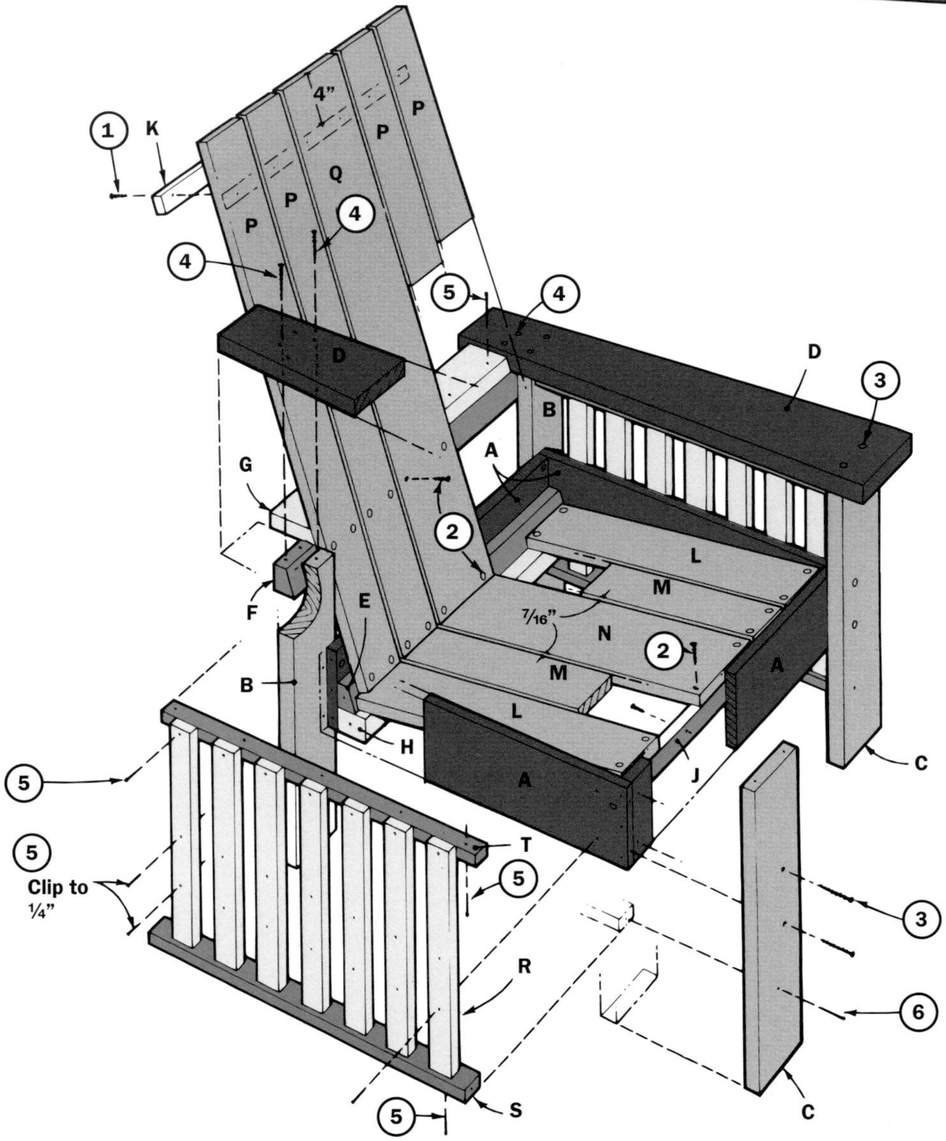
K
P
P
Q
P
P
4"
D
D
B
A
G
F
E
B
H
L
M
N
M
L
A
A
J
C
T
R
S
C
7/16"
Clip to ¼"

### ARM REST (D)

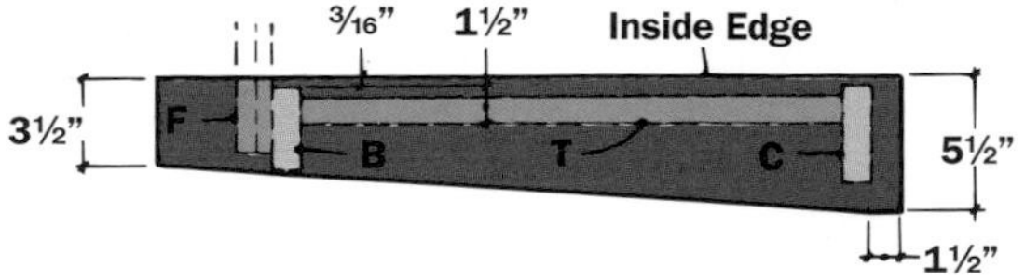
3/16"
1½"
Inside Edge
3½"
F
B
T
C
5½"
1½"

### MIDDLE BACK BRACE

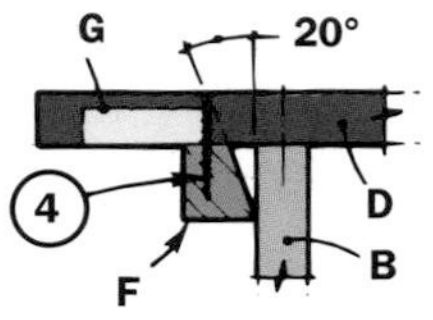
G
20°
D
F
B

### LOWER BACK BRACE

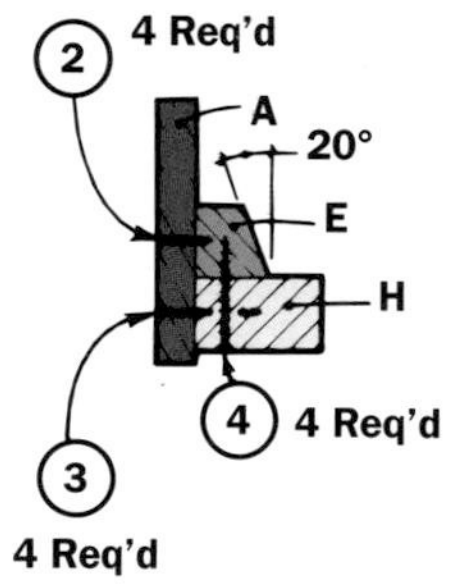
4 Req'd
A
20°
E
H
4 Req'd
4 Req'd

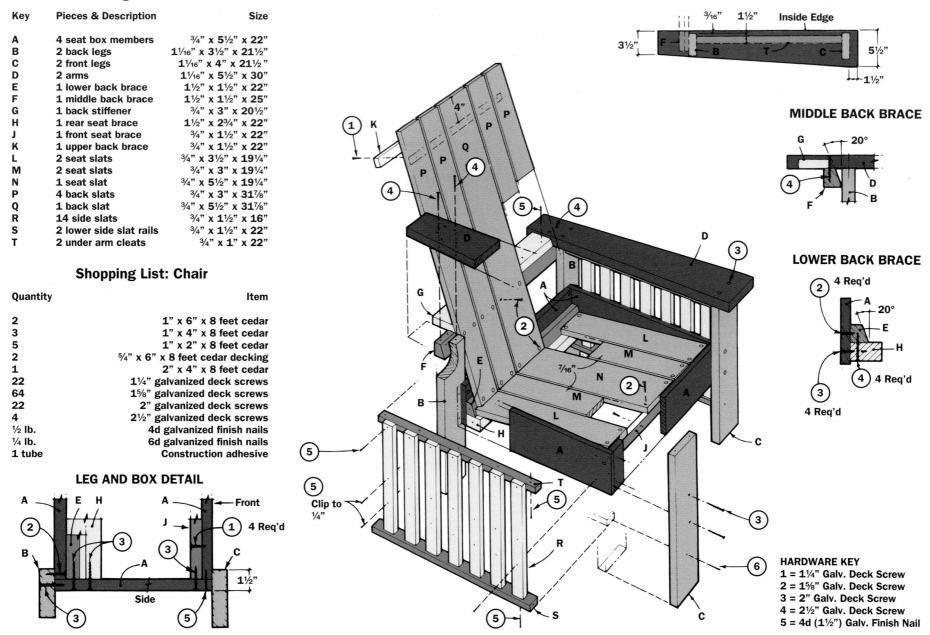

**HARDWARE KEY**
1 = 1¼" Galv. Deck Screw
2 = 1 5/8" Galv. Deck Screw
3 = 2" Galv. Deck Screw
4 = 2½" Galv. Deck Screw
5 = 4d (1½") Galv. Finish Nail

# Mission Loveseat, Chair, and Table

The design of this furniture lets you build it even without the luxury of a home wood shop. There's no fancy joinery (most parts are just screwed together) so even if you don't have a lot of tools, this outdoor set is easily within your grasp. Each piece will take only a day or so for you to make — even if you're a novice.

The only difference between the loveseat (shown on this page) and chair (facing page) is the number of seat and back slats and the length of some parts. The table has even fewer parts — you won't find step-by-step instructions for building it because the table is nothing more than a box with legs and top.

You have many choices of wood to use, but the straightforward elegance of the design demands a harmonious material. The chair shown here is western cedar, which has a natural beauty and resistance to decay. Cypress is another excellent choice if it's available in your area. Redwood is a good choice, but it's the most expensive choice among softwoods.

If you decide to use cedar, the boards may only be available smooth on one side and rough on the other. Your lumberyard or a local cabinet shop may be able to plane the rough side for you; if not, use a belt sander and a 36-grit belt to smooth it.

## Chair

### Cutting List: Chair

| Key | Pieces & Description | Size |
|---|---|---|
| A | 4 seat box members | ¾" x 5½" x 22" |
| B | 2 back legs | 1 1/16" x 3½" x 21½" |
| C | 2 front legs | 1 1/16" x 4" x 21½" |
| D | 2 arms | 1 1/16" x 5½" x 30" |
| E | 1 lower back brace | 1½" x 1½" x 22" |
| F | 1 middle back brace | 1½" x 1½" x 25" |
| G | 1 back stiffener | ¾" x 3" x 20½" |
| H | 1 rear seat brace | 1½" x 2¾" x 22" |
| J | 1 front seat brace | ¾" x 1½" x 22" |
| K | 1 upper back brace | ¾" x 1½" x 22" |
| L | 2 seat slats | ¾" x 3½" x 19¼" |
| M | 2 seat slats | ¾" x 3" x 19¼" |
| N | 1 seat slat | ¾" x 5½" x 19¼" |
| P | 4 back slats | ¾" x 3" x 31⅞" |
| Q | 1 back slat | ¾" x 5½" x 31⅞" |
| R | 14 side slats | ¾" x 1½" x 16" |
| S | 2 lower side slat rails | ¾" x 1½" x 22" |
| T | 2 under arm cleats | ¾" x 1" x 22" |

### Shopping List: Chair

| Quantity | Item |
|---|---|
| 2 | 1" x 6" x 8 feet cedar |
| 3 | 1" x 4" x 8 feet cedar |
| 5 | 1" x 2" x 8 feet cedar |
| 2 | 5/4" x 6" x 8 feet cedar decking |
| 1 | 2" x 4" x 8 feet cedar |
| 22 | 1¼" galvanized deck screws |
| 64 | 1⅝" galvanized deck screws |
| 22 | 2" galvanized deck screws |
| 4 | 2½" galvanized deck screws |
| ½ lb. | 4d galvanized finish nails |
| ¼ lb. | 6d galvanized finish nails |
| 1 tube | Construction adhesive |

### LEG AND BOX DETAIL

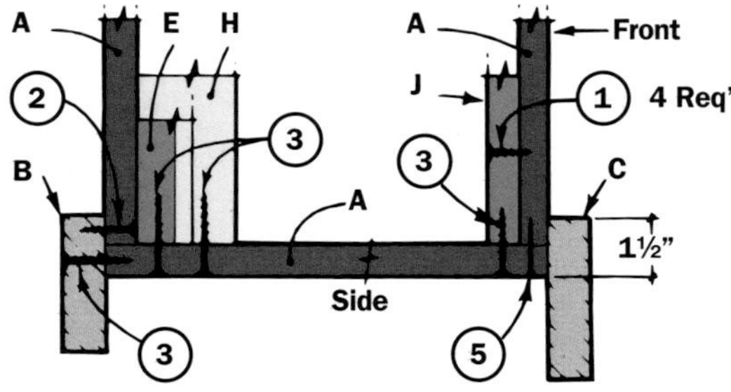


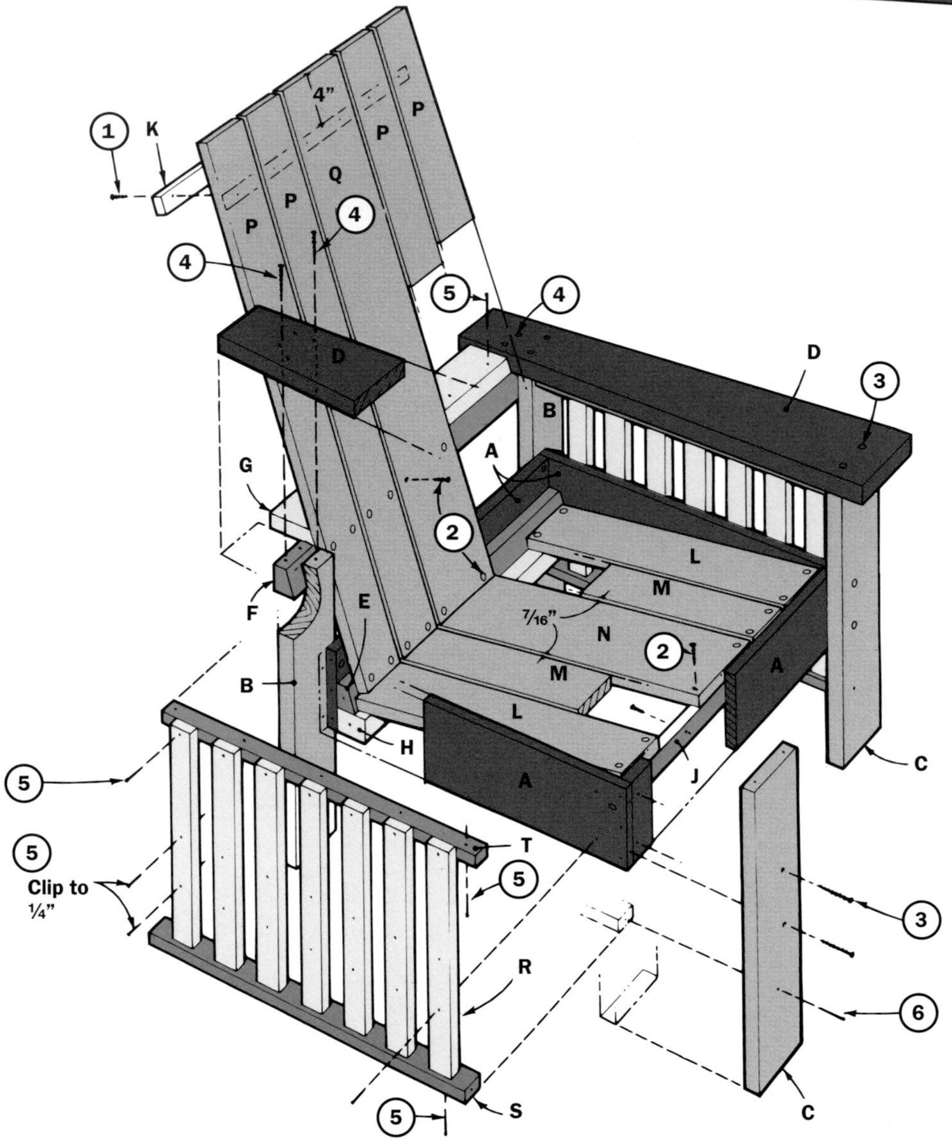


### ARM REST (D)

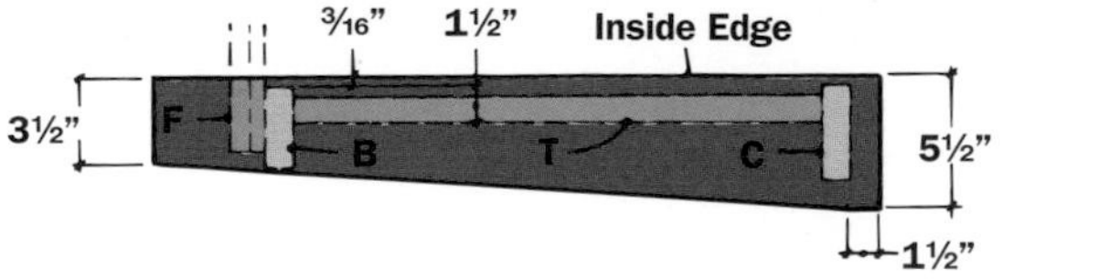


### MIDDLE BACK BRACE

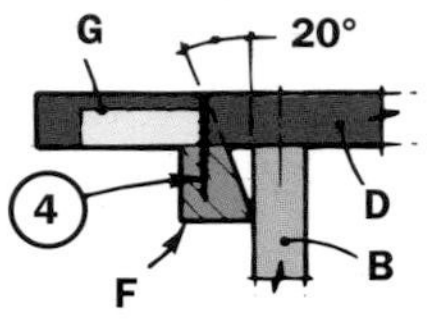


### LOWER BACK BRACE

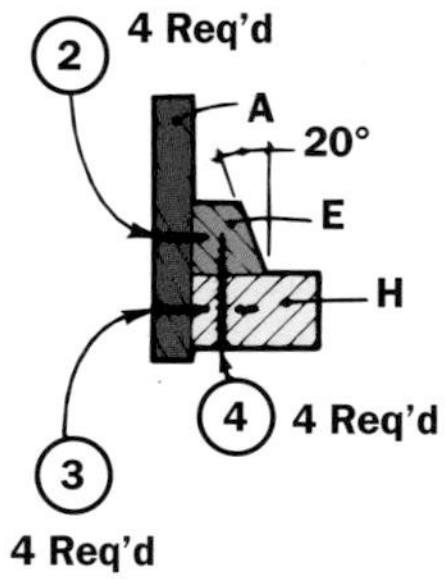


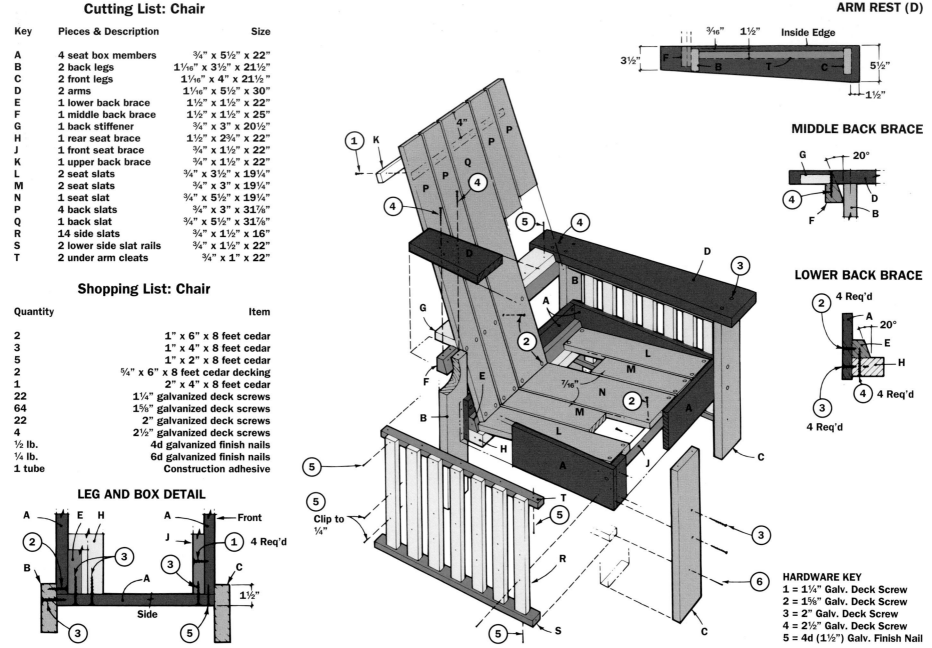

**HARDWARE KEY**
1 = 1¼" Galv. Deck Screw
2 = 1⅝" Galv. Deck Screw
3 = 2" Galv. Deck Screw
4 = 2½" Galv. Deck Screw
5 = 4d (1½") Galv. Finish Nail

# Loveseat

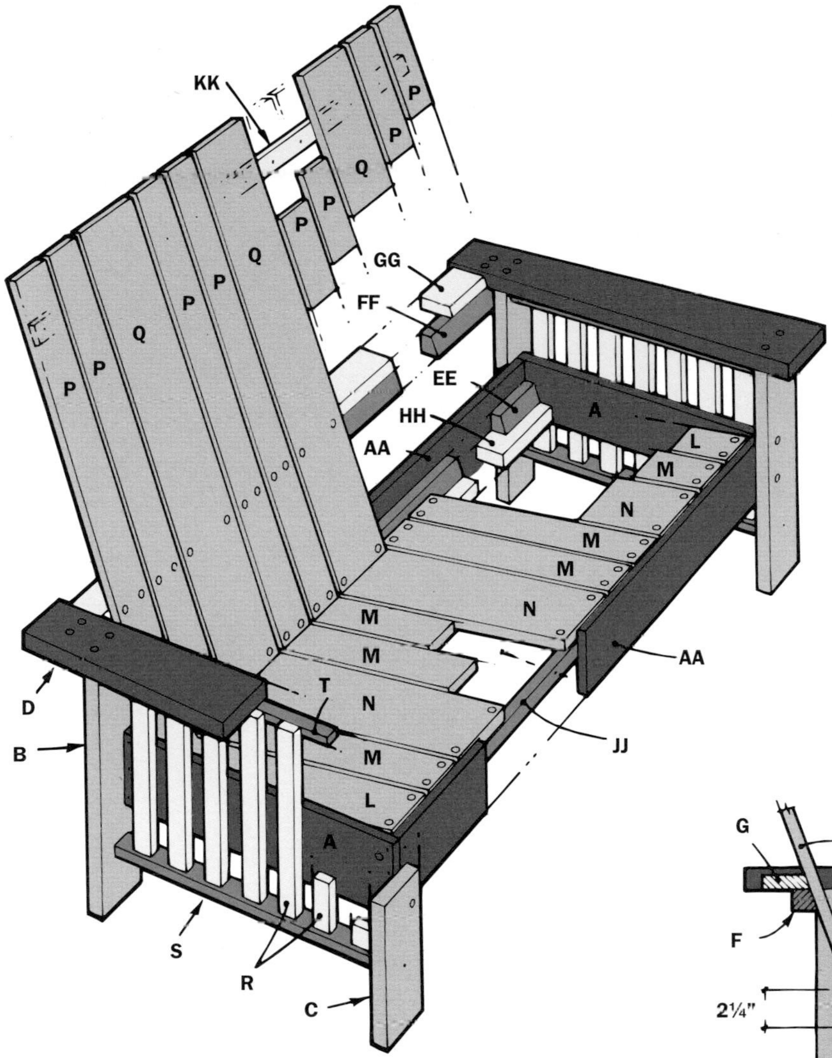


## Cutting List: Loveseat

| Key | Pieces & Description | Size |
|---|---|---|
| A | 2 seat box members | ¾" x 5½" x 22" |
| AA | 2 seat box members | ¾" x 5½" x 47¾" |
| B | 2 back legs | 1¹⁄₁₆" x 3½" x 21½" |
| C | 2 front legs | 1¹⁄₁₆" x 4" x 21½" |
| D | 2 arms | 1¹⁄₁₆" x 5½" x 30" |
| EE | 1 lower back brace | 1½" x 1½" x 47¾" |
| FF | 1 middle back brace | 1½" x 1½" x 51¼" |
| GG | 1 back stiffener | ¾" x 3" x 45¾" |
| HH | 1 rear seat brace | 1½" x 2¾" x 47¾" |
| JJ | 1 front seat brace | ¾" x 1½" x 47¾" |
| KK | 1 upper back brace | ¾" x 1½" x 43¼" |
| L | 2 seat slats | ¾" x 3½" x 19¼" |
| M | 6 seat slats | ¾" x 3" x 19¼" |
| N | 3 seat slats | ¾" x 5½" x 19¼" |
| P | 8 back slats | ¾" x 3" x 31⅞" |
| Q | 3 back slats | ¾" x 5½" x 31⅞" |
| R | 14 side slats | ¾" x 1½" x 16" |
| S | 2 lower side slat rail | ¾" x 1½" x 22" |
| T | 2 under arm cleats | ¾" x 1" x 22" |

## Shopping List: Loveseat

| Quantity | Item |
|---|---|
| 5 | 1" x 6" x 8 feet cedar |
| 6 | 1" x 4" x 8 feet cedar |
| 6 | 1" x 2" x 8 feet cedar |
| 2 | 5/4" x 6" x 8 feet cedar decking |
| 1 | 2" x 4" x 10 feet cedar |
| 120 | 1⅝" galvanized deck screws |
| 10 | 1¼" galvanized deck screws |
| 20 | 2" galvanized deck screws |
| 8 | 2½" galvanized deck screws |
| ½ lb. | 4d galvanized finish nails |
| ¼ lb. | 6d galvanized finish nails |

CROSS SECTION VIEW: CHAIR AND LOVESEAT

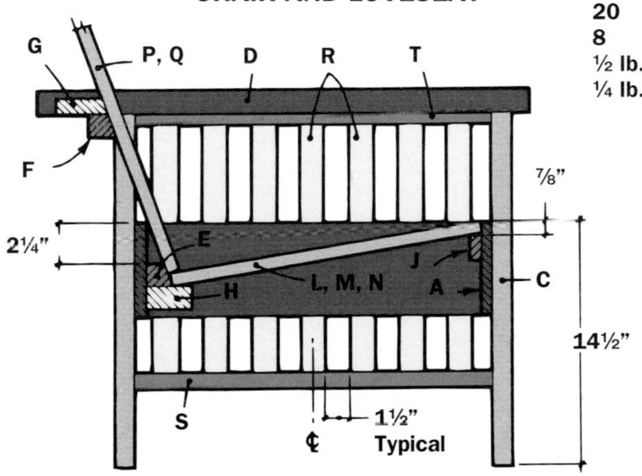

## Cutting List: Table

| Key | Pieces & Description | Size |
|-----|---------------------|------|
| A | 4 upper box members | ¾" x 1½" x 16" |
| B | 4 lower box members | ¾" x 2½" x 16" |
| C | 4 legs | ¾" x 2½" x 18" |
| D | 4 top slats | ¾" x 3½" x 19½" |
| E | 1 middle top slat | ¾" x 5½" x 19½" |
| F | 4 shelf slats | ¾" x 3½" x 17½" |
| G | 10 side slats | ¾" x 1½" x 16" |
| H | 2 bottom side slat rails | ¾" x 1½" x 16" |

## Shopping List: Table

| Quantity | Item |
|----------|------|
| 1 | 1" x 3" x 10 feet cedar |
| 2 | 1" x 4" x 8 feet cedar |
| 1 | 1" x 6" x 2 feet cedar |
| 3 | 1" x 2" x 8 feet cedar |
| 28 | 1⅝" galvanized deck screws |
| 8 | 1¼" galvanized deck screws |
| ½ lb. | 4d galvanized finish nails |

**HARDWARE KEY**
1 = 1¼" galv. deck screw
2 = 1⅝" galv. deck screw
3 = 2" galv. deck screw
4 = 4d (1½") galv. finish nail

**CORNER DETAIL**

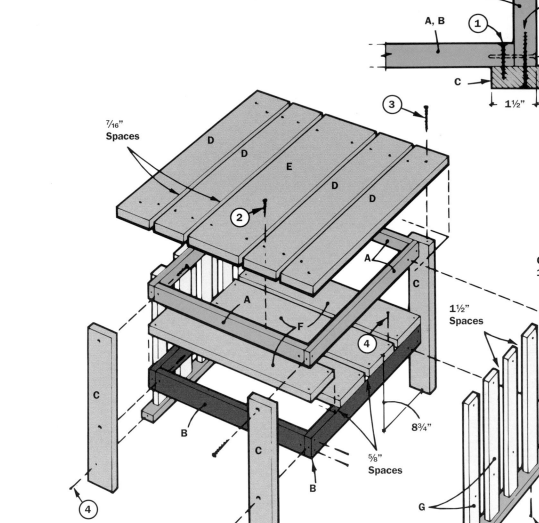

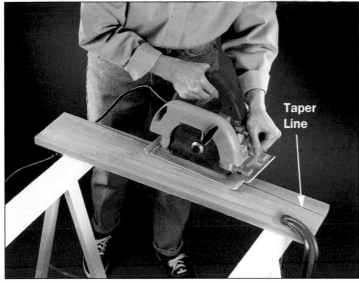

**Figure 1:** Cut the chair parts with your circular saw. Make tapered cuts for the arms of the chair.

**Figure 2:** Nail together a box to begin the chair assembly. Nail through the sides and into the front and back pieces.

The building method for the table is similar to that used for the chair. Build two boxes from parts A and B, then attach legs just as you did for the chair. To finish the job, just nail on the shelf slats and screw on the top slats.

## Cutting the chair and loveseat parts

- Begin by cutting all of the pieces listed in the cutting list, with the exception of the back stiffener (G), lower side slat rails (S), and under arm cleats (T). These parts must be cut later to fit the chair when it's partially assembled.
- Take particular care to cut the side slats (R) exactly the same length. These slats must fit against a rail (S), and any differences in length will result in gaps.
- Cut the arms of the chair and loveseat (D) with a 2-inch taper from front to back (Figure 1).
- When cutting the lower back brace (E), middle back brace (F), and back stiffener (G) set the blade angle of your circular saw to 20 degrees.

## Building the basic frame

- You can see from the photos that the whole chair is built around a simple box. The legs, seat, and back are attached to this basic structure.
- Nail the seat box parts (A) together with 4d galvanized finish nails (Figure 2). Notice that the sides overlap the ends of the front and back boards.
- Glue and screw each of the legs (B and C) onto the box you've just built. The box overlaps each leg 1½ inches and the top of the box is 14½ inches from the bottom of the legs. To make juggling these parts a little easier, mark reference lines on the legs and box.
- Lay the back legs flat on the floor and align the box with the marks on the legs. Drill pilot holes and glue and screw the box to the back legs, as shown in the plan.
- Turn the assembly and fasten the box to the front legs.
- To complete this phase of the assembly, screw through each leg into the corners of the box as shown in the plan.

**Figure 3:** Screw the arms to the tops of the legs after attaching the legs to the box frame. Also use waterproof glue on all joints.

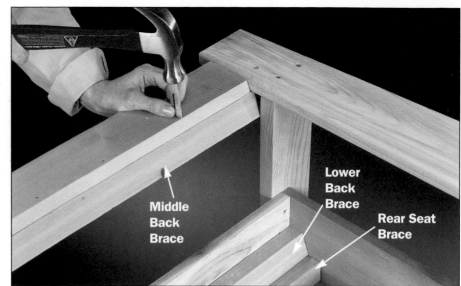

**Figure 4:** Glue and nail the middle back brace between the arms. Seat and back supports are glued and nailed inside the box frame.

## Attaching the arms and braces

- Predrill and then screw the arms onto the legs. The chair really starts to take shape now (Figure 3). Be sure that each arm overhangs the front and back legs as shown in the plan.
- Glue and screw the lower back brace (E), middle back brace (F), and the rear seat brace (H) as shown in the plan. Be sure that E, H, and the front seat brace (J) are screwed from the sides of the chair box as well as the front and back. All this gluing and fastening with screws may seem like overkill, but strong joints here will help relieve stress on other joints.

- Measure and cut the back stiffener (G) to fit between the back of the arms and onto the middle back brace (F), then glue and nail G onto F (Figure 4).
- Look over the chair to make sure all the legs are in contact with the floor. Clean off any glue that's oozing out of the joints, and check for any screws or nails that may have been left out — this is by far the easiest time to correct problems.

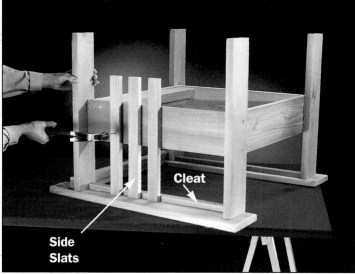

**Figure 5:** Attach the side slats with the chair upside down. Start in the middle, and leave a 1½ inch space between slats.

**Figure 6:** Add back and seat slats, starting in the middle and working out. Keep the slats square to the frame.

Don't postpone the final sanding and finishing. If you wait too long, the sun will dry out the wood and leave cracks at the ends of the boards. If you don't have time to finish your furniture right away, store it in a shaded area.

To smooth the wood before finishing, use a sanding block and 100-grit paper. Then retrace your steps with 150-grit. Be careful to remove saw marks from the edges of boards. Sand all the corners to make them comfortable and to keep them from splintering.

Use a wood sealer that protect decks and outdoor furniture from water and sun damage. Look for one that offers ultraviolet (UV) protection. The chair on these pages uses a mixture of a UV-blocking exterior deck sealer and boiled linseed oil in equal amounts. The sealer protects the wood and the linseed oil gives it a warm, natural glow.

After finishing, wait at least 24 hours before relaxing in your chair. Put on another coat of finish after the first season of use, and as needed after that.

## Attaching the side slats

- To install the slats, turn the chair upside down and cut the cleats (T) to fit under the arms between the front and back legs (Figure 5).
- Glue and nail part T onto the underside of each arm, making sure it is 1½ inches from the inside edge of the legs, just as the box was (Figure 5). The side of part T should line up with the side of the box, so the slats rest tightly on both (see the plan detail on page 16).
- Before nailing on the side slats, clip about ⅛ inch off the ends of the 4d nails, using a side cutter.
- Glue and nail the side slats into the box and undcrarm cleats (T), starting with the center slat positioned in the middle of the box. Then move out in each direction, leaving a 1½-inch space between the slats.
- Measure the distance between the front and back leg and cut the lower side slat rail (S) to fit into place. Center S over the slats and nail through the bottom of S into each slat.
- Nail into S from the front and back legs with two 6d galvanized finishing nails.

## Securing the seat and back slats

- Center the wide seat slat (N) inside the box. Drill and screw it in place using two screws on each end.
- Set the remaining slats, L and M, in position, leaving a 7/16-inch space between the slats. Screw them down.
- Position the wide center back slat (Q) on top of the center seat slat N and use a square (Figure 6) to mark the correct vertical position so that all of the slats will be perfectly upright. Screw Q into place. Repeat the process for the remaining back slats.
- Glue and screw upper back brace (K) into the back slats using one screw in each narrow slat and two in the middle slat. Be sure to use 1¼-inch screws.

# Adirondack Chair and Table

## What You Need

Table saw or circular saw
   with rip and crosscut
   blades
Jig saw or band saw
Belt or drum sander
Flat file

Electric drill with
   countersink bit
Clamps
Hacksaw
Vise

The Adirondack chair originated at the camps and resorts of New York's Adirondack mountains during the late 1800s. The "camps" were in fact large estates, and leisure comfort, not roughing it, was the goal of wealthy owners. Of course, the Adirondacks were remote from civilization then, and these chairs had to be built with the tools and materials at hand. This chair was the solution to comfort-in-the-wild, and it has become an outdoor classic today.

This version, like its forebears, is designed for maximum comfort. This chair has a deep seat with a rounded front edge, spacious arms, and a curved back. When you want to take a nap, the matching footrest fits your contour, and at lunch-time you have a small table by your side. When summer's gone, you can fold up the chair and footrest and disassemble the table for easy moving and storage.

The furniture shown here is made of clear fir, which is strong, light, moderately priced, and takes paint, stain, or varnish well. You can build your pieces from a variety of woods. Redwood, cedar, or lauan (Philippine mahogany) would be good choices if the furniture is to stay outdoors most of the time. The pieces can be left unfinished to weather gracefully, or given a clear preservative finish. Oak, maple, and fir are stronger, but must receive a weatherproof finish. Pine isn't as strong, but is acceptable if painted.

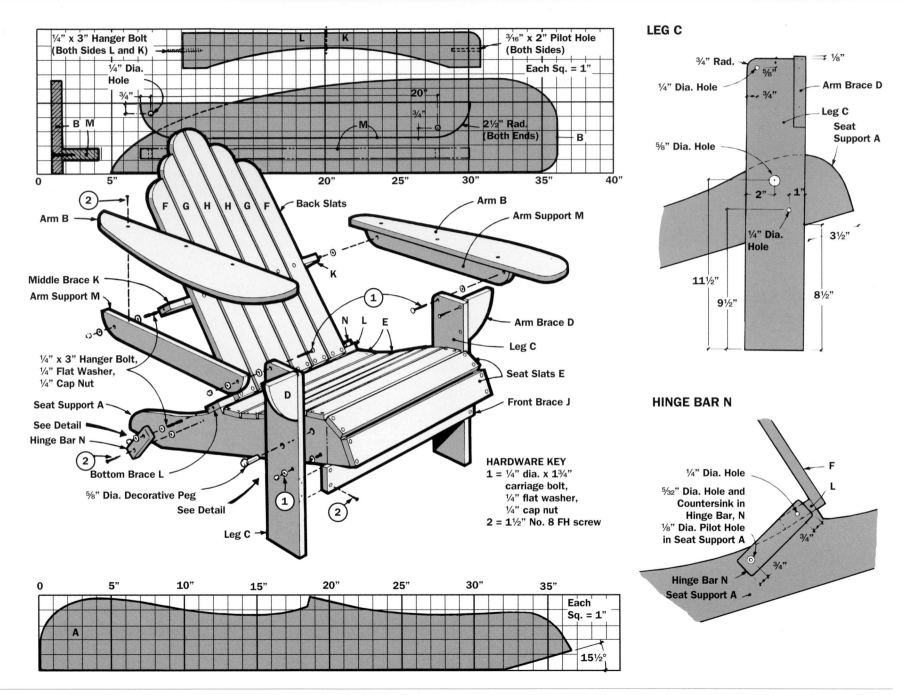

¼" x 3" Hanger Bolt (Both Sides L and K)

¼" Dia. Hole

¾"

B M

L K

³⁄₁₆" x 2" Pilot Hole (Both Sides)

Each Sq. = 1"

20"

¾"

M

¾"

2½" Rad. (Both Ends)

B

0    5"    20"    25"    30"    35"    40"

2

Arm B

Middle Brace K

Arm Support M

¼" x 3" Hanger Bolt, ¼" Flat Washer, ¼" Cap Nut

Seat Support A

See Detail

Hinge Bar N

2

Bottom Brace L

⅝" Dia. Decorative Peg

See Detail

Leg C

F G H H G F    Back Slats

Arm B

Arm Support M

K

1

N L E

Arm Brace D

Leg C

Seat Slats E

Front Brace J

1

D

2

**LEG C**

¾" Rad.

⅝"

¼" Dia. Hole

⅝" Dia. Hole

2"

¼" Dia. Hole

11½"

9½"

⅛"

¾"

Arm Brace D

Leg C
Seat Support A

1"

3½"

8½"

**HINGE BAR N**

¼" Dia. Hole

⁵⁄₃₂" Dia. Hole and Countersink in Hinge Bar, N
⅛" Dia. Pilot Hole in Seat Support A

Hinge Bar N

Seat Support A

F

L

¾"

¾"

**HARDWARE KEY**
1 = ¼" dia. x 1¾" carriage bolt, ¼" flat washer, ¼" cap nut
2 = 1½" No. 8 FH screw

0    5"    10"    15"    20"    25"    30"    35"

Each Sq. = 1"

A

15½°

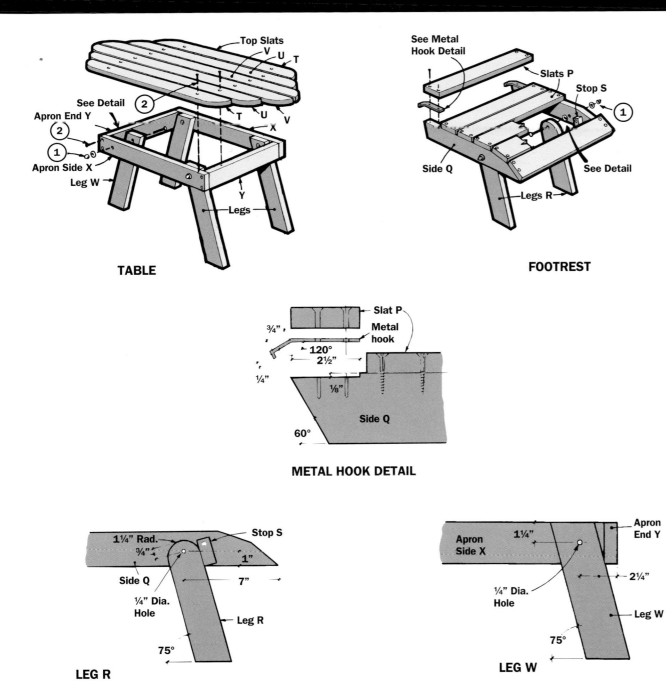

**TABLE**

- Top Slats V U T
- See Detail (2)
- Apron End Y (2)
- (1)
- Apron Side X
- Leg W
- T U V
- X
- Y
- Legs

**FOOTREST**

- See Metal Hook Detail
- Slats P
- Stop S
- (1)
- Side Q
- See Detail
- Legs R

**METAL HOOK DETAIL**

- Slat P
- Metal hook
- ¾"
- 120°
- 2½"
- ¼"
- ⅛"
- Side Q
- 60°

**LEG R**

- 1¼" Rad.
- Stop S
- ¾"
- 1"
- Side Q
- 7"
- ¼" Dia. Hole
- Leg R
- 75°

**LEG W**

- Apron End Y
- 1¼"
- Apron Side X
- 2¼"
- ¼" Dia. Hole
- Leg W
- 75°

## Cutting List

| Key | Pieces & Description | Size |
|---|---|---|
| A | 2 seat supports | ¾" x 5" x 36½" |
| B | 2 arms | ¾" x 6¾" x 31" |
| C | 2 legs | ¾" x 4" x 20" |
| D | 2 arm braces | ¾" x 4" x 5" |
| E | 8 seat slats | ¾" x 2½" x 20" |
| F | 2 back slats | ¾" x 2½" x 27" |
| G | 2 back slats | ¾" x 2½" x 29½" |
| H | 2 back slats | ¾" x 2½" x 32" |
| J | 1 front brace | ¾" x 2½" x 21⅝" |
| K | 1 middle brace | ¾" x 2½" x 21½" |
| L | 1 bottom brace | ¾" x 2½" x 20" |
| M | 2 arm supports | ¾" x 2½" x 23" |
| N | 2 hinge bars | ¾" x 1½" x 6" |
| P | 6 slats | ¾" x 2½" x 16" |
| Q | 2 sides | ¾" x 2½" x 16" |
| R | 2 legs | ¾" x 2½" x 9½" |
| S | 2 stops | ¾" x ¾" x 2" |
| T | 2 top slats | ¾" x 2½" x 21" |
| U | 2 top slats | ¾" x 2½" x 26" |
| V | 2 top slats | ¾" x 2½" x 31" |
| W | 4 table legs | ¾" x 2½" x 15" |
| X | 2 apron sides | ¾" x 2½" x 18" |
| Y | 2 apron ends | ¾" x 2½" x 13½" |

## Shopping List

| Quantity | Item |
|---|---|
| 6 feet | 1" x 8" clear fir for the chair |
| 30 feet | 1" x 6" clear fir for the chair |
| 7 feet | 1" x 6" clear fir for the footrest |
| 12 feet | 1" x 6" clear fir for the table |
| 10 | ¼" x 1¾" carriage bolts |
| 26 | ¼" flat washers |
| 14 | ¼" cap nuts |
| 4 | ¼" x 3" hanger bolts |
| 110 | No. 8 x 1½" FH screws |
| 1 foot | ⅛" x ¾" steel or brass bar stock |
| 2 | ⅝" diameter decorative pegs |

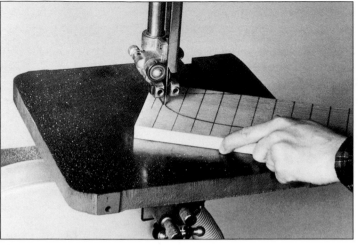

**Figure 1:** Use a band saw or jig saw to cut the curved pieces.

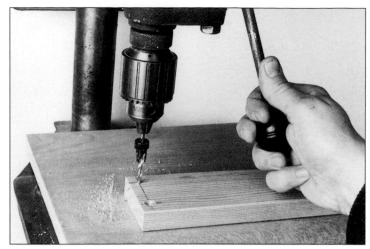

**Figure 2:** A drill with a countersink bit helps make consistent holes when drilling the slats. Use a drill guide or a drill press.

## Building the chair

- Rip the boards and then crosscut all the parts to length according to the plan and cutting list. With a jig saw or band saw, cut all the curved pieces (Figure 1). Use a 1-inch grid of pencil lines to transfer the pattern (see page 24).
- Sand the curved edges with a belt sander or drum sander chucked into an electric drill. Sand all the parts.
- Drill holes in all the parts that need them, except for the holes in the seat supports (A) where they attach to the legs (C). In each seat slat (E), drill two holes ½ inch from each end (see the plan on page 25).
- A combination drill and countersink, used in a drill press or drill guide, will enable you to make quick and consistent holes on the slats (Figure 2).
- Screw the hanger bolts into the ends of the braces (K, L). Clamp the boards to prevent the wood from splitting (Figure 3 on page 27).
- Screw the slats (E) to the seat supports (A). Start with the slat farthest back, then do the one at the front. Space out the remaining slats and screw them in place. You may want to file flat surfaces on the curved edge of the seat supports underneath the first few slats.

- Assemble the back. Screw the slats to the bottom brace (L), then attach the middle brace (K) 10¼ inches above the bottom brace (Figure 4).
- Screw the arms (B) to the arm supports (M), and the arm braces (D) to the legs (C), being sure to leave the braces protruding above the tops of the legs (see the seat leg detail in plan on page 24).
- Bolt the hinge bars (N) to the back assembly (see the plan detail on page 24). Use washers between the wooden pieces.
- Bolt the arm supports (M) to the legs (C) and back, and clamp the legs to the seat assembly. Then screw the hinge bars to the seat supports.
- Adjust the legs (C) so they are square, then drill through the holes in the leg and into the seat supports (A) (Figure 5). The peg must have a firm fit in its hole, so be sure to make a test hole first on scrap. Bolt the legs to the seat, insert the pegs, and screw on the front brace (J).
- Attach the front brace (J) to the legs.
- Fill imperfections in the wood with an exterior filler before giving a final sanding. You may want to secure the cap nuts with a bit of paint or glue on the bolt threads.

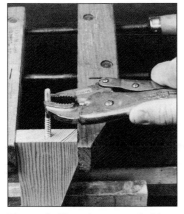

**Figure 3:** Use clamps to hold the ends of the braces (K, L) when screwing in the hanger bolts. This will keep the wood from splitting.

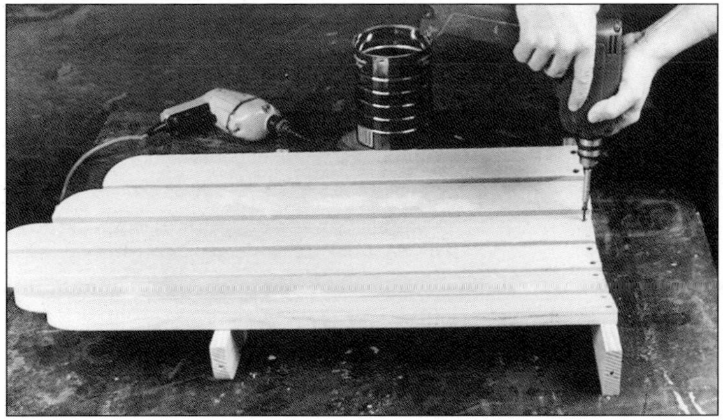

**Figure 4:** Screw the back slats to the lower brace first, then attach the middle brace 10¼ inches above it.

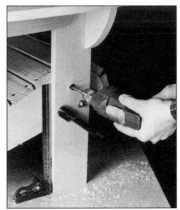

**Figure 5:** Make sure the legs are square to the ground before drilling the bolt holes.

## Finishing

**Fill holes, cracks, and other imperfections in the wood before finishing it. Then apply the finish you have decided on. Whether you use paint, varnish or stain, be sure to thoroughly soak all the end grain, especially the bottoms of the legs and seat supports, to prevent moisture penetration.**

## Building the footrest

- Cut all pieces to size, then cut and sand the curves as you did those of the chair.
- Cut the angled ends of the legs (R). Drill screw holes in the slats, bolt holes in the sides, and chop a shallow mortise for the metal hooks (see the plan detail on page 24).
- Bend the hooks in a metal vise, cut them off with a hack saw, and file or grind smooth. Use a slat (P) as a guide for drilling clearance holes for the screws.
- Screw the slats and hooks to the sides (Q) and bolt on the legs (R). As with the seat, you may need to file flat surfaces on the curved edges of the sides so the slats rest firmly. Do not insert screws too close to the narrow ends of the sides.
- Hook the footrest to the chair and adjust the legs so they are flat on the ground. Clamp them there. Screw the stops (S) to the inside so that when the legs are unfolded the stops will keep them in position (see the plan detail on page 24).

## Building the table

- Cut all the pieces to length and width and round the ends of the top slats (T, U, V).
- Cut the angled ends of the legs (W) (see the plan detail on page 24). Drill the ends of the apron sides (X) for screws, but don't drill the bolt holes quite yet. Screw the apron sides to the ends (Y).
- Place the evenly spaced slats on top of the apron, with the short slats (T) centered over the apron sides (X). Drill the slats and screw them on. Make sure that when you screw the short slats (T) to the apron sides, you avoid the horizontal screws already fastened into the apron sides and ends.
- Turn the table over and clamp the legs so they are butted firmly against the ends of the apron (see the plan detail on page 24). Drill the bolt holes and insert the bolts.

# A–frame Picnic Table

There are good reasons why this is considered the classic picnic table, the one that defines the breed. It's sturdy enough for a gang of unruly teenagers; it's cheap, it's about as easy to build as any project you'll find, and its built-in benches are convenient — you don't need anything else except food and a sunny day.

You can build an A–frame table in a morning, and you don't need a shop. Sawhorses work fine as a workbench and portable tools such a circular saw and electric drill will do the job as well as larger shop tools. Even if you have a shop, build your table outside — fresh air spices up the building as well as the eating.

This version is 6 feet long and will seat six large adults easily, or eight adults with a bit of togetherness. Traditionally, many parts of a table like this would be nailed on. But you'll lend even greater strength to the A–frame's rock-solid design if you use your electric drill and a Phillips head driver bit to screw the bench together with weatherproof deck screws.

Build your table from materials such as redwood, cedar, or pressure-treated lumber, or any other wood that will resist rot and insect damage. A redwood table will cost a bit more than cedar. Pressure-treated lumber will be the least expensive, but carries a penalty of less convenient use. Because of the preservative chemicals, you should never put food directly on the treated wood — use plates and cutting boards.

## Cutting List

| Key | Pieces & Description | Size |
|---|---|---|
| A | 4 legs | 2" x 6" x 34" |
| B | 2 seat supports | 2" x 6" x 58½" |
| C | 2 table top supports | 2" x 4" x 29½" |
| D | 9 seat boards | 2" x 6" x 72" |
| E | 2 diagonal braces | 2" x 4" x 28¼" |
| F | 1 center brace | 2" x 4" x 28" |

## Shopping List

| Quantity | Item |
|---|---|
| 11 | 2" x 6" x 6 feet |
| 1 | 2" x 6" x 10 feet |
| 2 | 2" x 4" x 8 feet |
| 12 | ⅜" x 3½" galvanize carriage bolts |
| 12 | ⅜" galvanized washers |
| 50 | 2½" galvanized deck screws |

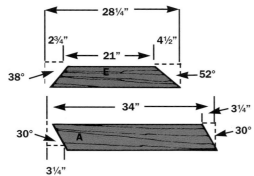

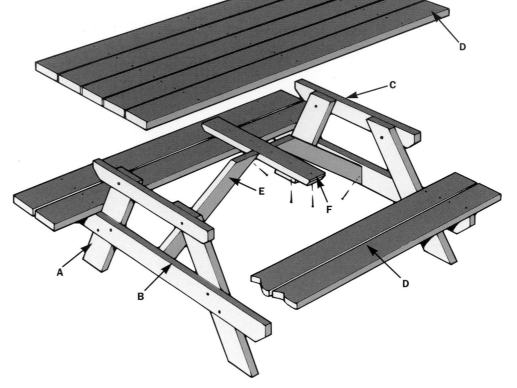

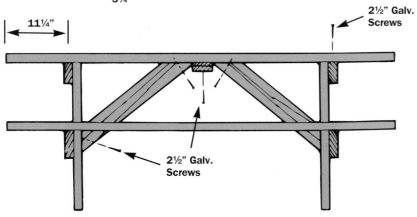

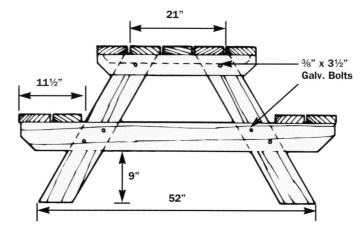

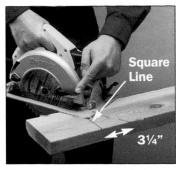

Figure 1: Cut all the parts to size first. You don't need a protractor for an angled cut like this one, simply measure away from a square line.

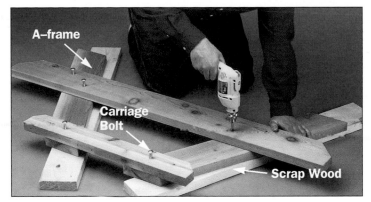

Figure 2: Assemble the A–frames on the ground, with scrap wood underneath to protect your drill bit as you drill the holes. Insert the bolts as you finish the holes to keep pieces in alignment.

Figure 3: Start with the outer seats when assembling the table, lining them up flush with the ends of their supports. Then add the other boards, spacing them evenly.

## Keep in Mind ...

For most of the projects in this book, dimensions in the cutting list are actual sizes of the wood used. For this bench (and a couple of other projects) the difference between actual measurements and nominal wood sizes is unimportant to construction, so nominal dimensions are used.

Pick out the lumber for this project carefully so you get boards that are all about the same color without splits and splinters. Most lumberyards will cut the boards for the top and seats for you at little or no cost.

## Cutting the pieces

• Cut all the pieces with square ends (B, C, and D) to length.
• To avoid having to measure an angle (which requires another tool), the plan shows the measurements so you can mark your cutting line. Use a tape measure (Figure 1) to mark off and cut the angles on one leg (A) and one brace (E).
• Lop off the outside edges of B and C at a 45-degree angle.
• Mark and cut the remaining pieces using the first as guides.

## Assembling the frame

• On a flat surface, assemble the A–frames that form the ends of the table. First, make a mark on seat support (B) 11½ inches from each end.
• Lay the legs on pieces of scrap wood and hold a board tight against their bottom ends to get the angles right. Then measure the distance between the outside edges of the legs at the bottom — it should measure 52 inches.
• Hold the top support (C) so it is centered at the top of the A–frame. Position the seat support (B) so each end extends 11½ inches beyond a leg. When everything is lined up, drill through the overlapping pieces (Figure 2).
• After you complete a hole, insert a bolt so the pieces stay in alignment. When all the bolts are in place, put on the washers and nuts and tighten.

## Assembling the seats and top

• Mark a line across all your top and seat boards, 11¼ inches from each end. Start a pair of screws along that line.
• Hold up one A–frame and screw a seat board onto the support, flush with the outside edge of the support (Figure 3). Drive in only one of the two screws you started. Attach the other seat board the same way, then screw both seats to the second A–frame.
• Use your square to adjust the seat boards perpendicular to the seat support. Then put on the remaining seat boards, leaving a uniform gap between them. Use only one screw at each end for now.
• Set all the top boards in place so the outer boards are flush with the ends of the top supports (C). When everything looks good — ends flush, boards square to the supports and gaps uniform — screw the top boards down and drive the remaining screws in the seat boards.
• Turn the table upside down and arrange the diagonal braces (E) and center brace (F). Part F has a 45-degree bevel cut at the bottom edge of each end to avoid sharp corners beneath the table. Screw all three braces in place, then turn the table right side up.
• Use a file or sandpaper to round over the cut edges of the boards, and apply a water-repellent finish or exterior stain.

# Pedestal Picnic Table

## What You Need

| | |
|---|---|
| Circular saw | Straightedge |
| Hole saw | Clamps |
| Hand saw | Hammer |
| Carpenter's square | Nail set |
| Adjustable square (optional) | Electric drill |

This pedestal table's interesting octagonal shape and cedar construction will complement any house or deck. The design is also very practical; it eliminates the leg-banging crisscross supports of more conventional picnic tables and makes it easy to disassemble the table for winter storage. The design includes single-person benches to go with the table so no one will be trapped in the center of a long seat.

Pedestal tables usually have an aptly named "spider" that connects the tabletop to the pedestal. In this design the spider is also used as a work surface for laying out and building the tabletop. This and other features make the table less complicated to build than it might look. It's put together with screws and butt joints throughout, and you only need a few basic carpentry tools to build it.

The table and benches shown on the facing page were built from an almost knot-free grade of cedar that produces a minimum of waste. If you choose the less expensive knotty grade, anticipate purchasing more material. The rule of thumb is true for any species you may use: Clear grades result in less waste. As with most outside furniture, any good grade of rot-resistant wood can be used. However, this elegant design will be shown off best by an equally elegant wood and careful craftsmanship.

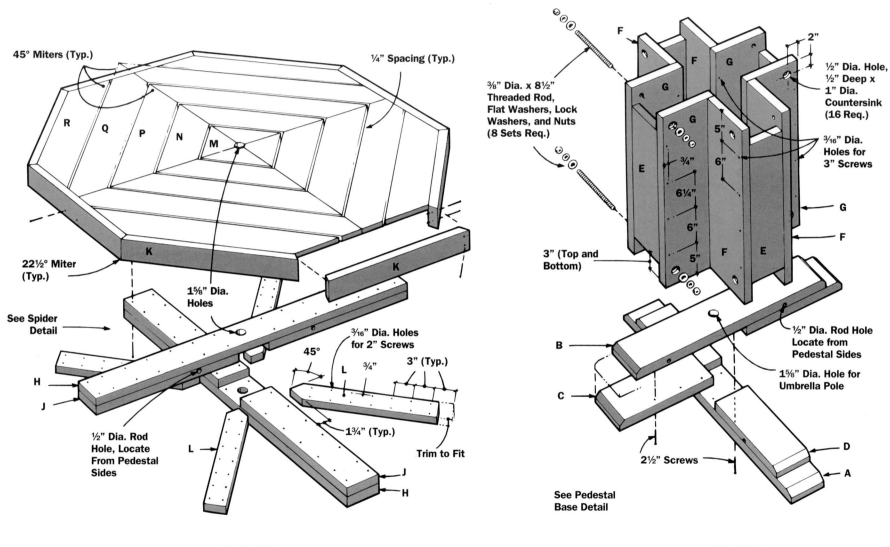

45° Miters (Typ.)

¼" Spacing (Typ.)

R  Q  P  N  M

22½° Miter (Typ.)

K

K

See Spider Detail

1⅝" Dia. Holes

H

J

½" Dia. Rod Hole, Locate From Pedestal Sides

L

45°

L  ¾"

3" (Typ.)

³⁄₁₆" Dia. Holes for 2" Screws

1¾" (Typ.)

Trim to Fit

J

H

**TABLETOP**

⅜" Dia. x 8½" Threaded Rod, Flat Washers, Lock Washers, and Nuts (8 Sets Req.)

F

F  G

G

G

2"

½" Dia. Hole, ½" Deep x 1" Dia. Countersink (16 Req.)

³⁄₁₆" Dia. Holes for 3" Screws

E

¾"

5"

6"

6¼"

6"

G

F

3" (Top and Bottom)

5"

F  E

B

C

½" Dia. Rod Hole Locate from Pedestal Sides

1⅝" Dia. Hole for Umbrella Pole

2½" Screws

D

A

See Pedestal Base Detail

**PEDESTAL**

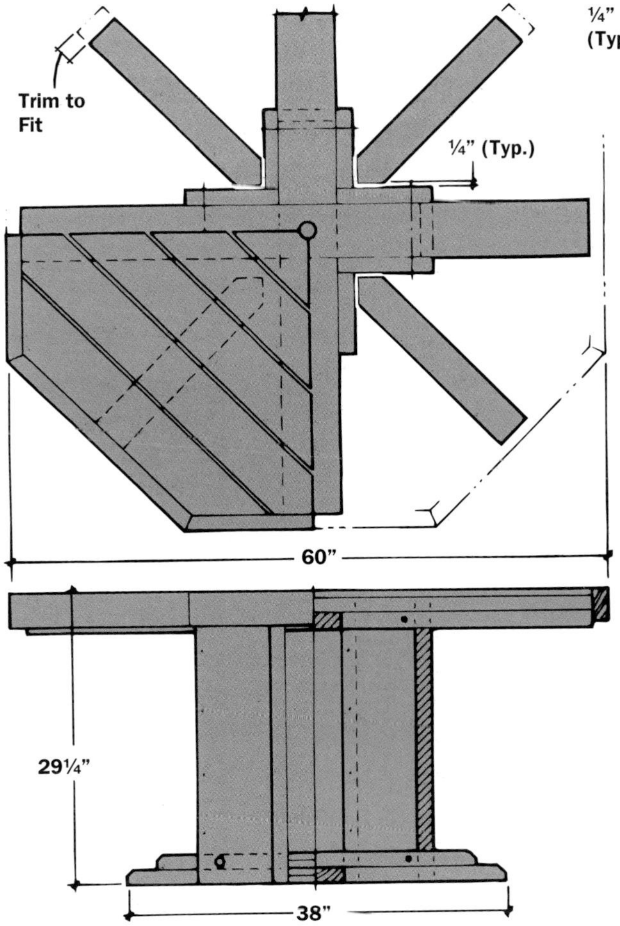

Trim to Fit
¼" (Typ.)
60"
29¼"
38"


**TABLE SIDE AND FRONT VIEWS**

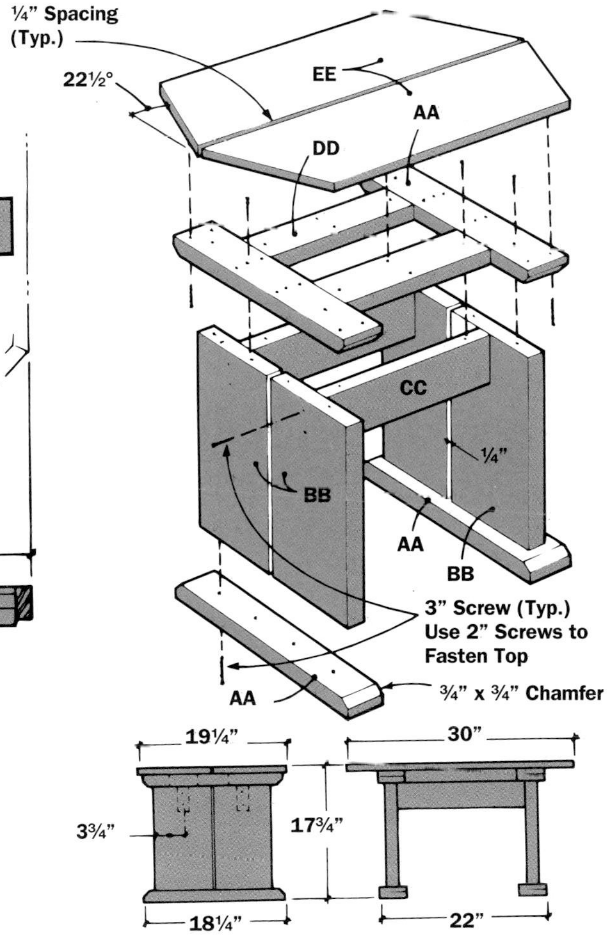

¼" Spacing (Typ.)
22½°
EE
AA
DD
CC
¼"
BB
AA
BB
3" Screw (Typ.) Use 2" Screws to Fasten Top
AA
¾" x ¾" Chamfer
19¼"
30"
3¾"
17¾"
18¼"
22"


**BENCH SIDE AND FRONT VIEWS**

## Cutting List

**Table**

| Key | Pieces & Description | Size |
|---|---|---|
| A | 1 pedestal base | 1½" x 5½" x 8" |
| B | 1 pedestal base | 1½" x 5½" x 32" |
| C | 2 pedestal base | 1½" x 5½" x 16¼" |
| D | 2 pedestal base | 1½" x 5½" x 13¼" |
| E | 4 pedestal sides | 1½" x 5½" x 22¼" |
| F | 4 pedestal sides | 1½" x 7½" x 28¼" |
| G | 4 pedestal sides | 1½" x 9½" x 28¼" |
| H | 2 tabletop spider | 1½" x 5½" x 60" |
| J | 4 tabletop spider | 1½" x 5½" x 27¼" |
| K | 8 tabletop edging | 1½" x 3½" x 24½" |
| L | 4 tabletop cleats | 1½" x 3½" x 24" |
| M | 4 tabletop inner ring | ¾" x 5½" x 11" |
| N | 4 tabletop second ring | ¾" x 5½" x 22½" |
| P | 4 tabletop third ring | ¾" x 5½" x 34" |
| Q | 4 tabletop fourth ring | ¾" x 5½" x 45½" |
| R | 4 tabletop outer ring | ¾" x 5½" x 45½" |
| S | 8 threaded rods | ⅜" x 8½" |

**Benches (8)**

| | | |
|---|---|---|
| AA | 32 feet & leg tops | 1½" x 3½" x 18¼" |
| B | 32 legs | 1½" x 7½" x 14" |
| CC | 16 cross supports | 1½" x 3½" x 17" |
| DD | 16 seat cleats | 1½" x 3½" x 15" |
| EE | 16 bench tops | ¾" x 9½" x 30" |

## Shopping List

**Table**

| Quantity | Item |
|---|---|
| 6 | 1" x 6" x 8 feet cedar |
| 2 | 1" x 6" x 10 feet cedar |
| 4 | 2" x 4" x 8 feet cedar |
| 6 | 2" x 6" x 8 feet cedar |
| 1 | 2" x 8" x 10 feet cedar |
| 1 | 2" x 10" x 10 feet cedar |
| 2 lbs. | #6 x 2" galvanized deck screws |
| 1 lb. | #6 x 2½" galvanized deck screws |
| 2 lbs. | #6 x 3" galvanized deck screws |
| 100 | 3" galvanized finish nails |
| 2 | 36" x ⅜" threaded rod |
| 16 | ⅜" nuts |
| 16 | ⅜" lock washers |
| 16 | 5/16" flat washers |
| 3 qts. | Exterior wood sealer |

**Benches (8)**

| | |
|---|---|
| 6 | 1" x 10" x 8 feet cedar |
| 12 | 2" x 4" x 8 feet cedar |
| 6 | 2" x 8" x 8 feet cedar |

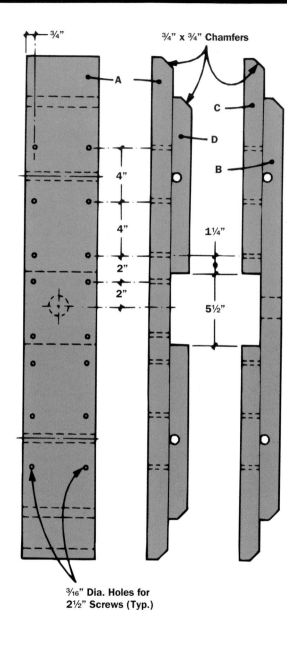

¾"

¾" x ¾" Chamfers

A

C

D

B

1¼"

4"

4"

2"

2"

5½"

**³⁄₁₆" Dia. Holes for
2½" Screws (Typ.)**

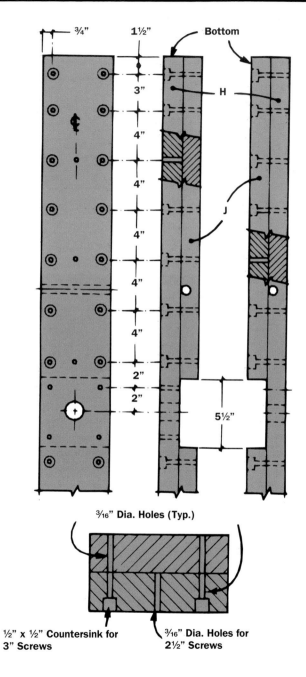

¾"   1½"   Bottom

3"

H

4"

J

4"

4"

4"

4"

2"

2"

5½"

**³⁄₁₆" Dia. Holes (Typ.)**

**½" x ½" Countersink for
3" Screws**

**³⁄₁₆" Dia. Holes for
2½" Screws**

## Cutting the table parts

- To ensure that the pedestal slips easily over the pedestal base and the tabletop spider, measure the widths of your 2x6 stock and cut the pedestal sides (E) from the widest boards, then cut the pieces for the pedestal base (A, B, C, and D), the pedestal sides (F, G), the tabletop spider (H, J), and the cleats (L) to length.
- The tabletop is built using mitered 1x6s of equal length to make square and concentric rings. Cut the ring pieces (M, N, P, Q, and R) 1 inch longer than the dimensions shown in the cutting list. Choose lumber of equal width for the four boards in each ring. Cut the ends square for now.
- Cut the tabletop edging pieces (K) approximately 1 inch longer than the dimension shown on the cutting list. Cut the ends square and set them aside.

## Building the pedestal base

- Lay out and drill all assembly holes in parts A, B, C, and D (see Pedestal Base Detail, facing page). With a hole saw, cut a $1\frac{5}{8}$-inch hole in the center of piece (B) for the umbrella pole.
- With a hand saw or a circular saw set at 45 degrees, chamfer the top sides of both ends of pieces A and B and one end of pieces C and D. Align pieces A and B and use a carpenter's square to check that they are 90 degrees to each other and that they cross at their center points (see Pedestal Base Detail). Screw A to B with 2 ½-inch screws. Flip the base over and screw on the two C pieces. Flip the base back over and screw on the D pieces.
- Lay out and drill all assembly holes in the pedestal sides (F, G). Make four pedestal side assemblies by screwing pieces F and G together and set them in position against the pedestal base. Rest the pedestal side pieces (E) on top of the pedestal base, and screw them to the assembled (F, G) pieces.
- Using the holes in the pedestal sides as guides, drill holes through the pedestal base for the threaded rods. Drill from both sides until the holes meet in the middle.
- Mark the lengths for the eight threaded rods (S) on the rod stock. Thread nuts onto the rod stock and place them below the marks for the cuts. Using a hacksaw, cut the rod pieces to length. File the rod ends (Figure 1) and then unscrew the nuts to clean the cut threads.

- Put a flat washer, lock washer, and nut on one end of each threaded rod. Drive each rod through its passageway by tapping on the nuts so you don't damage the threads on the ends. Put washers and nuts on the other ends and tighten to secure the pedestal to the base. Set the pedestal aside.

## Building the spider

- The spider and cleats are cut long so they can be trimmed to fit after the outer top ring is attached.
- Lay out and drill the holes in the spider pieces (H) for the screws that connect the H pieces together and the H pieces to the J pieces (see Spider Detail, facing page). Screw the pieces together just as you did with pieces A and B of the pedestal base. Align two of the pieces (J with H) and screw them together (see Spider Detail). Flip the spider over and screw the remaining two pieces (J) to the spider. Don't drill the hole for the umbrella pole yet.
- Countersink and drill holes for the 3-inch screws that attach the tabletop rings to the spider. Set the spider into the top of the pedestal and drill holes for the threaded rods. Remove the spider from the pedestal and set it on saw horses so you can drive the 3-inch screws.

## Building the table top

- Draw center lines along the length of the H pieces on the top side of the spider. Build the tabletop by screwing on the inner ring first, and progressively adding rings. All but the outer ring are aligned to these center lines and screwed through the holes in the spider. The outer ring is attached by screwing through the cleats (L).
- You can make a 45-degree mitering jig to use with your circular saw to cut the ends of the ring boards (Figure 2), or you can use an adjustable square.
- Miter one end of all the M, N, P, and Q pieces. Place one M piece on the spider, mark its length, and cut that miter. Match the other three M pieces to the finished one. Align and screw the four M pieces to the spider.
- Make eight ¼-inch spacers from scrap wood to maintain uniform gaps between the tabletop rings. Set two ¼-inch spacers against one edge of the inner ring. Place one N piece against the spacers.

**Figure 1:** File cut ends of threaded rod to remove the burr. Backing the nut off will clean the threads.

**Figure 2:** A miter jig will help you cut the mitered ends of all the tabletop boards.

**Figure 3:** Check pieces for square as you assemble the top. Spacers keep a uniform gap between the boards.

• Align the mitered end with the center line on the spider. Mark the other end of the N piece, and cut the miter. Match the other three N pieces to the finished one.

• Align and screw one N piece to the spider. Use the ¼-inch spacers as gap guides to align the remaining three N pieces on the spider. Check the pieces' position for square with a carpenter's square (Figure 3).

• Adjust the gaps, if necessary, until the ring is square. Then screw it to the spider.

• Fit and assemble the remaining tabletop rings (P, Q). Flip the top over to attach the cleats.

• The four cleats under the tabletop hold the rings flat and support the outer ring. Cut one end of all the cleats (L) to a point, making sure you maintain the length of the cleat from the point to the squared end. Drill holes for the 2-inch screws that secure the cleats to the rings. Screw the cleats onto the underside of the top. Leave room for the pedestal to slip over the spider. Turn the top over and mount it to the pedestal with the threaded rods.

• Tape two ¼-inch spacers to each edge of the fourth ring (Q). Center and screw the outer ring pieces (R) to the cleats. Trim these ends when you cut the octagon.

## Cutting the octagon

• Cut the octagon by laying a long straightedge across the table so it goes through the center point. Use a framing square to adjust the straightedge so it is perpendicular to the outside edge of the last ring (R). Mark where the straightedge crosses the outer edges of the last ring (this will give you the centers of two sides of the octagon). Turn the straightedge 90 degrees and repeat this procedure.

• Next, mark points on the edge 11¾ inches on each side of your center marks. Do this to all four sides of the outer ring.

• Using your straightedge, draw lines connecting these points. These lines mark the remaining four sides of the octagon. Measure the lengths of the eight sides of the octagon to check that they are equal. The sides of the table shown measure 23½ inches. If necessary, make minor adjustments until all sides are equal.

• Clamp a straightedge to the top to guide your circular saw while trimming the ends of rings Q and R (Figure 4).

• With a handsaw, cut off the protruding ends of the spider and cleats. Drill the 1⅝-inch hole for the umbrella pole in the center of the top.

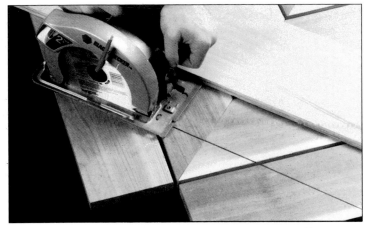

**Figure 4:** Trim corners to make the top into an octagon. Use a straightedge guide to obtain a nice straight cut.

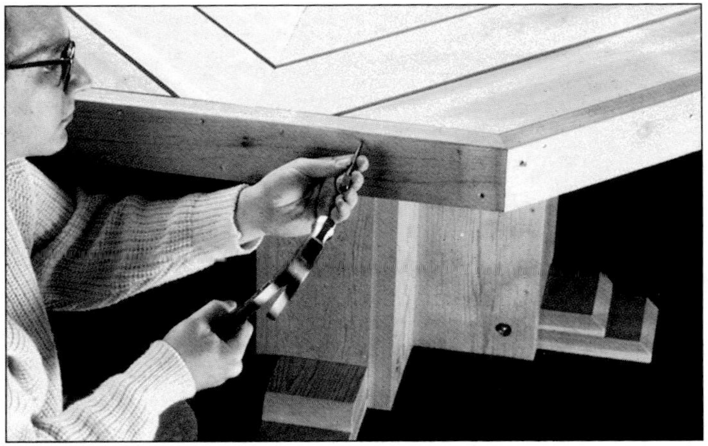

**Figure 5:** Attach edging with galvanized finish nails to the top boards, toenail the corners, and set below the wood surface.

## Finishing

**The project shown here uses a wood preservative designed for cedar siding and decks. Read the directions on the can before buying a finish because some finishes require that the wood weather outside for six months first.**

## Attaching the edging

- Set your circular saw to 22 ½ degrees. Miter one end of all the edging pieces (K). Align one piece (K) on an outside edge of the top. Mark the length, and cut the second miter. Check the fit and attach the edging to the top with 3-inch galvanized finish nails. Continue this process around the top of the table until all the edging is applied.
- Toenail the mitered corners together and drive a few nails through the sides into the ends of the cleats and spider. Set all nail heads below the surface with a nail set (Figure 5).
- Sand away any pencil marks or other surface marks and remove the sharp edges. Set the table aside now and build the eight benches.

## Building the benches

- Prepare yourself for lots of repetition — there are 112 pieces of wood needed to make 8 benches. Don't let your mind wander while sawing or you'll have an accident.
- Cut pieces AA, BB, CC, and DD to length. Chamfer the ends of the feet and leg tops (AA), and drill assembly holes.
- Cut the pieces for the bench tops (EE) 1 inch longer than shown on the cutting list. Lay out and cut the 22 ½-degree mitered ends on one EE piece. Use this piece as a template for the 15 remaining bench top pieces. Cut all mitered ends on the bench tops.
- Screw the legs, feet, and leg tops (AA and BB) together and screw the assembled legs and cross supports (CC) together. Screw the seat cleats (DD) on top of the cross supports. Align the bench tops on the assembled benches and screw down the tops with 2-inch screws.
- The table and benches are now complete except for a protective exterior finish.

# Porch Glider

| | |
|---|---|
| Table saw | Screwdriver |
| Circular saw | Blanket |
| Jigsaw | Sanding block |
| Electric drill | Paintbrush |
| Pencil | Belt sander |
| Compass | Wrenches |

This sturdy glider seats three in comfort and requires only basic carpentry skills and tools to build. In fact, this is a deceptively easy project, providing a big payoff for a relatively small investment. What makes it easy? There are no joints to cut and the glider is put together entirely with bolts and screws, so you don't need to glue and clamp.

Building the glider is an excellent way to become familiar with some advanced skills, such as making and using templates, accurately marking and cutting repeated patterns, and tracing a smooth curve. This is a boatbuilder's trick, involving the use of a thin strip of wood called a "batten" to connect the ends and middle of the curve. It's easy and guaranteed foolproof, once you've done it the first time.

For the glider to be as strong and durable as possible, you can build it of oak. This wood is fairly expensive, so to keep the costs down, buy the lumber rough and in random widths. You can have it planed to the required thickness at the lumberyard and then rip the boards to final widths on your table saw. This process is more work than buying planed dimension lumber, but it saves considerable money.

You could also save money by building a fine glider from a softwood, such as pine, fir, cedar, or redwood. But you'll need to increase the thicknesses of several key parts to make up for softwood's lower strength. See the advice in "Keep in Mind" on page 44 for these changes.

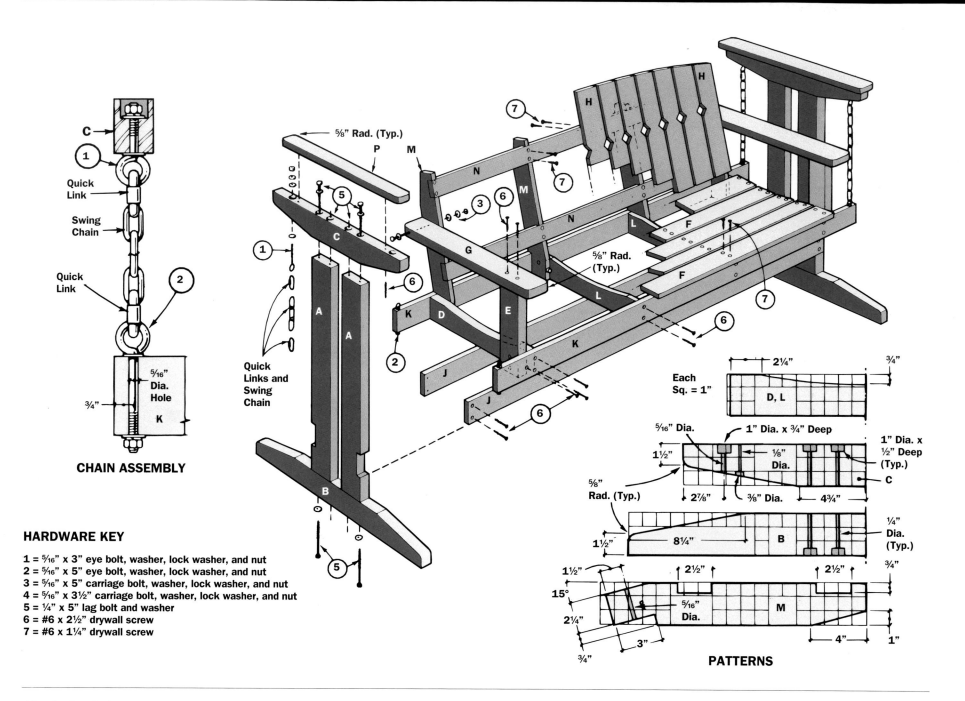

C

1

Quick Link

Swing Chain

Quick Link

2

5/16" Dia. Hole

3/4"

K

**CHAIN ASSEMBLY**

5/8" Rad. (Typ.)

P    M

H

H

7

N

7

M

6

3

N

L

F

1

G

5/8" Rad. (Typ.)

6

F

2

K    D    E

7

J    L

K

6

J    5

6

**HARDWARE KEY**

1 = 5/16" x 3" eye bolt, washer, lock washer, and nut
2 = 5/16" x 5" eye bolt, washer, lock washer, and nut
3 = 5/16" x 5" carriage bolt, washer, lock washer, and nut
4 = 5/16" x 3½" carriage bolt, washer, lock washer, and nut
5 = ¼" x 5" lag bolt and washer
6 = #6 x 2½" drywall screw
7 = #6 x 1¼" drywall screw

Quick Links and Swing Chain

A    A

B

5

Each Sq. = 1"

2¼"    ¾"

D, L

5/16" Dia.    1" Dia. x ¾" Deep

1½"

⅛" Dia.

1" Dia. x ½" Deep (Typ.)

C

5/8" Rad. (Typ.)

2⅞"    ⅜" Dia.    4¾"

8¼"    B    ¼" Dia. (Typ.)

1½"

1½"    2½"    2½"    ¾"

15°

5/16" Dia.    M

2¼"

3"    4"    1"

¾"

**PATTERNS**

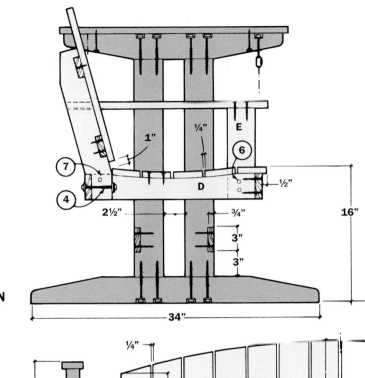

**CROSS SECTION**

1"

¼"

E

6

7

4

2½"

¾"

16"

3"

3"

D

½"

34"

## Cutting List

| Key | Pieces & Description | Size |
|---|---|---|
| A | 4 legs | 1½" x 3½" x 26" |
| B | 2 feet | 1½" x 3" x 34" |
| C | 2 tops | 1½" x 3" x 26" |
| D | 2 seat supports | 1½" x 3" x 19½" |
| E | 2 arm supports | 1½" x 3" x 11" |
| F | 5 seat slats | ¾" x 3½" x 55¼" |
| G | 2 arms | ¾" x 3½" x 24" |
| H | 14 back slats | ¾" x 3½" x 19" |
| J | 2 stretchers | ¾" x 3" x 65¼" |
| K | 2 seat rails | ¾" x 3" x 65¼" |
| L | 2 seat supports | ¾" x 3" x 19½" |
| M | 4 back supports | ¾" x 3" x 19" |
| N | 2 back battens | ¾" x 2½" x 52¼" |
| P | 2 caps | ¾" x 2½" x 27" |

## Shopping List

| | |
|---|---|
| 25 | board feet of 2" oak |
| 50 | board feet of 1" oak |
| 4 | feet of 200-lb.-test swing chain |
| 4 | 5/16" x 3" eye bolts with washers, lock washers, and nuts |
| 4 | 5/16" x 5" eye bolts with washers, lock washers, and nuts |
| 2 | 5/16" x 3" carriage bolts with washers, lock washers, and nuts |
| 4 | 5/16" x 3½" carriage bolts with washers, lock washers, and nuts |
| 16 | ¼" x 5" lag bolts with washers |
| 8 | Quick Links (chain repair links) |
| 40 | #6 x 2½" drywall screws |
| 120 | #6 x 1¼" drywall screws |
| 6 | 12-ounce aerosol cans of exterior white primer |
| 6 | 12-ounce aerosol cans of exterior white paint |

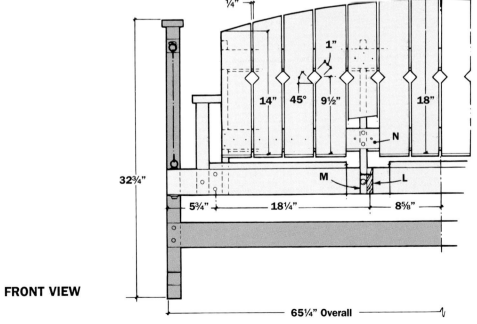

**FRONT VIEW**

¼"

1"

14"   45°   9½"

18"

N

M

L

32¾"

5¾"   18¼"   8⅝"

65¼" Overall

If you are building with softwood, double the thickness of the seat rails (K), seat supports (L), and back supports (M) to 1½ inches, and change the dimensions of mating parts and the location of bolt and screw holes accordingly.

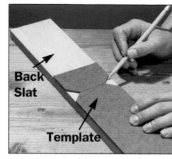

**Figure 1:** A template is a fast and easy way to draw the triangular cutouts, and it ensures that all the cutouts will be identical.

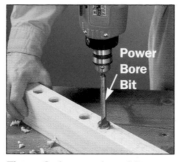

**Figure 2:** A power bore bit or spade bit makes the flat-bottom holes that you need to countersink the eye bolts and carriage bolts.

**Figure 3:** A dowel jig will ensure straight bolt holes through the arms and other parts. If you do it by eye, line up the bit with a square.

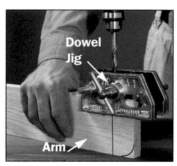

**Figure 4:** The back supports are screwed to the seat supports, then bolted to the rear seat rails to make a strong joint.

## Cutting the pieces

- Make and cut out templates for the feet and tops (B and C), seat supports (D and L), back supports (M), and the cutouts of the back slats (H).
- Trace the shapes from the templates onto the appropriate parts (Figure 1). Use a compass to draw the corners of the arms (G) and caps (P). Don't cut the curves yet.

## Drilling the assembly holes

- Drill 1-inch-diameter countersunk holes in the feet (B) and tops (C) for the lag bolts and eye bolts (Figure 2).
- Drill the eye bolt holes in the seat rails (K) and the carriage bolt holes in the arms (Figure 3). Lay out and drill all the remaining screw and bolt holes except for the carriage bolt

holes at the bottom of the back supports (M). Cut out the curved shapes and sand the sawn edges smooth.

## Assembling the seat and back

- Label the pieces as you assemble them so they can be reassembled the same way later, after they're painted.
- Screw the seat rails (K) to the seat supports (D and L), and attach the eye bolts to the rails. Screw the arm supports (E) and the back supports (M) in place.
- Screw the back battens (N) to the back supports. Bolt the arms (G) to the outer back supports, then screw the arms to the arm supports.
- Drill through the carriage bolt holes in the rear seat rail

Figure 5: After the back is in place, draw a smooth curve at the top of the back by following a flexible strip of wood, called a "batten," clamped at the center and ends.

**Thin Wood Strip**

Figure 6: Cut the curve at the top of the back with a jigsaw and fine-toothed blade. Cut as close to the line as you can without cutting it away.

Figure 7: Sand the sawn edges of the back slats with a belt sander. Hold the sander firmly to keep the curve smooth.

**Quick Link**

Figure 8: A Quick Link, also called a chain repair link, is a fast and secure way to connect the eye bolts to the swing chain.

To provide your glider with a weatherproof, long lasting finish, begin by completely disassembling the glider and frame. Finish sand all the pieces and smooth any sharp edges.

Coat the inside surfaces that can't be reached once the parts are assembled. The glider shown here was painted with aerosol spray cans of exterior white enamel. You could also use a clear finish on your glider, but if you do, replace the drywall screws with brass, bronze or stainless steel screws for a better appearance.

Reassemble the glider and frame. Finish the remaining uncoated surfaces, rehang the glider in its frame, and you're ready to relax.

and through the back supports to complete the bolt holes. Attach the carriage bolts (Figure 4).

- To attach the seat and back slats, first screw the seat slats (F) to the seat frame. Then cut a 1-inch x 1-inch x 55-inch spacer from scrap wood. Place this spacer strip on the rear seat slat and against the back supports.
- Set the back slats (H) on top of the spacer and against the back battens. Align the back slats so the gaps between them are equal, then screw them to the back battens.

## Cutting the curved back

- To lay out and cut the curved back, use a thin, flexible strip of solid wood, at least 55 inches long, as a guide for drawing

the curve. Mark the finished height of the back at the center and ends. Clamp the drawing stick to the marked points and draw the curve (Figure 5).

- Remove the waste (Figure 6) and sand the edges (Figure 7).

## Assembling the frame

- Cut notches in the legs (A) for the stretchers (J). Bolt the feet and tops to the legs. Screw the stretchers to the legs. Attach the eye bolts to the tops, then screw on the caps (P).
- Remove the caps and tops from the legs of the frame. Set the glider on the stretchers. Reattach the tops and caps.
- Cut four 9- to 10-inch lengths of chain. Connect the chain, Quick Links, and eye bolts (Figure 8).

# Backyard Lawn Glider

This glider is all that its name implies: a vehicle for swinging freely through a summer afternoon. This version also provides an attractive focal point for your backyard — a symbol of relaxing times from a bygone era. You will also swing freely through construction of the glider, because you need to use only simple techniques and easily obtainable materials.

Most of the structural frame pieces are cut from ⁵⁄₄ pressure-treated pine decking boards. The actual thickness of these boards can vary from ¹¹⁄₁₆ inch to ¹³⁄₁₆ inch, so select boards at the lumberyard that are, as much as possible, of consistent thickness. These ⁵⁄₄ boards come with rounded bullnose edges. They look good on a deck, but when you rip them to the widths you need, you will cut off the rounded edges.

All other frame parts are 1x3 pine (actual size: ¾ inch x 2 ½ inches). If you can't find good-quality 1x3s, buy 1x6s and rip them to the required width. Be sure to inspect all pieces of wood carefully for any flaws, such as knots, that could result in structural weakness.

*One word of caution*: This glider is for genteel rocking. It's not a rough-house climbing or swinging toy for kids — especially young ones. With exuberant swinging, an arm, leg, or head could be caught between the moving glider and the outer frame, causing serious injury. Children should use the glider only with adult supervision.

## HARDWARE KEY

1 = ¼" x 2" carriage bolt, locknut and washer
2 = ¼" x 2½" machine bolt, locknut and washers
3 = ⅜" x 2½" machine bolt, locknut and washers (2)
4 = ⅜" x 2½" machine bolt, locknut and washers (2)
5 = 1¼" galvanized deck screw
6 = 1⅝" galvanized deck screw
7 = 2" galvanized deck screw

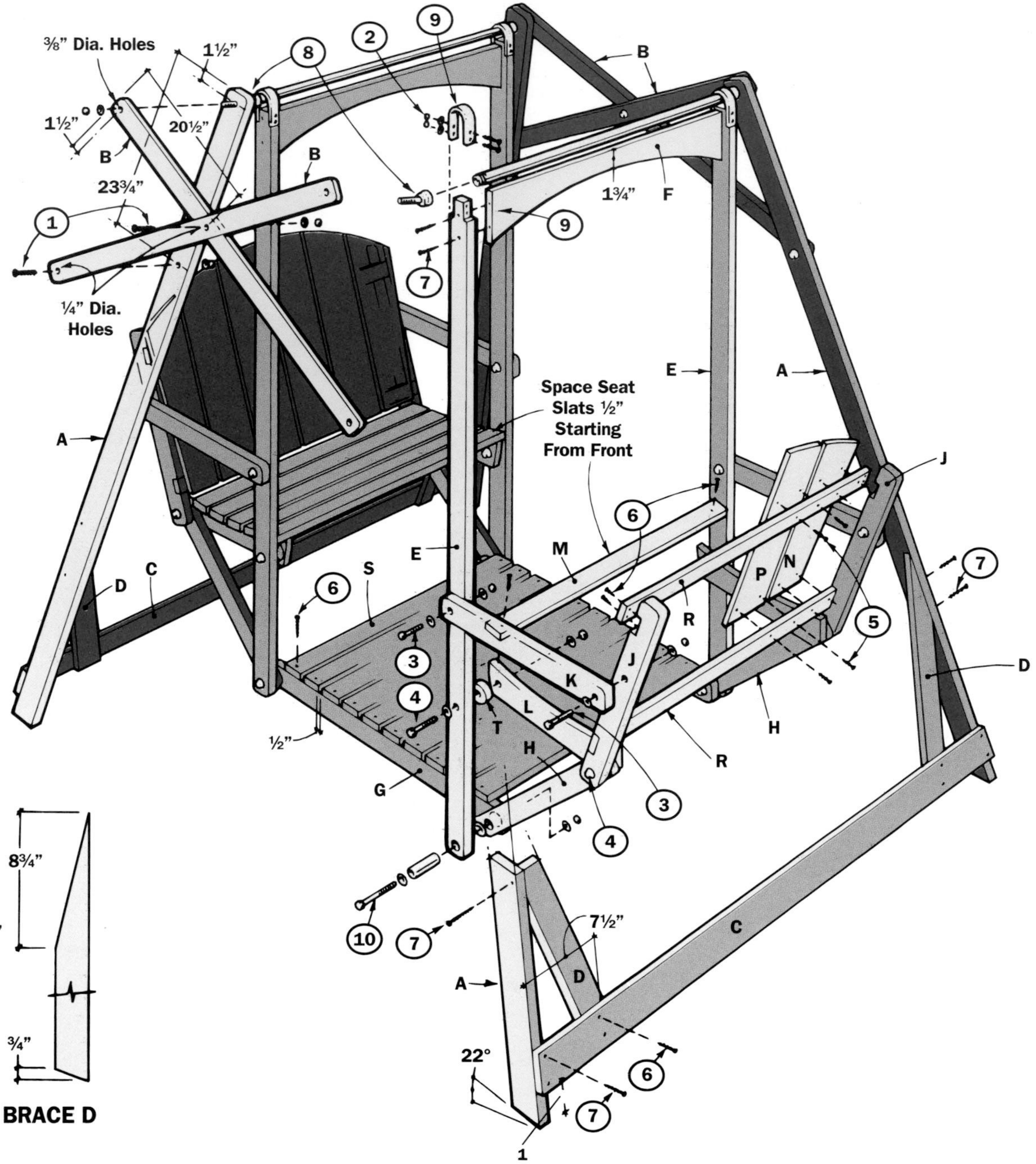

⅜" Dia. Holes
1½"
1½"
20½"
23¾"
B
¼" Dia. Holes
1¾"
F
E
A
Space Seat Slats ½" Starting From Front
J
M
P
N
R
S
C
D
K
L
T
H
G
½"
7½"
22°


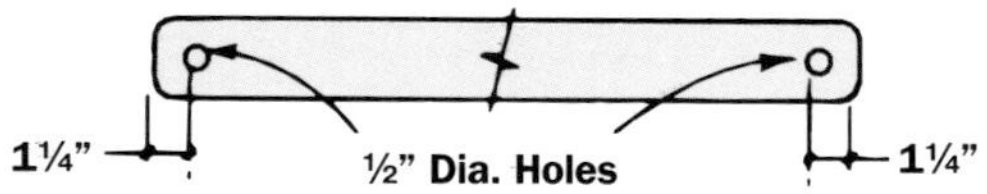

1¼"
½" Dia. Holes
1¼"

PLATFORM RAIL G

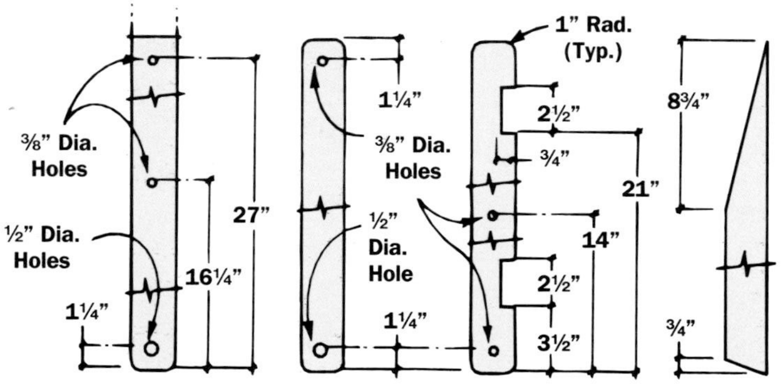

⅜" Dia. Holes
½" Dia. Holes
1¼"
27"
16¼"
1¼"
⅜" Dia. Holes
½" Dia. Hole
1¼"
1" Rad. (Typ.)
2½"
¾"
21"
14"
2½"
3½"
8¾"
¾"

POST E BRACE H BRACE J BRACE D

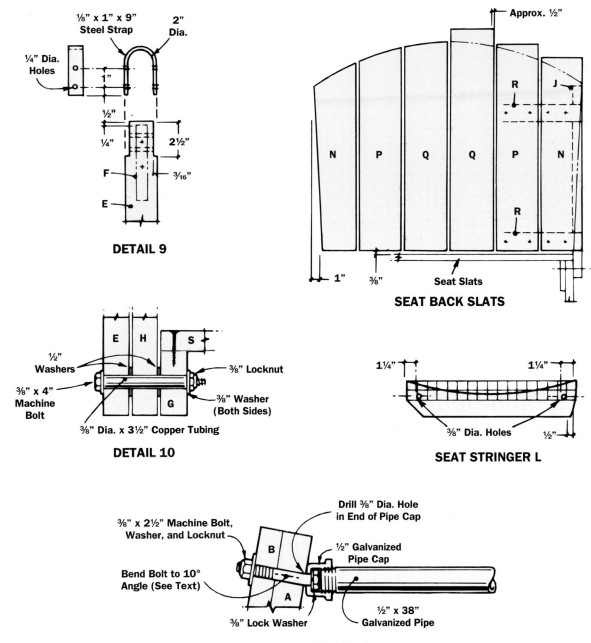

**DETAIL 9**

¹⁄₈" x 1" x 9"
Steel Strap

2" Dia.

¹⁄₄" Dia. Holes

1"

¹⁄₂"

¹⁄₄"

2¹⁄₂"

³⁄₁₆"

F

E

---

**SEAT BACK SLATS**

Approx. ¹⁄₂"

R J

N P Q Q P N

R

1" ³⁄₈" Seat Slats

---

**DETAIL 10**

E H S

¹⁄₂" Washers

³⁄₈" x 4" Machine Bolt

³⁄₈" Dia. x 3¹⁄₂" Copper Tubing

³⁄₈" Locknut

³⁄₈" Washer (Both Sides)

G

---

**SEAT STRINGER L**

1¹⁄₄" 1¹⁄₄"

³⁄₈" Dia. Holes ¹⁄₂"

---

**DETAIL 8**

³⁄₈" x 2¹⁄₂" Machine Bolt, Washer, and Locknut

Drill ³⁄₈" Dia. Hole in End of Pipe Cap

B

¹⁄₂" Galvanized Pipe Cap

Bend Bolt to 10° Angle (See Text)

A

³⁄₈" Lock Washer

¹⁄₂" x 38" Galvanized Pipe

---

## Cutting List

| Key | Pieces & Description | Size |
|---|---|---|
| A | 4 legs | ⁵⁄₄" x 3¹⁄₄" x 83⁷⁄₈" |
| B | 4 cross braces | ³⁄₄" x 2¹⁄₂" x 47⁷⁄₈" |
| C | 2 lower frame stretchers | ³⁄₄" x 3¹⁄₂" x 65³⁄₄" |
| D | 4 diagonal frame braces | ⁵⁄₄" x 2¹⁄₄" x 26¹⁄₂" |
| E | 4 vertical swing posts | ⁵⁄₄" x 2¹⁄₄" x 71" |
| F | 2 arched headers | ³⁄₄" x 5¹⁄₂" x 34" |
| G | 2 platform rails | ⁵⁄₄" x 2¹⁄₄" x 34" |
| H | 4 diagonal seat brace | ⁵⁄₄" x 2¹⁄₄" x 22¹⁄₂" |
| J | 4 seat back braces | ⁵⁄₄" x 2¹⁄₄" x 26" |
| K | 4 arm braces | ⁵⁄₄" x 2¹⁄₄" x 21" |
| L | 4 seat stringers | ³⁄₄" x 3¹⁄₂" x 17" |
| M | 10 seat slats | ³⁄₄" x 2¹⁄₂" x 33¹⁄₂" |
| N | 4 back slats | ³⁄₄" x 5¹⁄₂" x 26" |
| P | 4 back slats | ³⁄₄" x 5¹⁄₂" x 28" |
| Q | 4 back slats | ³⁄₄" x 5¹⁄₂" x 30" |
| R | 4 back stringers | ³⁄₄" x 2¹⁄₂" x 36" |
| S | 10 deck slats | ³⁄₄" x 2¹⁄₂" x 31³⁄₈" |
| T | 4 spacer blocks | ⁵⁄₄" x 2¹⁄₈" square |

## Shopping List

| Quantity | Item |
|---|---|
| 1 | ⁵⁄₄" x 6" x 8-foot treated pine decking |
| 4 | ⁵⁄₄" x 6" x 14-foot treated pine decking |
| 2 | 1" x 3" x 8-foot pine |
| 1 | 1" x 4" x 8-foot pine |
| 1 | 1" x 4" x 12-foot treated pine |
| 1 | 1" x 6" x 6-foot pine |
| 4 | 1" x 3" x 12-foot pine |
| 3 | 1" x 3" x 8-foot pine |
| 3 | 1" x 6" x 10-foot pine |
| 6 | ¹⁄₄" x 2" carriage bolts |
| 8 | ¹⁄₄ x 2¹⁄₂" bolts |
| 1 | 36" x ¹⁄₈" x 1" steel strap |
| 14 | ¹⁄₄" washers |
| 12 | 1³⁄₈" x 2¹⁄₂" bolts |
| 8 | ³⁄₈" x 3¹⁄₂" bolts |
| 4 | ³⁄₈" x 4" bolts |
| 1 | 14" x ³⁄₈" soft copper tubing |
| 8 | ¹⁄₂" washers |
| 4 | ³⁄₈" lock washers |
| 44 | ³⁄₈" washers |
| 14 | ¹⁄₄" locknuts |
| 24 | ³⁄₈" locknuts |
| 24 | 2" galvanized deck screws |
| 64 | 1⁵⁄₈" galvanized deck screws |
| 48 | 1¹⁄₄" galvanized deck screws |
| 4 | ¹⁄₂" galvanized pipe caps |
| 2 | ¹⁄₂" x 38" galvanized pipe threaded on both ends |

All the parts are either bolted or screwed together. At each bolted joint, use washers between the wood and the bolt heads and nuts. Use locknuts to secure all the bolts; they have plastic inserts at the thread ends to prevent loosening.

Wherever wood parts are screwed together, drill pilot holes for the screws to prevent the wood from splitting. Also drill countersink recesses for the screw heads so they rest slightly below the wood surface. A combination drill bit and countersink can save you time here.

You can also save time by using two drills — one for drilling holes, the other for driving screws — so you won't have to keep changing bits.

**Figure 1:** Rip the rounded bullnose edges from ⁵⁄₄ decking boards using a rip-guide attachment on your circular saw. Then rip the boards again to final width.

**Figure 2:** Notch a ¾-inch cutout into the seat back braces for the horizontal back support. Make several ¾-inch cuts, then chisel out the waste and file smooth.

## Getting started

• Begin by ripping all the ⁵⁄₄ lumber to width, using your circular saw and rip guide (Figure 1). In the process, remove the rounded edges from all of the ⁵⁄₄ lumber.
• Cut all the pieces to the correct length.
• Cut all the ¾-inch-thick pieces to size.
• Round the corners of all the ⁵⁄₄ pieces except for the bottom of the legs (A), which require a 22-degree angle. Cut the rounded corners with a jigsaw after drawing a 1-inch radius on each corner. File the cuts or smooth them with coarse sandpaper.
• Drill all the ⅜-inch and ½-inch holes in the frame pieces, as shown in the plan. Also drill the ¼-inch holes in the cross braces (B).

• Mark the curves on the arched headers (F) and seat stringers (L). Use a flexible stick to mark these curves using the same method, shown in Figure 8 on page 53, that is used to cut the curve on the back seat slats.
• Cut these curves with a jigsaw. Be sure to cut the L pieces carefully because they form the curvature of the seat. You can smooth the curves with a drum sanding attachment on your drill or with a few strokes of a wood rasp or file.
• Notch the seat back braces (J) to receive the stringers (R). Mark the end points of each notch, then make several ¾-inch-deep cuts with a circular saw. Carefully chisel out the notches with a ¾-inch chisel (Figure 2). Clean up the notches with a wood file.

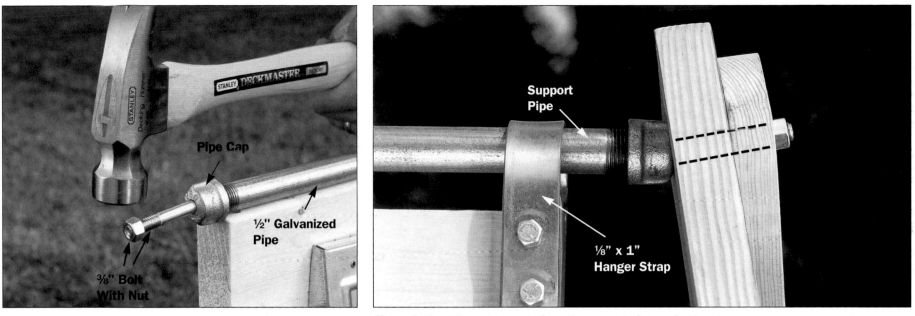

**Figure 3:** Assemble the swing support pipes from ½-inch galvanized pipe. Drill holes in caps for bolts. Bend the bolt 10 degrees to match the glider's leg angles.

**Figure 4:** Hang the swing posts from the support pipes using hanger straps. Form these from standard galvanized steel ⅛-inch x 1-inch strapping 9 inches long, then drill holes.

## Assembling the hardware

- Take a break from the woodworking and begin forming the metal hardware. Hold the ½-inch galvanized pipe caps firmly in a vise or pliers with the inside threads facing up. Drill a ⅜-inch hole through the center of each cap.
- Put together the pipe assembly by inserting the ⅜-inch x 2½-inch bolt, with a lock washer, into the pipe cap holes, as shown in Detail 8 of the plan on page 49. With the bolt in place, tighten the cap securely onto the galvanized pipe. With a nut protecting the threads, use a hammer to bend the bolt to a 10-degree angle (Figure 3).
- Make the steel hanger straps (Detail 9 of the plan and Figure 4) by cutting four 9-inch pieces from the galvanized steel strap. File the edges smooth. This strap is a stock item in most hardware stores.

- Mark the middle of each piece and form it into a U shape by bending the strap around any cylindrical object that's approximately 2 inches in diameter.
- Mark where the holes are to be drilled in the straps with a center punch or large nail and drill two ¼-inch holes through the legs of each strap. Make sure all four straps are identical so the swing will be balanced and hang evenly.
- Chisel out the tops of the vertical swing posts (E) as shown in Detail 9. Clamp the straps in place and drill bolt holes through the strap holes into parts E. Bolt the straps temporarily to parts E.

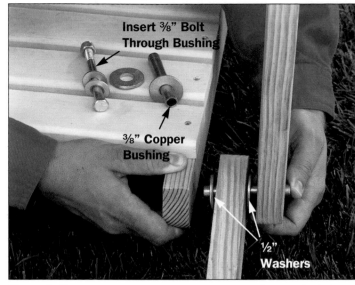

Figure 5: Place washers between moving parts. Secure the bolt with a locknut.

Figure 6: Attach the swing platform at each corner using bushings cut from ⅜-inch copper tubing with bolts inserted through the tubing.

## Assembling the frame

- Find a large flat area on your lawn or driveway to begin assembling the main frame of the swing. Lay the legs (A) and cross braces (B) flat on the work area.
- Use the ¼-inch bolts to join parts A and B as shown in the plan. After you bolt each side together, get a helper to hold the assemblies while you mount the pipes.
- Insert the bolts that protrude from the pipe caps through the top holes of A and B. Put on the washers and locknuts and tighten them down.
- Install the lower frame stretchers (C) by measuring up 2 inches from the bottom of the frame, drilling the pilot holes, and screwing parts C to A.
- Square up the frame by screwing the diagonal frame braces (D) onto C and A as shown in the plan. (See the plan detail on page 48 for the angles to cut at the ends of parts D.)

## Assembling the moving parts

- The mechanical parts of the swing may look confusing, but the only connecting parts that actually move are the straps that wrap around the pipes and the platform corners where the bushings are located, as shown in Detail 10 of the plan.
- Screw the arched headers (F) to each pair of the vertical swing posts (E) as shown in the plan. Position the screws so they'll miss the strap bolts already in parts E.
- Unbolt the straps on parts E and hang them from the galvanized pipes on each side of the frame, then reinstall the straps through parts E.
- Assemble the platform as shown in the plan. Keep the ends of the deck slats (S) flush with the platform rails (G).
- Cut the 3¼-inch bushings from ⅜-inch copper tubing with a hacksaw or tubing cutter. Then insert the bushings through holes drilled in parts E, G, and the diagonal seat braces (H), placing a ½-inch washer between adjacent

**Figure 7:** Position the seat back slats using a ⅜-inch spacer resting on the seat. Space the slats evenly, with about a ½-inch gap between each slat.

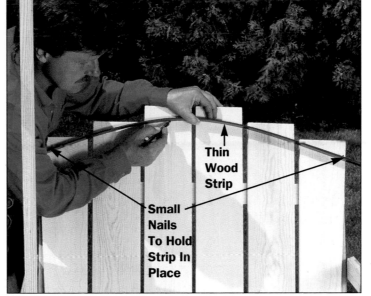

**Figure 8:** Mark the arc on the back slats using a thin strip of wood bent evenly between small nails near the edges of the outside slats. Unbolt the back and cut the arc with a jigsaw.

## Finishing

Sand all the sharp and rough edges with 100-grit sandpaper to reduce splintering. Paint the glider with a good grade of oil primer, topped with an oil-based or latex gloss or semigloss enamel.

You'll find that painting goes easier if you disassemble all the bolted-together sections, then reassemble them after the paint is dry.

parts (Detail 10 and Figures 5 and 6). Tighten the nut onto the bolt just enough to make the nut snug and to allow the joint to move freely.

- Cut out the spacer blocks (T) using a 2¼-inch hole saw, or cut a 2¼-inch square block of wood and round the corners.
- Bolt the seat stringers (L) to the vertical swing posts (E), placing the spacer blocks (T) between them.
- Bolt parts J to H and L, then tighten.
- Bolt the arm braces (K) to E and J on each side.
- Screw the back stringers (R) into the notches that you previously cut in J. Make sure the ends of the stringers are flush with the sides of J.
- Screw the seat slats (M) onto the seat stringers (L). Start at the front of the seat and work your way back, leaving a ½-inch space between slats.
- Taper the two outside back slats (N) by cutting them 1 inch

back from the bottom corners. Place a ⅜-inch spacer (Figure 7) on the back seat slat, then lay out all the back slats (N, P, Q) on the spacer. Position them so there is about a ½-inch gap between slats. Mark their positions and screw them into place from the back side of R.

- Mark the curve along the top of the back slats. Tack a small finish nail ½ inch from the edge of N on each side. Use the ⅜-inch spacer from the previous step and gently bend it to form an arc (Figure 8) for marking the curves.
- Unbolt the backs, place them on sawhorses and cut the curves with your jigsaw.
- Reassemble the backs. The straps may squeak where they hang on the pipe above, but don't do any lubricating just yet. Wait until all the finishing work is done, then use a waterproof grease, available at your hardware store, to lubricate the straps.

# Tree Bench

What better way to enjoy a warm summer day: a cool drink, and a seat in the shade of a spreading tree? Here's a sturdy, easy-to-build bench that encircles your favorite shade tree.

The tree bench is made from four separate sections, each of which goes a quarter of the way around the tree. The sections are connected with cleats on the underside of the seat. The diameter of the bench is 48 inches and it will fit around a tree up to 16 inches in diameter.

The bench shown here is made out of pressure-treated pine painted white, but you could give yours an exterior stain, which is easier to maintain, or no finish at all, which is easier yet. Cedar or redwood would also look good, but these woods would also be more expensive.

You can build this bench in a shop or right out in the yard. However, it's easier to make the tapered slats for the seat with a table saw, using the two taper jigs included in the plan. If you don't have a table saw, you can cut the slats with a jigsaw; you'll get the same results, but it will take a bit longer.

This is not a complicated project by any means. But you will have to concentrate on each step, and take care in cutting the parts. The reason lies in the bench's simplicity: Because it is made of four identical sections, you will find yourself cutting the same shape over and over again.

# Tree Bench

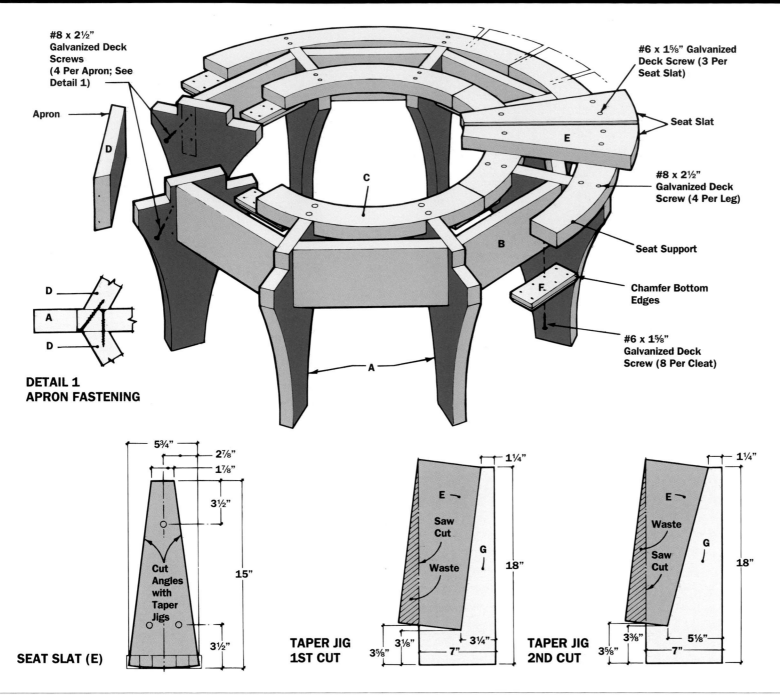

#8 x 2½" Galvanized Deck Screws (4 Per Apron; See Detail 1)

Apron

D

DETAIL 1
APRON FASTENING

D
A
D

#6 x 1⅝" Galvanized Deck Screw (3 Per Seat Slat)

Seat Slat

E

#8 x 2½" Galvanized Deck Screw (4 Per Leg)

Seat Support

Chamfer Bottom Edges

#6 x 1⅝" Galvanized Deck Screw (8 Per Cleat)

C

B

F

A

**SEAT SLAT (E)**

5¾"
2⅞"
1⅞"
3½"
15"
Cut Angles with Taper Jigs
3½"

**TAPER JIG 1ST CUT**

1¼"
E
Saw Cut
Waste
G
18"
3⅝"
3⅛"
3¼"
7"

**TAPER JIG 2ND CUT**

1¼"
E
Waste
Saw Cut
G
18"
3⅝"
3⅜"
5⅛"
7"

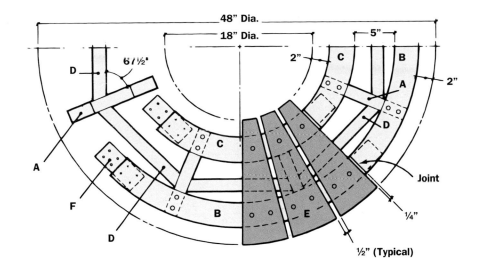

## Cutting List

| Key | Pieces & Description | Size |
|-----|---------------------|------|
| A | 8 legs | 1½" x 11" x 14½" |
| B | 4 seat supports | 1½" x 8⁹⁄₁₆" x 31⅛" |
| C | 4 seat supports | 1½" x 6¼" x 19¾" |
| D | 8 apron | 1½" x 5" x 12⅞" |
| E | 24 seat slats | ¾" x 5¾" x 15" |
| F | 8 cleats | ¾" x 2½" x 6" |
| G | 2 taper jigs | ¾" x 7" x 18" scrap plywood |

## Shopping List

| Quantity | Item |
|----------|------|
| 2 | 2" x 12" x 8-foot treated pine |
| 2 | 2" x 10" x 8-foot treated pine |
| 1 | 2" x 8" x 8-foot treated pine |
| 5 | 1" x 8" x 8-foot treated pine |
| 104 | #6 x 1⅝-inch galvanized deck screws |
| 64 | #8 x 2½-inch galvanized deck screws |
| 1 qt. | Oil-based enamel primer |
| 2 qts | Oil-based enamel paint |

**TREE BENCH PLAN VIEW**

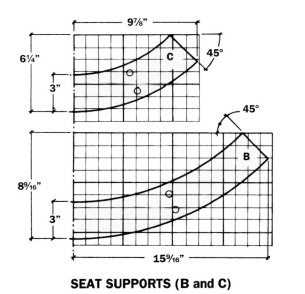

**SEAT SUPPORTS (B and C)**

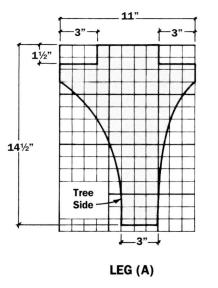

**LEG (A)**

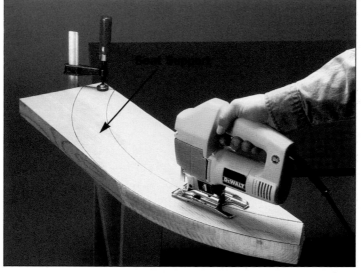

**Figure 1:** Cut curved parts with a jigsaw after enlarging the shapes from the grids in the drawing. Cut one example of each curved part, then use it as a template to mark all similar ones.

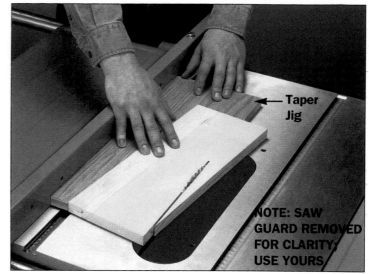

**Figure 2:** Cut the tapered seat slats using plywood taper jigs as described in the plans. You can also cut these slats with a jigsaw, although it's more time consuming.

## Cutting the parts

- You'll need a jigsaw or band saw to cut the curved parts and either a belt sander or a stationary disc sander to sand some of the parts.
- Cut all the pieces for the bench, including the taper jigs, to the sizes given in the cutting list.
- Make templates for the curved parts, A, B and C, by enlarging their shapes from the grids in the plan onto pieces of thin scrap plywood or hardboard. Drill ⅛-inch holes in the seat support templates so you can mark where the screw holes will be on your finished pieces.
- Using the templates, trace the shapes of the seat supports (B and C) and the legs (A) onto the wood, then cut them out using a band saw or jigsaw (Figure 1).
- Make the two taper jigs as shown in the plan detail. On a table saw, cut one side of all 24 seat slats (E) using jig No. 1, then cut the other edge of all pieces using jig No. 2 (Figure 2). Be sure to use the blade guard on your table saw. If you don't have a table saw, cut all the seat slats out with a circular saw or jigsaw, then plane or sand the edges smooth.

## Assembling the supports

- Mark the screw hole location on the seat supports (B and C) using the templates you made earlier. Countersink first, then drill clearance holes for the screws (or use a combination bit that does both at the same time). Countersink and drill screw holes in one seat slat, then use that as a template to mark the rest of the slats. Countersink and drill them, and then drill the holes in the cleats (F).
- Using a belt sander or a stationary disc sander, shape the curved front edge of all the seat slats (Figure 3).
- Chamfer the bottom edges of the cleats (F) and cut a 67 ½-degree bevel on each end of all the apron pieces (D).
- Sand all pieces and round over all sharp edges.

**Figure 3:** Sand the front ends of the seat slats to a curve using either a disc sander, as shown here, or by clamping each piece in a vise and using a belt sander.

**Figure 4:** Assemble the base of the bench around your tree after painting all the parts. The base is made of four sections, joined underneath with cleats.

**Figure 5:** Screw the seat slats onto the base, spacing them evenly on each quarter section. A spacer helps maintain a consistent gap between slats.

## Assembling the legs

- Screw together the legs (A) and seat supports (B and C), making sure you don't install the legs backwards (see leg detail in plan, page 57).
- Join the four parts of the bench around the tree, attaching them with the cleats.
- Position an apron piece (D) between every other pair of legs, drill through the legs, and screw them on.
- Position the remaining apron pieces, then drill and screw them on (Figure 4). The screws must enter at an angle through the ends of the apron pieces and into the legs (see detail 1 in plan, page 56).

## Assembling the seat

- Screw on the seat slats. Begin by attaching two slats on each side of the joints between the quarter sections. The side of each slat should rest ¼ inch from the joint and the front should overhang the front supports by 2 inches. Space the remaining slats evenly in the gaps, then screw them down. It'll help to use a ½-inch spacer between the slats (Figure 5).
- Paint the exposed screw heads, clean up, grab a cool drink and enjoy the shade.

# Garden Bench

## What You Need

Table saw or radial arm saw
Router with rounding-over bit
Portable jigsaw or band saw
Electric drill or drill press
Pipe clamps
Dowel jig
Electric sander

Jointer (optional)
Square
Files
Sanding block
Chisels
Mallet
Plug cutter
Paintbrush
Water sealer
Waterproof glue

Traditionally made of teak, these benches grace hundreds of English parks and gardens, aging beautifully through years of use and weather. This version is made of redwood, which is naturally rot-resistant like teak, but less expensive, more readily available, and easier to work with. You could also use cedar or cypress. Whatever wood you use, it's a good idea to finish your bench with a clear, water-repellent preservative.

This project uses traditional mortise and tenon construction (see plan detail) for extra durability. Normally, you might try to avoid this type of joinery in favor of easier methods, such as dowels or drywall screws, but the extra strength of a mortise and tenon joint will enable your bench to stand up to years of rugged use, and it is consistent with the bench's classic character. If you've never made a mortise and tenon joint, don't be scared off — you'll find it's surprisingly easy. This project is perfect for learning this joint, because redwood compresses easily (unlike oak or other hardwoods), so the joint will fit together well even if it's not perfectly cut.

Other skills you will learn (if you are not already an accomplished woodworker) are face-gluing and the accurate drilling and fitting of dowelled joints. Face gluing of the boards that make up this bench's legs is not difficult if you follow the instructions on page 65. Dowelling requires care and patience, more than anything else. Just remember when assembling the back of the bench that all slats should be fitted to the bottom rail before the top rail is put on.

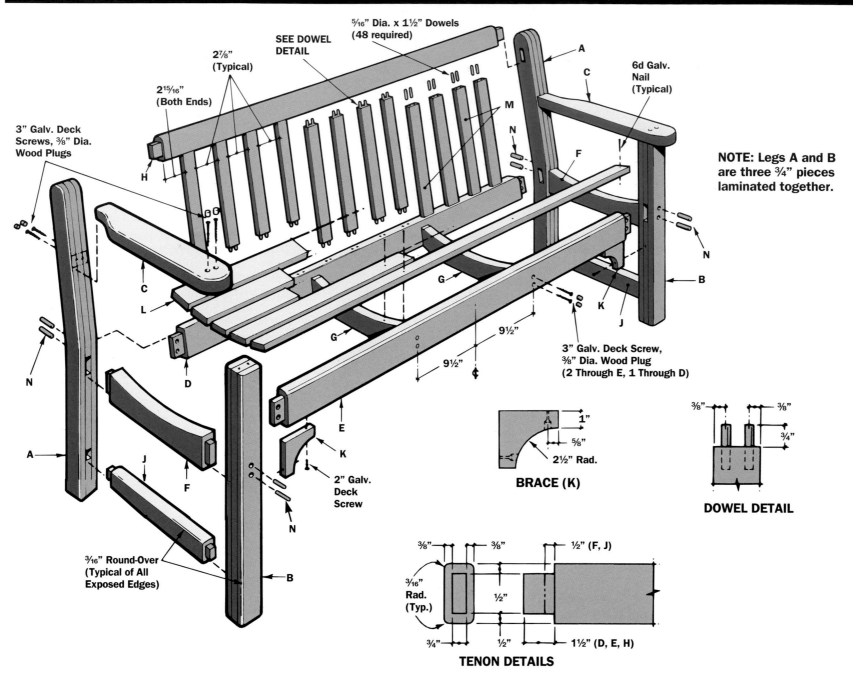

5⁄16" Dia. x 1½" Dowels
(48 required)

SEE DOWEL
DETAIL

2⅞"
(Typical)

2¹⁵⁄₁₆"
(Both Ends)

A

C

6d Galv.
Nail
(Typical)

3" Galv. Deck
Screws, ⅜" Dia.
Wood Plugs

H

M

N

F

NOTE: Legs A and B
are three ¾" pieces
laminated together.

C

L

G

G

N

B

K

J

N

D

E

9½"

9½"

3" Galv. Deck Screw,
⅜" Dia. Wood Plug
(2 Through E, 1 Through D)

A

J

F

K

2" Galv.
Deck
Screw

N

B

3⁄16" Round-Over
(Typical of All
Exposed Edges)

**BRACE (K)**

1"

5⁄8"

2½" Rad.

⅜"    ⅜"

¾"

**DOWEL DETAIL**

⅜"    ⅜"    ½" (F, J)

3⁄16"
Rad.
(Typ.)

½"

½"

¾"    ½"    1½" (D, E, H)

**TENON DETAILS**

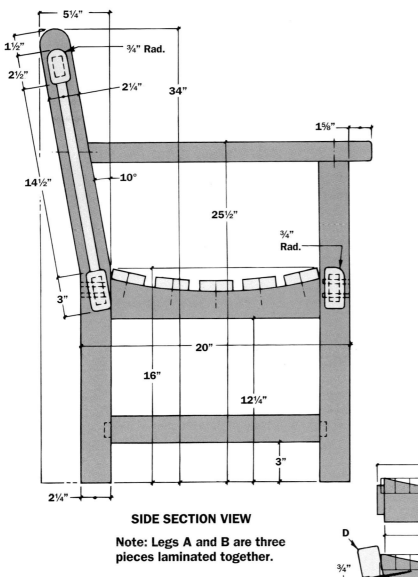

**SIDE SECTION VIEW**

5¼"
1½"
2½"
¾" Rad.
2¼"
34"
14½"
10°
25½"
1⅝"
¾" Rad.
3"
20"
16"
12¼"
3"
2¼"

**Note: Legs A and B are three pieces laminated together.**

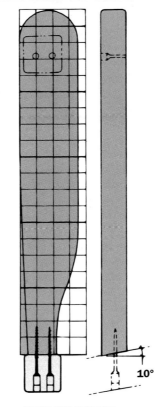

**ARM (C) DETAIL**

10°

## Cutting List

| Key | Pieces & Description | Size |
|---|---|---|
| A | 2 back legs | 2¼" x 5¼" x 34" |
| B | 2 front legs | 2¼" x 2¼" x 24" |
| C | 2 arms | 1½" x 3½" x 21" |
| D | 1 back seat rail | 1½" x 3" x 58½" |
| E | 1 front seat rail | 1½" x 3" x 58½" |
| F | 2 side seat rails | 1½" x 3" x 16½" |
| G | 2 seat supports | 1½" x 3" x 16¼" |
| H | 1 top rail | 1½" x 2½" x 58½" |
| J | 2 leg braces | 1½" x 2" x 16½" |
| K | 2 front rail braces | ¾" x 3½" x 3½" |
| L | 5 seat slats | ¾" x 2½" x 60" |
| M | 12 back slats | ¾" x 1½" x 14½" |
| N | 8 tenon pins | ¼"-diameter x 2" birch dowels |

## Shopping List

| Quantity | Item |
|---|---|
| 4 | 2" x 4" x 8-foot clear redwood |
| 6 | 1" x 6" x 8-foot clear redwood |
| 16 | #8 x 3" galvanized deck screws |
| 4 | #8 x 2" galvanized deck screws |
| 20 | 6d galvanized finish nails |
| 48 | ⁵⁄₁₆" x 1½" dowel pins |
| 1 | ¼" x 18" birch dowel rod |
| 1 qt. | wood preservative finish |

**Each Sq. = 1"**

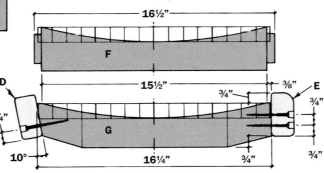

16½"
F
15½"
D
¾"
⅜"
E
¾"
G
¾"
¾"
10°
16¼"
¾"
¾"

**DETAIL OF SEAT RAIL (F) AND SUPPORT (G)**

## Building the legs and frame

- Cut both front legs (B) from a single lamination of two 1x6s. Each back leg (A) requires its own, heavier, lamination of three 1x6s.
- After the glue is dry, finish one edge of the glued-up piece flat and square with the face. You can get the best results using a jointer or plane, but you can hand-sand the edge.
- Cut out the legs, using either a band saw, a jigsaw with a long blade, or even a hand saw to cut the angled part of the back legs (see side section view, page 63).
- Cut out the curved parts — the seat supports (G), side seat rails (F), arms (C), front rail braces (K) — enlarging the patterns off the grids shown in the plan.

## Cutting the mortises and tenons

- Lay out and cut tenons on the ends of the rails (D, E, F, and H) and leg braces (J). You can cut these entirely with a hand saw, but you will get more accurate results by using a router to remove the waste from the "cheeks" (flat sides) of the tenon (Figure 2 on page 65).
- Cut the tenons to width with a small hand saw. Cut them a little oversize, then file them to fit the mortises.
- Pencil in the outlines of the mortises in the legs, drill ⅝-inch holes inside the outlines to clear out most of the waste, and then chisel out the sides and ends. A drill press or drill guide will ensure that your holes are vertical. Otherwise, you can hold a square against the wood to guide the drill.
- Test the fit of each tenon in its corresponding mortise, and file the tenon or chisel the mortise to adjust the fit. The tenon should be snug and hard to push in by hand, but easily tapped in (not pounded) with a mallet.

## Assembling the bench

- Drill holes for the plugs and clearance holes for the screws in the arms, front and back seat rails (D and E), front rail braces (K), and back legs (A). Drill dowel holes for the back slats (M), using a dowel jig (Figure 3 on page 65).
- Using a router and ³⁄₁₆-inch rounding-over bit, round the edges of the legs (A and B), the leg braces (J), the bottom edges of side seat rails (F), and the exposed edges of the front rail braces (K). Also round the edges of back slats (M), the top edges of the seat slats (L) including the ends, the bottom edges of the top rail (H), the top and bottom edges of back seat rail (D) and all edges of the front seat rail (E) except the front top edge. Rout slowly to avoid splintering as you cut. Finish sand all pieces.
- Assemble the end pieces (A, B, F, and J). Use waterproof glue, and clamp the joints tightly until the glue dries. Don't attach the arms yet.
- The mortises in the legs for the back and front rails will be blocked at the bottom by the tenons of the side rail you just glued. Chisel this little piece of tenon out, along with any squeezed-out glue.
- Assemble the back by gluing the slats into one rail first. Test fit the other rail, then glue it on.
- Using a ¾-inch rounding-over bit or a rasp and file, round over the top edges of the top rail (H) and the front top edge of part (E), the front rail.
- Finish sand the remaining rails, the arms (C), the seat supports (G), and the front rail braces (K).
- Glue and clamp together the rails, back assembly, and end assemblies. Drill pilot holes, then screw on the seat supports (G) and braces (K).
- After drilling pilot holes, nail on the seat slats (L) and set the nail heads below the surface. Drill the holes for the dowel pins that lock the tenons, and glue in the dowels. Attach the arms. Cut redwood plugs with a plug cutter and glue them over the screws attaching the arms.
- Give your bench a final sanding and apply a waterproof finish to protect the wood.

**Figure 1:** Fabricate the thick material for the back legs by laminating three thicknesses of ordinary ¾-inch lumber. Use a waterproof glue and align the edges of the boards.

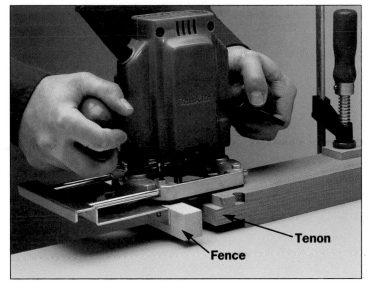

Tenon

Fence

**Figure 2:** Cut tenons with a router equipped with a straight bit and "outrigger" fence. Rout back and forth, starting at the end of the board. The fence will ensure an accurate shoulder.

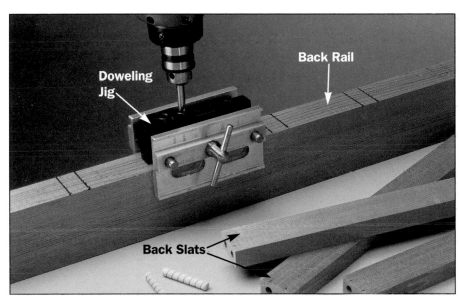

Doweling Jig

Back Rail

Back Slats

**Figure 3:** Dowel the back slats to the back rails. Don't glue them all at once, though. Glue the slats to one rail first, let the glue dry, then glue on the other rail.

Routing a splintery wood like redwood, you may have trouble with the wood chipping out along the length of a cut, especially when you're rounding over the edges. You can reduce tearing out by routing very slowly, using a sharp bit, and cutting in several shallow passes until you reach the desired depth.

Your clamps might not be long enough for the final assembly of the bench. If you have some shorter pipe clamps, you can hook two together or buy a threaded plumbing coupler to screw the two pipes together. Another approach is to extend the reach of a single clamp with a long piece of plywood. Screw a block of wood onto it at one end to bear against the bench, and cut a hole in the other end of the plywood to house the "foot" end of the clamp (the one without the handle).

# Small Structures

Both children and adults need places and spaces where they can pursue their own kinds of activities. These four projects provide space for boisterous play, quiet reading, and storage of tools and equipment.

# Arbor and Swing

## What You Need

Circular saw with rip fence

Jigsaw

Electric drill with twist bits

Post-hole digger

Hammer

Hacksaw

Screwdriver

Chisels

Hand saw

Carpenter's level

Sandpaper or drum sander

Resorcinol glue

Exterior wood putty

Here's a do-it-yourself arbor with plenty of style and just the right amount of shade. And it can be home for fragrant roses, delicate morning glories, or just about any climbing plant. An old-fashioned porch swing is the arbor's perfect complement.

Feel free to consider this plan as a starting point for your own design. It can be made deeper or wider to house a table and chairs or bench underneath. Instead of the painted, pressure-treated lumber shown on these pages, you could build your arbor from unpainted redwood or cedar and leave it to weather, or you might want to give it a clear water-repellent finish. Stay away from dark paints, however, because they absorb heat from the sun, making the surfaces hot enough to burn plants.

The swing is made almost completely from 1x4s, joined with screws and bolts. For strength, build this swing from Philippine mahogany or oak. You can also use pressure-treated yellow pine, though in that case you should construct the frame that supports the seat and back from 1-inch, rather than ¾-inch-thick lumber. In all, you will need 75 feet of 1x4 boards.

The bolts for the swing are used not only to make it easier to build. Porch swings are designed to flex and bend. Unless it is built of gargantuan timbers, a moving swing loaded down with 300 pounds of people has to flex or it will break. The single bolts holding this swing at critical joints allow that safe movement.

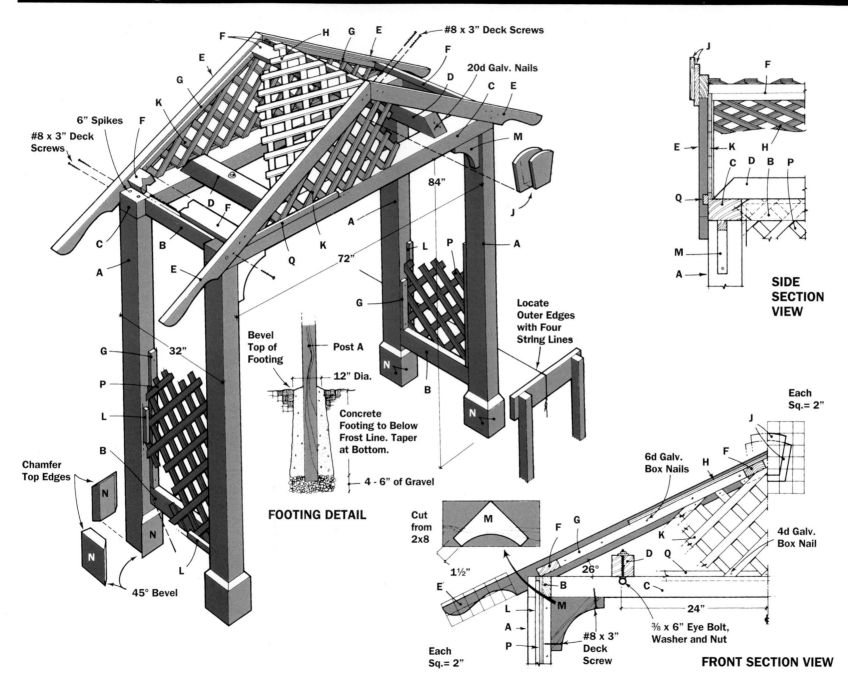

F H G E

#8 x 3" Deck Screws

E

G

20d Galv. Nails

K

F

6" Spikes F

D

#8 x 3" Deck Screws

C E

M

84"

D F

J

C

B

A

E

A

K

A

Q

P L P A

72"

G

B

Locate Outer Edges with Four String Lines

N

G 32"

P

Bevel Top of Footing

Post A

N

L

12" Dia.

B

Chamfer Top Edges

N

Concrete Footing to Below Frost Line. Taper at Bottom.

N

N

4 - 6" of Gravel

45° Bevel

**FOOTING DETAIL**

J

F

Cut from 2x8

M

6d Galv. Box Nails

H

F

Each Sq.= 2"

G

K

4d Galv. Box Nail

1½"

F G

D Q

26°

E

B

C

L

M

A

24"

P

Each Sq.= 2"

#8 x 3" Deck Screw

⅜ x 6" Eye Bolt, Washer and Nut

**FRONT SECTION VIEW**

J

F

E

K

H

Q

C D B P

M

A

**SIDE SECTION VIEW**

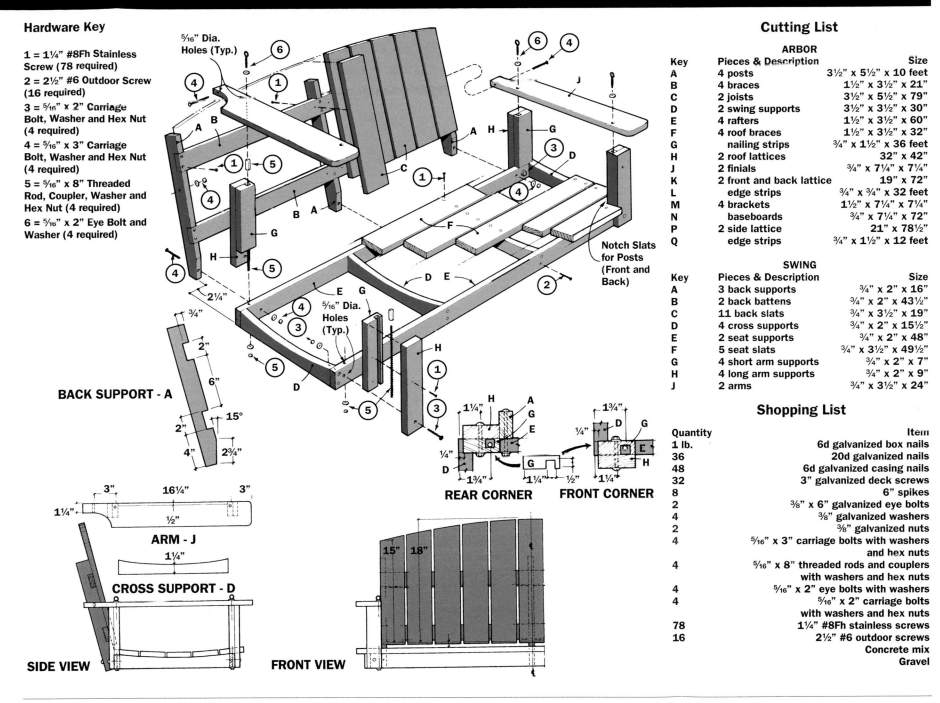

**Hardware Key**

1 = 1¼" #8Fh Stainless Screw (78 required)

2 = 2½" #6 Outdoor Screw (16 required)

3 = ⁵⁄₁₆" x 2" Carriage Bolt, Washer and Hex Nut (4 required)

4 = ⁵⁄₁₆" x 3" Carriage Bolt, Washer and Hex Nut (4 required)

5 = ⁵⁄₁₆" x 8" Threaded Rod, Coupler, Washer and Hex Nut (4 required)

6 = ⁵⁄₁₆" x 2" Eye Bolt and Washer (4 required)

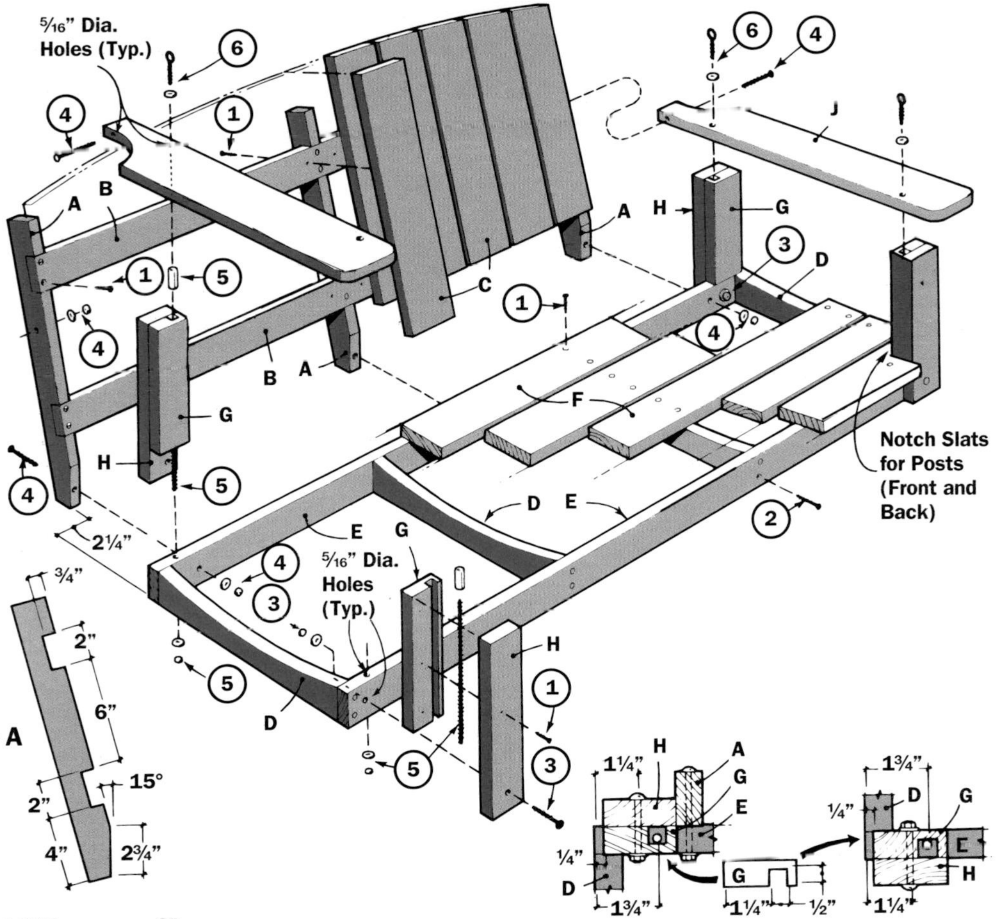
⁵⁄₁₆" Dia. Holes (Typ.)
⁵⁄₁₆" Dia. Holes (Typ.)
Notch Slats for Posts (Front and Back)
2¼"
¾"
2"
6"
15°
2"
4"
2¾"
BACK SUPPORT - A
1¼"
¼"
1¾"
1¼"
½"
REAR CORNER
1¾"
¼"
1¼"
FRONT CORNER

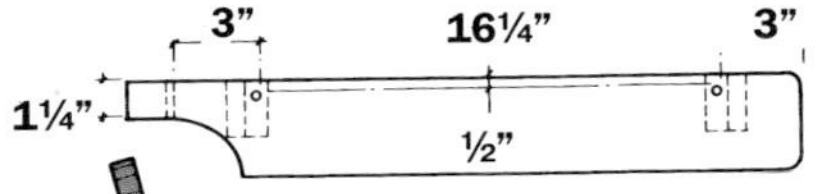
3"
16¼"
3"
1¼"
½"

ARM - J

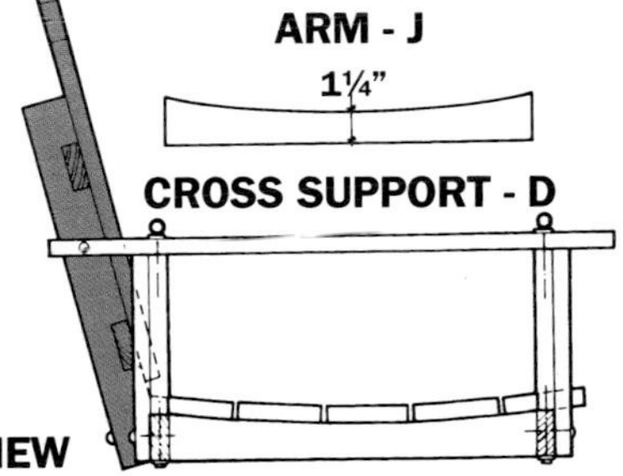
1¼"
CROSS SUPPORT - D

SIDE VIEW

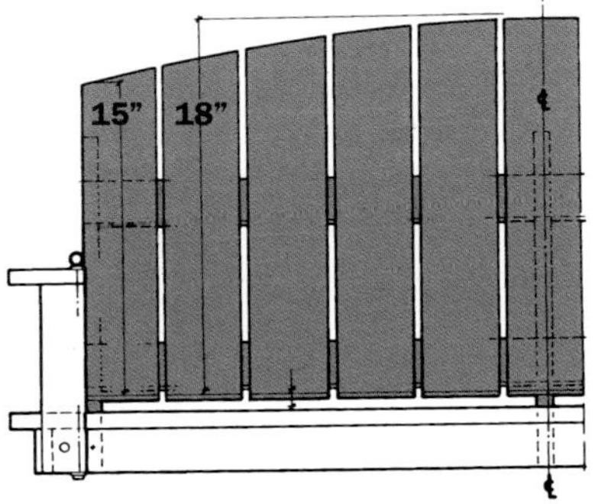
15"
18"

FRONT VIEW

## Cutting List

**ARBOR**

| Key | Pieces & Description | Size |
|---|---|---|
| A | 4 posts | 3½" x 5½" x 10 feet |
| B | 4 braces | 1½" x 3½" x 21" |
| C | 2 joists | 3½" x 5½" x 79" |
| D | 2 swing supports | 3½" x 3½" x 30" |
| E | 4 rafters | 1½" x 3½" x 60" |
| F | 4 roof braces | 1½" x 3½" x 32" |
| G | nailing strips | ¾" x 1½" x 36 feet |
| H | 2 roof lattices | 32" x 42" |
| J | 2 finials | ¾" x 7¼" x 7¼" |
| K | 2 front and back lattice | 19" x 72" |
| L | edge strips | ¾" x ¾" x 32 feet |
| M | 4 brackets | 1½" x 7¼" x 7¼" |
| N | baseboards | ¾" x 7¼" x 72" |
| P | 2 side lattice | 21" x 78½" |
| Q | edge strips | ¾" x 1½" x 12 feet |

**SWING**

| Key | Pieces & Description | Size |
|---|---|---|
| A | 3 back supports | ¾" x 2" x 16" |
| B | 2 back battens | ¾" x 2" x 43½" |
| C | 11 back slats | ¾" x 3½" x 19" |
| D | 4 cross supports | ¾" x 2" x 15½" |
| E | 2 seat supports | ¾" x 2" x 48" |
| F | 5 seat slats | ¾" x 3½" x 49½" |
| G | 4 short arm supports | ¾" x 2" x 7" |
| H | 4 long arm supports | ¾" x 2" x 9" |
| J | 2 arms | ¾" x 3½" x 24" |

## Shopping List

| Quantity | Item |
|---|---|
| 1 lb. | 6d galvanized box nails |
| 36 | 20d galvanized nails |
| 48 | 6d galvanized casing nails |
| 32 | 3" galvanized deck screws |
| 8 | 6" spikes |
| 2 | ⅜" x 6" galvanized eye bolts |
| 4 | ⅜" galvanized washers |
| 2 | ⅜" galvanized nuts |
| 4 | ⁵⁄₁₆" x 3" carriage bolts with washers and hex nuts |
| 4 | ⁵⁄₁₆" x 8" threaded rods and couplers with washers and hex nuts |
| 4 | ⁵⁄₁₆" x 2" eye bolts with washers |
| 4 | ⁵⁄₁₆" x 2" carriage bolts with washers and hex nuts |
| 78 | 1¼" #8Fh stainless screws |
| 16 | 2½" #6 outdoor screws |
| | Concrete mix |
| | Gravel |

If you want the arbor in a sunny spot, be careful about what direction it faces. Avoid facing it into the afternoon summer sun.

Some perennial vines you might plant for the arbor, such as wisteria, are heavy and pull at their supports; use slats of 1x2 or 2x2 instead of lattice, and set your posts in concrete.

A common mistake is to enclose the entire bottom of a post in concrete. Water will collect between the concrete and the post and rot the wood. If you use concrete, cover the bottom of the hole with gravel first. Set and plumb the post, then pour the concrete around it.

If you encounter a large rock while digging the post holes, be prepared to move your site.

You can use chain or rope to hang your swing. Chain is much easier to work with, although it's not as handsome as rope. If you use rope, avoid nylon unless it specifically claims to be nonstretching. A book on knots can help you make the loops and eyes.

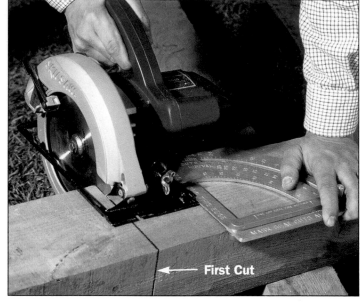

**Figure 1:** Cut tops of posts with two passes of your circular saw. Be sure to use a square to guide the saw, and practice on scrap first. Caution: wear a dust mask when cutting and sanding treated lumber.

**Figure 2:** Tamp gravel around the bottom of the post, then brace it to stay plumb and against the layout line. Fill hole with concrete.

## Building the arbor

- Lay out four string lines so they cross where the outer edges of the posts (A) will be located (see plans). Check the corner-to-corner measurements to be sure the lines are at right angles. Dig the post holes.
- Cut the four posts (A) to length (Figure 1). Sand them to get a smooth paint finish. Nail on a pair of braces at ground level to hold the posts at the right height (Figure 2).
- Line the holes with 2 to 3 inches of gravel, tamp it down firmly with a 2x4, and set the posts into the holes. Add or remove gravel so all the posts are the same height.

- Make sure the posts are plumb, then nail on two diagonal braces per post. The braces should be nailed from adjacent sides of the post to stakes in the ground.
- When the posts are plumb, the sides lined up, and the tops at the same height, add an additional 3 to 4 inches of gravel and tamp it down (Figure 2). Mix concrete and pour it into the post holes. Allow it to cure for several days.

**Paper Template**

**Figure 3:** Cut rafter ends with a jigsaw, using a paper template to get the shape.

**Figure 4:** A sanding drum chucked in an electric drill speeds sanding.

**Figure 5:** Support lattice panels with scrap plywood for cutting. A carbide blade will cut through the staples without dulling.

**Figure 6:** Paint lattice panels with a paint sprayer. You can paint on the ground or paint the whole arbor after completion.

## Constructing the roof frame

- Measure from post to post, then cut the joists (C) to length. Pre-drill holes, then drive spikes almost all the way through the joists while they are still on the ground, then hoist them up and spike them to the posts. Cut the swing supports (D) and nail them to the joists.
- Attach the edge strips (L), nailing strips (G), braces (B). Cut the side lattice (P) and attach (Figure 5).
- Make the angled cuts at the peak of the rafters (E) and cut the scrolled ends with a jigsaw (Figure 3). Sand with a drum sander chucked in a drill (Figure 4).

- Cut the remaining parts of the roof and assemble it, except the front lattice (K).
- Lift the roof onto the posts, center it, and screw it on. Nail on the lattice and edging strip (L).
- Cut the corner brackets (M), finial (J), and baseboard (N), then nail them.
- If you are using treated lumber, let it weather for a month before painting. If using redwood or cedar, brush or spray on several coats of water-repellent preservative (Figure 6).

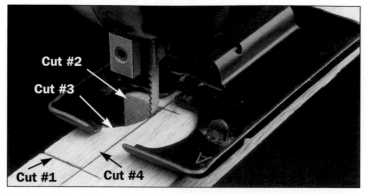

**Figure 7:** Cut 1x4 notches in the back supports using a jigsaw. The easiest way is to make four cuts in the order shown.

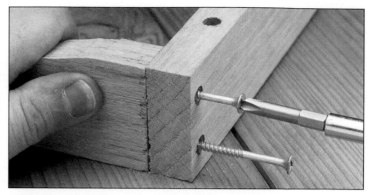

**Figure 8:** Frame pieces are held together with long rustproof deck screws. Fill screw holes with exterior putty or wooden plugs.

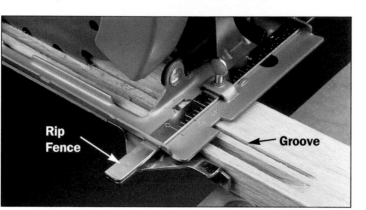

**Figure 9:** Cut a groove by making several passes in a long board with a circular saw, then cut off what you need. Use a rip fence.

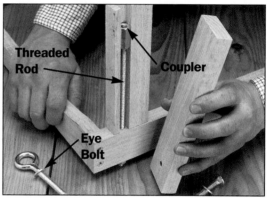

**Figure 10:** Two-part arm supports house the threaded rod that transfers weight from the seat to the eye bolts in the arms.

## Building the swing

• Cut the parts for the back (A, B, and C), leaving the back slats (C) extra long. Cut lap joints in the vertical supports (A, Figure 7), and cut their angled ends. Drill all holes.
• Screw together parts A, B, and C (Figure 8).
• Draw the curve for the top of the back and cut it with a jigsaw. Sand the ends smooth.
• Cut parts D and E for the seat and screw them together.
• Use a circular saw and rip guide to cut the groove in part G (Figure 9), then cut off the lengths you need. Glue and screw it to part H, then drill bolt holes.

• Cut the arms with a jigsaw; sand the edges with a drum sander in an electric drill and drill the bolt holes.
• Cut the threaded rod and file the cut ends.
• Bolt the back, then the arm support (G and H), to the seat. Screw the couplers to the threaded rod, pass it through the supports, and attach the bolt and washer under the seat (Figure 10). Bolt on the arms and tighten the screw eyes.
• Cut the seat slats (F) and screw them on.
• Sand, then soak the entire swing with several coats of water-repellent preservative. Then spray-paint or stain it.

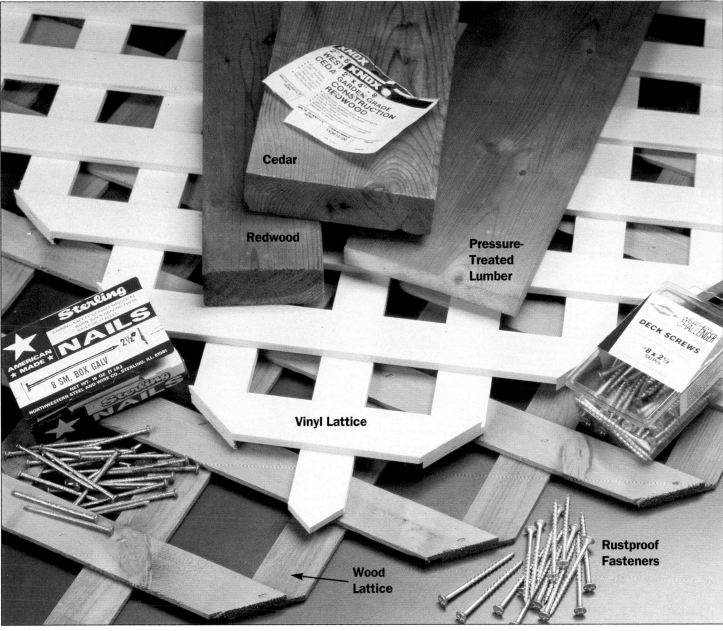

Cedar

Redwood

Pressure-
Treated
Lumber

Vinyl Lattice

Wood
Lattice

Rustproof
Fasteners

## Defeating the Weather

Whatever outdoor construction you are doing, here are a few tips on buying supplies and comments on some of the materials shown at left.

Use noncorroding fasteners. Galvanized bolts, stainless fasteners, and rustproof deck screws prevent the loss of strength, but also assume that rust streaks won't seep through paint and stain natural finishes.

Use water-repellent preservatives. Apply them liberally, especially on end grain, even if the wood is going to be painted.

Use waterproof resorcinol glue. This two-part purple glue is the only one truly suitable for outdoor use.

Keep up the maintenance. Repaint in the spring when temperatures are warming up and plants haven't yet covered the arbor.

Consider using vinyl lattice. It requires no maintenance.

You have many choices of materials to use to make your arbor and swing better able to stand up to the weather. Cedar and redwood are naturally resistant to rot, while pressure-treated lumber can survive many years exposed to the elements. Vinyl lattice is virtually maintenance-free. Wood lattice is available with pressure-treatment, but if you buy untreated lattice, be sure to give it a good coat of paint or water-repellent preservative. Rustproof nails and screws prevent ugly rust stains on your wood.

# Do-It-Yourself Gazebo

A gazebo for the do-it-yourselfer should be attractive, durable, and economical to build. It should be prefabricated, so you can put it up with a minimum of sawing and hammering. Finally, it should be adaptable.

Three features set this gazebo apart:

**Prefab walls.** The walls can be built ahead of time in the comfort of your workshop or garage. Rafters, roof blocking, and other parts can be precut, too. You can do a third of the work unhindered by the elements.

**Easy assembly.** All gazebos have a lot of angles — it's part of their appeal — but some designs require you to be part mathematician, part carpenter, and part juggler to build them. With this design, once the corners have been cut, the problem of building an eight-sided, odd-angled structure from four-sided lumber is solved. The walls and roof are self-spacing, self-bracing, and self-centering.

**Flexible design.** This gazebo is designed to be redesigned. The structure shown on these pages is a screened version with cedar siding and shingles, but yours could just as easily be a three-season model with windows or an open-air gazebo with fancy Victorian fretwork and gingerbread trim. The fill-in-the-blanks design makes modification simple — no architectural degree is required.

An advanced do-it-yourselfer should have no problem building this gazebo, and an intermediate do-it-yourselfer with determination will be able to rise to the occasion. For some additional information on what you'll need, turn to page 78.

# Planning and startup

Patience and moderate skill with power tools are the real prerequisites along with persistence, since the gazebo takes about 80 hours to build. A few parts of the project — setting up the walls and placing the rafters, in particular — require two people. Other jobs, such as installing the tongue-and-groove boards for the roof and shingling, will go faster with one person on the ground cutting and another on the roof measuring and nailing.

Gazebo construction can be divided into four stages: (1) building the walls and erecting them; (2) framing and sheathing the roof; (3) shingling, and (4) building the screens, doors, and miscellaneous trim pieces. Each step can be completed by two people in a weekend of serious work.

A table saw is mandatory for this project. You don't need a full-size model — a small, 8¼-inch benchtop saw will work just fine. Other must-haves are a router with a 3⅜-inch rabbeting bit, a circular saw and drill, and a belt sander to clean up the grading stamps and surface flaws you'll find on your lumber. Since there are many angled cuts in this gazebo, you may find it handy to guide your circular saw with a protractor-style saw guide, available at most home centers and hardware stores. A cordless screwdriver or drill will come in handy, too. A sturdy stepladder, a short extension ladder, a pair of roofing brackets and basic hand tools round out your tool needs.

The gazebo shown here was built of cedar (see the materials list on page 81) and finished with a clear water-resistant coating. If you paint your gazebo, you could build it from treated lumber, pine tongue-and-groove roof sheathing, and asphalt shingles. Just be sure to pick out the best material you can get — treated lumber can be pretty warped and ugly. (Whatever siding you use, be sure to nail it securely, because the base wall siding gives the gazebo much of its rigidity.)

If you plan to use your gazebo to escape from the hubbub of home, locate it as far from your house as you can. But stay within the property-line setback distances determined by your local zoning and building codes. Check with the building inspector.

If you plan to use your gazebo more for outdoor entertaining, you may want to locate it closer to your house. In that case, watch out for overhead electrical lines or views you may obstruct; the gazebo will be almost 12 feet tall.

The gazebo can be erected on either a concrete slab or a wood deck. (In cold climes, slabs and decks must rest on concrete footings that are below the frost line. Check with local building authorities for the required depth for footings in your area.) This one was built on a simple 17x17-foot deck that provides extra room for outdoor lounging. If you build on a deck, be sure to provide adequate support under the gazebo corners and put aluminum screen under the deck boards or across the underlying joists to help keep your gazebo pest-free.

## RIDGE CAPS

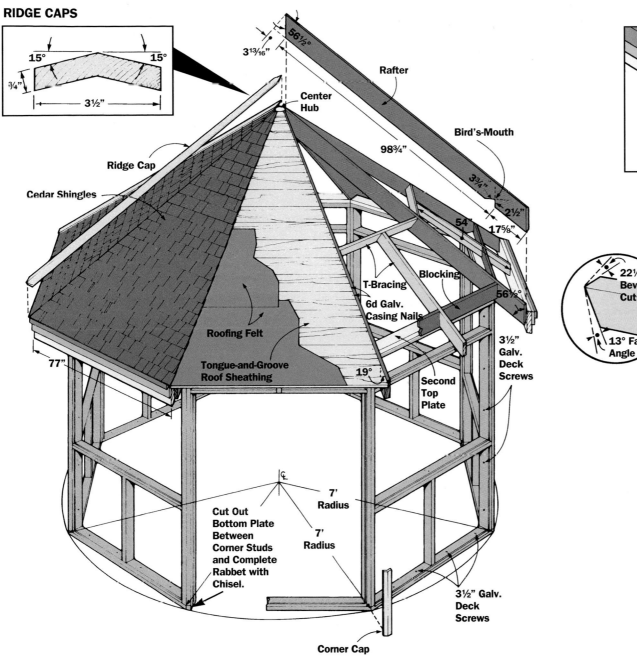

15° 15°

¾"

3½"

56½°

3¹³⁄₁₆"

**Rafter**

**Center Hub**

**Bird's-Mouth**

98¾"

3¾"

2½"

54"

17⅝"

**Ridge Cap**

**Cedar Shingles**

**T-Bracing**

**Blocking**

**6d Galv. Casing Nails**

**Roofing Felt**

**Tongue-and-Groove Roof Sheathing**

56½°

3½" Galv. Deck Screws

**Second Top Plate**

77"

19°

**Cut Out Bottom Plate Between Corner Studs and Complete Rabbet with Chisel.**

7' Radius

7' Radius

3½" Galv. Deck Screws

**Corner Cap**

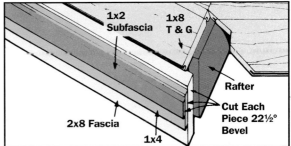

1x2 Subfascia

1x8 T & G

**Rafter**

2x8 Fascia

1x4

**Cut Each Piece 22½° Bevel**

## T-BRACING

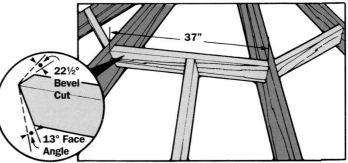

37"

22½° Bevel Cut

13° Face Angle

## BLOCKING

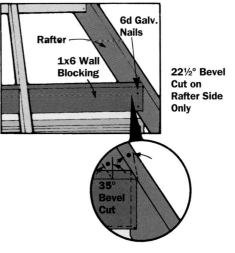

**Rafter**

6d Galv. Nails

1x6 Wall Blocking

22½° Bevel Cut on Rafter Side Only

35° Bevel Cut

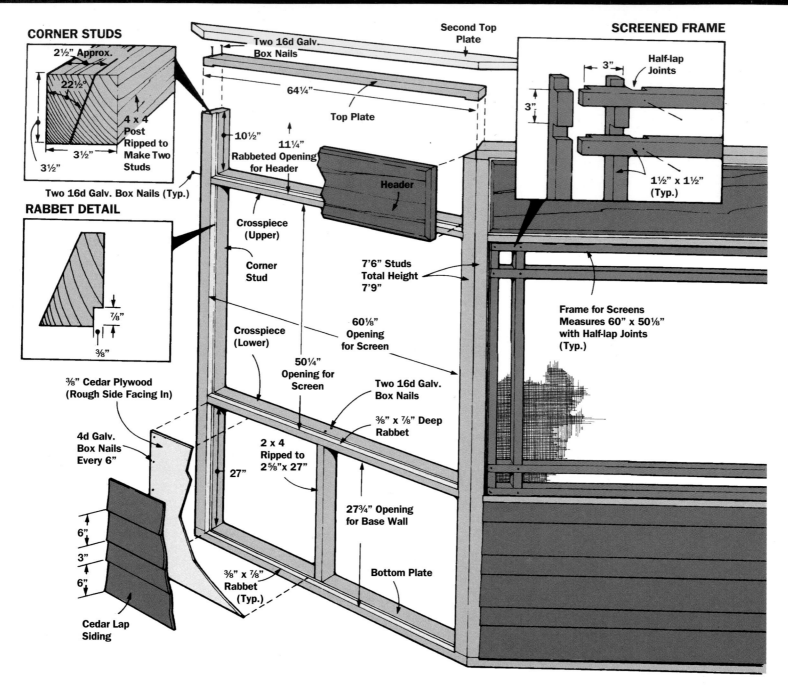

**CORNER STUDS**

2½" Approx.

22½°

4 x 4 Post Ripped to Make Two Studs

3½"

3½"

Two 16d Galv. Box Nails (Typ.)

**RABBET DETAIL**

⅞"

⅜"

⅜" Cedar Plywood (Rough Side Facing In)

4d Galv. Box Nails Every 6"

6"

3"

6"

Cedar Lap Siding

Two 16d Galv. Box Nails

Second Top Plate

64¼"

Top Plate

10½"

11¼" Rabbeted Opening for Header

Header

Crosspiece (Upper)

Corner Stud

7'6" Studs Total Height 7'9"

60⅛" Opening for Screen

Crosspiece (Lower)

50¼" Opening for Screen

Two 16d Galv. Box Nails

⅜" x ⅞" Deep Rabbet

27"

2 x 4 Ripped to 2⅝" x 27"

27¾" Opening for Base Wall

⅜" x ⅞" Rabbet (Typ.)

Bottom Plate

**SCREENED FRAME**

3"

Half-lap Joints

3"

1½" x 1½" (Typ.)

Frame for Screens Measures 60" x 50⅛" with Half-lap Joints (Typ.)

# Screen Door Construction

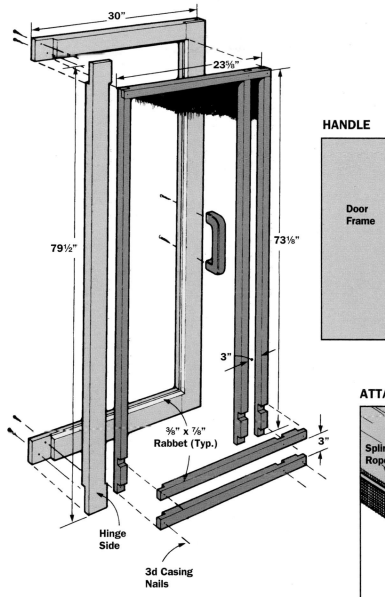

**30"**

**23⅝"**

**79½"**

**73⅛"**

**3"**

**3"**

**⅜" x ⅞"**
**Rabbet (Typ.)**

**Hinge**
**Side**

**3d Casing**
**Nails**

## HANDLE

**Door**
**Frame**

**3½"**

**2"**

**8"**

## ATTACHING SCREEN

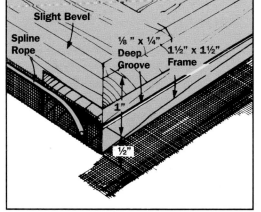

**Slight Bevel**

**Spline**
**Rope**

**⅛" x ¼"**
**Deep**
**Groove**

**1½" x 1½"**
**Frame**

**1"**

**½"**

## Materials List

| Item | Quantity |
| --- | --- |
| 35 | 2" x 4" x 16-foot cedar |
| 9 | 2" x 6" x 10-foot cedar |
| 4 | 2" x 8" x 14-foot cedar |
| 4 | 2" x 12" x 12-foot cedar |
| 8 | 4" x 4" x 8-foot cedar |
| 2 | 4" x 4" x 12-foot cedar |
| 5 | ⅜" x 4-foot x 9-foot rough-sawn cedar plywood |
| 120 linear feet | 4" clear lap siding |
| 120 linear feet | 8" clear lap siding |
| 4 | 1" x 2" x 14-foot cedar |
| 4 | 1" x 4" x 14-foot cedar |
| 3 | 1" x 6" x 16-foot cedar |
| 32 | 1" x 8" x 16-foot WP4 #3 tongue-and-groove cedar |
| 3 squares | 16" cedar shingles |
| 1 roll | 15-lb. roofing felt |
| 50 linear feet | fiberglass screen (5 feet wide) |
| 180 linear feet | ⅛" spline |
| 2 lbs. | 4d galvanized box nails |
| 1 lb. | 10d galvanized box nails |
| 5 lbs. | 16d galvanized nails |
| 5 lbs. | 1" galvanized roofing nails |
| 1 lb. | 3½" galvanized deck screws |
| 16 | 1¼" galvanized deck screws |

Follow the dimensions given for the walls and rafters exactly. Measure other parts, like the blocking above the walls and the T-bracing in the roof, for a tight fit and symmetry rather than rigidly adhering to the dimensions provided here.

Build one wall first, from start to finish, so you understand the techniques and tolerances involved. Then forge ahead and build the other seven walls in an assembly-line fashion. The only wall that is different is the one with the doors; it doesn't have a lower crosspiece.

Rome wasn't built in a day, and your gazebo won't be either, no matter how fast you work. Therefore, work carefully. Take the time to hand pick lumber that is straight and clean. The framework is exposed, so any bent nails, water stains, or accidental hammer marks will show.

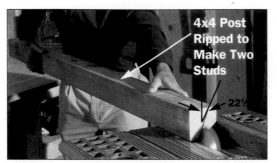

**Figure 1:** Cut two corner studs by ripping a 4x4 in half at 22½ degrees. It's a deep cut, so make one pass, rotate the 4x4, then make a second.

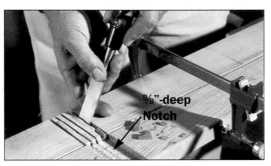

**Figure 2:** Cut notches in the corner studs that the crosspieces will fit into. Make several cuts with a circular saw, then chisel out the waste.

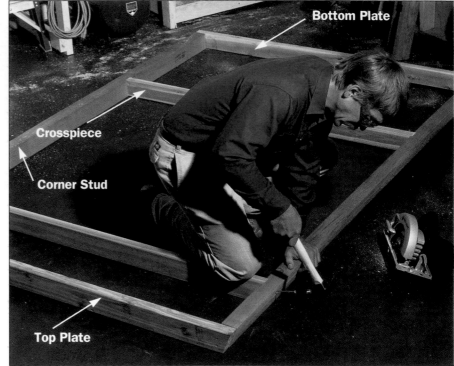

**Figure 3:** Nail top and bottom plates to the corner studs, then nail the crosspieces into their notches. Take care not to bow out the corner studs.

## Building the walls

• Make pairs of corner studs out of 4x4s. Trim the 4x4s to length, then rip them lengthwise (Figure 1) at a 22½-degree angle with your table saw fence set to produce two identical halves. The fence will be about 2½ inches from the blade, but to get the position exactly right, run a short piece of 4x4 scrap through the saw, rotate it, and run it through again — the cuts should meet exactly. Slight ridges that appear on the cut faces can be planed or sanded down. This ripping is easy as long as you have selected straight 4x4s.

• As you work, keep the ripped 4x4s in pairs. Clamp the pairs of ripped studs back to back, and notch them to accommodate the two crosspieces that will form the window openings (Figure 2).

• Cut the remaining wall pieces, and nail the walls together with 16d galvanized nails (Figure 3). Keep nails away from where the rabbets will be cut (Figure 4). Make certain the 22½-degree cuts on the plates align perfectly with the edges of the corner studs.

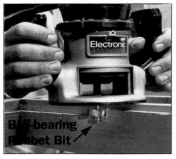

**Figure 4:** Rout a rabbet on the edge of each of the three wall openings. Make a shallow first pass, then a second deep one.

**Figure 5:** Square the corners of the rabbet using a sharp chisel. Then check the edges of the wall for square.

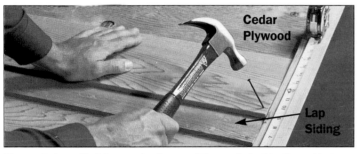

**Figure 6:** Install siding at the base of the wall, inside the rabbet. Cedar plywood goes in first, then lap siding is nailed on top of it.

**Figure 7:** Install a 2x12 header in the rabbet at the top of the wall, after beveling its edges with a router. Secure it with galvanized deck screws on all sides.

- Insert and fasten the two crosspieces. Make sure they're not forcing the corner studs to bow in or out. The wall where the doors go doesn't have a lower crosspiece, but you should build it with a bottom plate, which will be cut after the walls are erected.
- Use your router to cut a rabbet in the header space, the screen opening space, and the base wall space (plan detail and Figure 4). Use a ball-bearing-guided rabbeting bit, making two passes at increasing depths, the first to $\frac{7}{16}$ inch, the second to $\frac{7}{8}$ inch. Move your router clockwise within each opening and keep the base of the router flat.

When you're finished routing, use a chisel to make the rabbet corners square (Figure 5).
- Make certain your wall sections are square by measuring diagonally from corner to corner, then shifting the top of the wall to the left or right until the measurements are equal. Brace them in place.
- Install the $\frac{3}{8}$-inch cedar plywood, rough-sawn side facing in, and the cedar lap siding (Figure 6).
- Cut the 2x12 headers, bevel the outside edges with a router, and nail them to the wall (Figure 7).
- Repeat these steps for all eight of your walls.

**Figure 8:** Fasten wall sections together with 3½-inch galvanized screws. If the studs don't meet perfectly, clamp them tight first.

**Figure 9:** Set up wall sections, fastening them to the deck and to each other. A 14-foot-diameter circle acts as a guide for the corners.

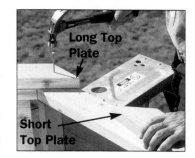

**Figure 10:** Nail on top plates to tie the tops of the walls together. The long top plate (71 ¼ inches between long points) overlaps the corner, and shorter ones (61 ⅜ inches between long points) fill in between.

## Erecting the walls

- Now you're ready to carry the walls outside and stand them up. To determine where to set the corners of your walls, draw a circle with a radius of 7 feet on your deck or slab. Mark off the locations of the gazebo corners at 64 ¼-inch intervals around this circle. When the layout is complete you should see a 14-foot-diameter circle with a perfect octagon inside, each of the octagon's eight points just kissing the circumference of the circle. It will pay to do this carefully because perfect layout means easy alignment.
- Erect the first wall. Its corners should rest on the corners of the octagon. Screw down the bottom plate with 3 ½-inch deck screws and brace the wall temporarily.

- Screw down the second wall, then screw the two walls' corner studs together (Figure 8). You may need to draw the walls together with clamps first. Install the remaining six walls in a similar fashion (Figure 9).
- Cut out the bottom plate of the door section only after all eight walls are screwed together.
- There are two types of top plates, short and long. Use 10d galvanized nails to install the four long top plates on alternating wall sections so they overlap the joint between the walls and tie the tops of the walls together (Figure 10). Fill in the remaining spaces with the four shorter top plates cut to fit the spaces.

**Figure 11:** Cut the roof hub from a 2-foot length of 4x4 cedar. Since the hub is short, make the four angled cuts, then trim it to length.

**Figure 12:** Cut one rafter, then check the length and angles. Cut the remaining seven rafters using the first as a pattern.

**Figure 13:** Join the hub and two rafters into an inverted "V". Lift and center it over two opposite corners, then toenail with two 16d galvanized nails.

## Framing the roof

- Cut the center hub for the rafters as shown in Figure 11. For safety, start with a 2-foot length of 4x4, bevel the sides at 45 degrees, then cut it to its final 6½-inch length.
- Cut a 33½ degree angle at each end of the rafters. A protractor will give you this angle. The distance from the bird's mouth to the rafter end must be exactly 98¾ inches.
- Cut one rafter very carefully, check it, then use it as a template for the remaining seven (Figure 12).
- On the ground, fasten two rafters and the hub to form a giant "V". Screw through the top point of each rafter into the hub, then put a second screw through the bottom of the hub into each rafter. Raise this inverted "V" onto the walls with the help of an assistant (Figure 13),

centering the rafters directly over the gazebo corners.
- Toenail each rafter to the top plate with two 16d nails.
- Install the remaining rafters in a similar fashion. Screw each one through the top point into the hub. Push the wall corners in or out slightly, so that all the rafters fit snugly.
- Install the 2x8 fascia boards connecting the outside tails of the rafters. With your circular saw base tilted to 22½ degrees, cut each 2x8 to fit as you work around the octagon.
- Install the two-piece T-braces (Figure 14) that lie within each pie-shaped roof section; measure and cut for a good fit, using the dimensions shown in the plan as guidelines only. The part of the T-brace that intersects the fascia simply rests on the top plate.

**Figure 14:** Install roof bracing, which is in the shape of a "T", after nailing 2x8 fascia boards to the ends of the rafters.

**Figure 15:** Install roof decking one section at a time. Let the boards run long at one end, then trim them after nailing. Note the roof brackets used for comfort and safety.

## Sheathing the roof

- Use simple roof brackets (Figure 15) to provide good footing when working on the roof. There are few worse pastimes than lying in bed with a broken leg, staring out at your almost-completed gazebo. Be careful.
- To install the tongue-and-groove roof sheathing, start at the bottom edge of the roof. Cut the first board with a 19-degree angle on the one end (see plan) and nail it on so the angled end extends halfway across one rafter and the other end runs a couple of inches beyond the other rafter. Drive two 6d galvanized casing nails through the roof sheathing at each end and at the T-bracing.
- Work up to the roof peak, trimming the long ends to the center of the rafter from time to time.

- After you've finished sheathing the first pie-shaped section, you'll have a rough idea of the length of each roof board. Your ground crew can cut seven more sets of boards to these approximate dimensions with a 19-degree angle on one end. By cutting all the longest boards first, then taking the cutoffs and turning them into intermediate-length and shorter boards, you can cut around bad knots and make economical use of your material.
- Install the 1x4 and 1x2 subfascia boards (see plan). They're not essential, but they do provide a drip edge to keep rain off the main fascia and they look nice, too.

**Figure 16:** Lay cedar shingles over the tarpaper. Use 1 inch nails to attach the shingles so the points won't come through on the inside of the gazebo.

Ridge Cap

**Figure 17:** Screw ridge caps along the roof seams with galvanized deck screws. Ridge caps are cut at a 15-degree angle from 4x4 cedar posts (see plan detail, page 79).

## Shingling

- Install 15-pound roofing felt (tarpaper), beginning from the bottom and working upwards. Make sure the end of each strip of felt overlaps the rafter joints, and maintain a minimum 6-inch overlap from one course to the next as you work toward the peak.
- Cedar shingles were used here to match the rest of the gazebo (Figure 16), but asphalt or fiberglass shingles would work just as well. (They'd go on faster and save you money, too.) When you nail on the shingles, be sure your nails don't go all the way through the roof sheathing or you'll be haunted by the ugly sight of hundreds of little nail tips staring at you from inside the gazebo. One-inch galvanized nails were used with these shingles.

- Follow the manufacturer's directions for nailing the shingles. At the ridges, cut the edges of the shingles at an angle of 19 degrees.
- Cut the ridge caps from cedar 4x4s, using a table saw and two intersecting cuts (plan detail, page 79). This is the same procedure shown in Figure 19 on page 88 for cutting the corner caps but the blade angle is set at 15 degrees to cut the roof ridge caps.
- Taper one end of each ridge cap by cutting a 19-degree angle that extends about 5¾ inches down each side (Figure 17).
- Lay a cone of felt at the peak, over the shingles and under the ridge caps. Fasten the caps with galvanized deck screws.

A cedar gazebo will naturally weather to a mellow, silvery gray. If you prefer to preserve its fresh cedar color, apply a clear exterior finish. The interior cedar roof boards will hold their color for a long time, but a coat of your exterior finish or Danish oil will make them glow. Just remember that you'll have to reapply the finishes every few years.

Fiberglass screen deteriorates in sunlight in 10 to 15 years, so you may want to remove your screens and store them inside over the winter.

**Figure 18:** Use blocking to cover gaps between the wall top and the bottom of the sheathing. Install two blocks per wall.

**Figure 19:** All eight corner caps are cut on the table saw from a single 2x6.

**Figure 20:** Install corner caps where the walls join.

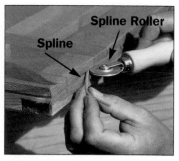

**Figure 21:** Screens consist of a wood frame, grooved around the edges, and a vinyl spline to hold the screen tightly.

**Figure 22:** Screw a finial to the hub and you're done.

## Adding screens, doors, and odds-and-ends

- To cover the 4-inch gap between the top of the wall and the bottom of the roof sheathing, fit in short pieces of 1x6 blocking (Figure 18). Then add the corner caps (Figures 19 and 20), which cover any gaps at the corners and give a finished appearance.
- Build the screens using a system of 2x2s and half-lap joints (plan detail, page 80). A radial arm saw with a dado blade works well for making the half-lap joints, but the score-and-chisel method will also work. Simpler screens can be made by eliminating the decorative inner set of 2x2s.
- Use a table saw with an ⅛-inch-wide blade to cut the screen spline groove (Figure 21) around the outer edges. Fiberglass screen is the easiest for a beginner to stretch and work with. Staples will secure the corners and keep the spline in place.
- Build the double doors shown in the plan, or buy ready-made 30-inch screen doors and cut an inch or two off the bottom so they fit. The routed rabbet acts as a stop for the closed door.
- Add a final decorative touch by screwing a cedar post finial (available at home centers) on the inside peak of the roof (Figure 22). With that done, you're finished.

### An Open-air Model

For maximum ventilation, you can eliminate the screens, but leave the base section of the walls intact. A gazebo that is all roof and no walls would be wobbly and dangerous.

The large space where the screen would go can be embellished accordingly to taste. This gazebo features some fancy fretwork in the Lone Star style (inset). If you like, use Victorian gingerbread and some white paint to turn your gazebo into a real Southern belle.

### A Three-season Model

Northerners may want to stretch their summers by enclosing their gazebos with operable storm windows. These will keep out the rain in summer, and you can use your gazebo to store lawn furniture, grills and outdoor toys when winter rolls around.

Order your windows before you cut the rabbets in the center section of your walls so you know how deep to make them (inset). You can buy custom windows from a dealer listed under "Storm Windows and Doors" in the phone book. A center divider helps proportion the space and keeps the windows to a manageable size.

# Backyard Playground

This playground has all the usual attractions — swings, a slide, and monkey bars — plus private spaces to get away and hide in and a challenging climber made from tires. It is designed to be one of the safest play structures you can make or buy. Plus, its deep footings will keep it solid for years, and building it yourself will save you quite a bit of money compared to commercial structures.

The plan follows guidelines for safety developed by the federal government. Recent changes in the guidelines dictate that all accessible openings on playground equipment must be less than 3½ inches or greater than 9 inches in order to prevent head entrapment and strangulation. For safety, therefore, it is strongly recommended that you replace the side guards with plywood panels 21 inches high. Because of this concern for potential entrapment hazards, the number and spacing of rungs on your ladder near the tires as well as the monkey bars will differ from the photos and illustrations. The dimensions and directions shown are accurate, however. In collaboration with a playground safety expert, several additional safety features for this play set were developed:

**Adequate handholds:** Many children fall from wooden play sets simply because grab-bars and handles are too large for them to grasp. This design features safe, easy-to-grab pipe handholds at critical places.

**A safer slide:** Most falls from slides occur at the top, where children jostle each other. This design includes guards.

**A better swing:** The chain that holds the swings is covered with garden hose, so fingers won't get pinched and there's less chance of strangulation.

## Before you begin

The cost for materials will depend on whether you use redwood (as shown here), cedar, or treated lumber. Treated lumber will last longest in damp ground. Any full-service lumberyard can give you a total cost based on the materials list on the facing page. The only specialized hardware is the swing seats, which are available by the pair through play equipment dealers. In your overall cost estimate, don't forget 16 cubic yards of soft landscape material for spreading underneath the play set.

For tools, you'll need a circular saw, router, belt sander, electric drill, and jigsaw, plus hand tools. An extra-long ⅜-inch drill bit is extremely useful. You'll also need a posthole digger, wheelbarrow, and 6-foot stepladder, and if you can get a power miter box, it'll make your work go faster and look better.

This is a project for an intermediate to advanced do-it-yourselfer. It's complex, and will require several weekends to complete, even with a helper or two.

When building the playset, keep in mind five key safety rules:
1. Corners and edges must be rounded to a ¼-inch radius.
2. Sharp hardware (bolt heads and nuts) must be recessed.
3. Place a 10-inch layer of cushioning material, such as sand, pea gravel, or shredded bark, under the play set (see plans for area). A landscape contractor can recommend an appropriate material for your area. Don't leave lawn underneath — when the grass wears off, the dirt will be as hard as asphalt. For the same reason, be sure to maintain the surfacing material.
4. Don't modify this design. Many of the dimensions are critical, and by changing them you could very easily create a safety hazard.
5. There's no substitute for supervision. Watch your kids on the playground, and check periodically to be sure it's sound and splinter free. Don't let them play with wires or ropes, or wear hoods or scarves around the equipment.

## Backyard Playground

**DETAIL 1**

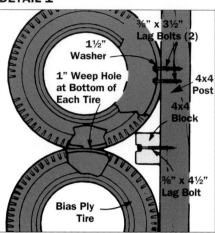

**DETAIL 2**

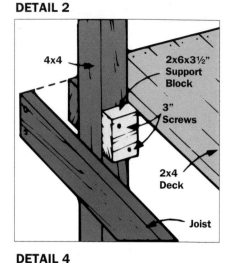

**DETAIL 3**

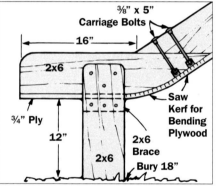

**DETAIL 4**

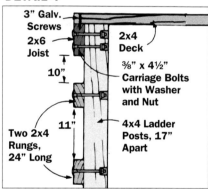

**DETAIL 5**

**DETAIL 6**

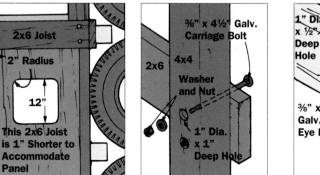

**DETAIL 7**

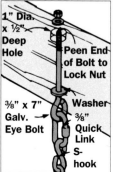

## Shopping List

| Quantity | Item |
|---|---|
| 1 | 4" x 8" x 16 feet |
| 12 | 4" x 4" x 12 feet |
| 10 | 2" x 6" x 10 feet |
| 12 | 2" x 4" x 8 feet |
| 14 | 2" x 4" x 6 feet |
| 1 sheet | ⅝" rough sawn plywood |
| 1 sheet | ¾" AC plywood |
| 1 | galvanized steel or plastic sheet, 24" x 10 feet |
| 28 feet | ¾" galvanized pipe |
| 10 | ¾" galvanized els |
| 12 | ¾" galvanized flanges |
| 8 | ¾" x 1½" galvanized nipples |
| 4 | ⅜" x 7" galvanized eye bolts |
| 2 | ⅜" Quick Links |
| 2 | belting swing seats and chains |
| 4 | used bias-ply (not steel-belted) tires |
| 24 feet | 1" plastic hose |

Screws, bolts, washers, nuts, other hardware, and concrete as required
Redwood, cedar, or treated lumber

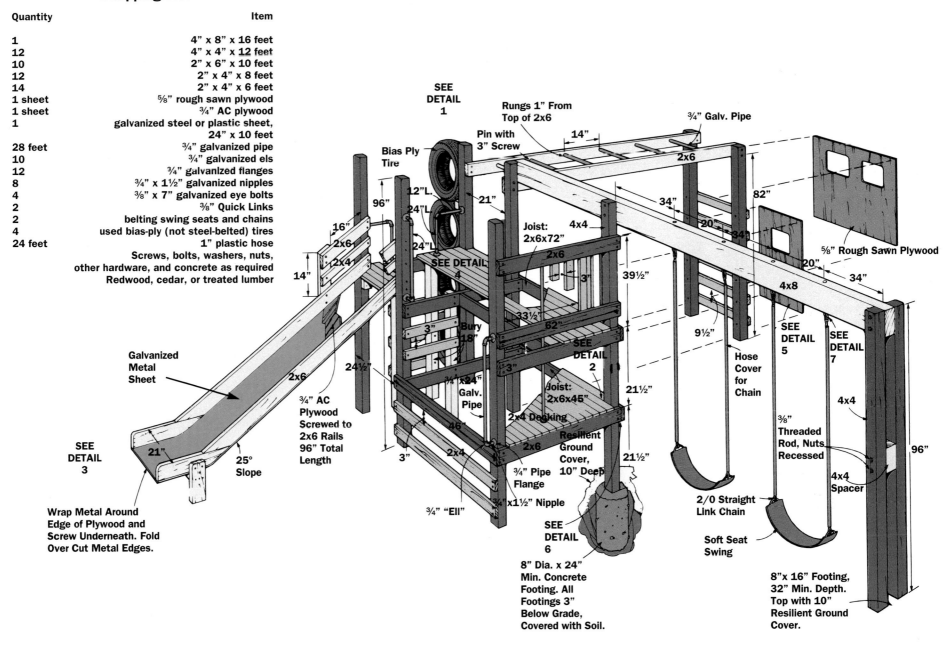

SEE DETAIL 1

Rungs 1" From Top of 2x6

¾" Galv. Pipe

Pin with 3" Screw

Bias Ply Tire

14"

2x6

96"

16"

2x6

12x4

14"

12"L.

24"L.

24"L

21"

SEE DETAIL 4

2x6

34"

82"

20"

34"

Joist: 2x6x72"

4x4

2x6

3"

39½"

20"

4x8

34"

⅝" Rough Sawn Plywood

Galvanized Metal Sheet

2x6

24½"

¾" AC Plywood Screwed to 2x6 Rails 96" Total Length

3"

Bury 18"

33½"

62"

SEE DETAIL 2

9½"

SEE DETAIL 5

SEE DETAIL 7

Hose Cover for Chain

SEE DETAIL 3

21"

25° Slope

¾"x24" Galv. Pipe

3"

Joist: 2x6x45"

21½"

46

2x4 Decking

Resilient Ground Cover, 10" Deep

4x4

⅜" Threaded Rod, Nuts Recessed

2x6

Wrap Metal Around Edge of Plywood and Screw Underneath. Fold Over Cut Metal Edges.

3"

2x4

2x6

21½"

¾" Pipe Flange

¾"x1½" Nipple

2/0 Straight Link Chain

4x4 Spacer

96"

¾" "Ell"

SEE DETAIL 6

Soft Seat Swing

8" Dia. x 24" Min. Concrete Footing. All Footings 3" Below Grade, Covered with Soil.

8"x 16" Footing, 32" Min. Depth. Top with 10" Resilient Ground Cover.

Watch out if your site isn't level. Rather than adjusting the plans, level the area. Build the structure before you lay down the cushioning ground cover under it.

Get the 4x4s that form the tower exactly plumb and in the right position. This is critical. If these posts are set correctly, everything else should follow without a problem. Use diagonal braces between posts and the ground, or between the posts themselves.

Measure a piece to be cut on the structure itself rather than relying slavishly on the plans. Warping or small differences in wood size can throw off even the most accurate measurements. As long as deviations are small (less than ½ inch) there will be no safety problems.

Whenever possible, attach boards with screws or clamps before cutting to length. Position the boards, then mark them and cut.

Round over the edges and corners of boards while they're on a bench, before you attach them — it's easier than routing them on the structure.

**Figure 1:** Use strings and stakes to lay out the six postholes for the tower. Check strings for square using the 3-4-5 method shown.

**Figure 2:** Brace the first post so it's plumb. Use screws or duplex nails for easy disassembly, and don't cut the posts to length yet.

## Erecting the support posts

- Using strings and stakes, lay out the overall structure on your site to make sure you have enough room all around. Then lay out the six postholes for the tower, measuring across the diagonal to be sure your strings are square (Figure 1). Dig the six holes.
- Cut the rim joists to length, and round over all edges and corners with a router. Don't forget that one of the joists is 1 inch short to accommodate a plywood panel that protects children on the slide platform (see plans).

- Round over edges of posts and treat one end of each with a wood preservative designed for below-ground use. The best way is to stand the post in a pail of preservative to let it soak into the end grain. Don't cut the posts yet.
- Set one corner post in its hole, and brace it plumb with two diagonal braces nailed to stakes in the ground (Figure 2).
- Put the remaining posts in their holes, and build a frame of 2x4s on the outside of the posts to space them correctly (Figure 3). Screw the posts to the frame.

**Figure 3:** The remaining posts are held in position by a temporary frame of 2x4s. As posts are plumbed, attach the rim joists.

**Figure 4:** Pour concrete after all the joists are in place and you have checked the posts and joists for plumb, level, and spacing.

- Plumb another post, and screw a rim joist between it and the first post to hold it. Screw where the bolt holes will be (see plans, page 93), and be sure the joists are level and at the right height above the ground (don't forget to add 10 inches for cushioning material). Continue plumbing the posts and bracing them. Add diagonal bracing as needed.
- Drill bolt holes in the posts and rim joists. The extra-long ⅜-inch drill bit will permit your helper to check that the hole is going in level by sighting from the side. Once the posts are plumb, bolt on the rim joists (Figure 3).

- Check the posts for plumb and spacing; be sure that the rim joists are level. Pour concrete in the holes, stopping 3 inches below ground level (Figure 4). Let the footings cure overnight, then cover with dirt.
- Dig holes for the three ladder posts, treat them as you did the other posts, and set them in place, tamping dirt around them rather than concrete. Bolt on the rungs. Use the plan dimensions as your guide, so you will space the rungs according to the latest guidelines.

**Figure 6:** Trim posts to length after the swing support beam is properly positioned. Then bolt the beam to the posts.

**Figure 7:** The monkey bars are pinned into the 2x6 rails by drilling a pilot hole and then driving in a 3-inch screw from the top side.

**Figure 5:** Attach decking with 3-inch weatherproof screws in pilot holes. Cleats are screwed on where extra support is needed.

## Building the deck and bars

- Screw on the cleats for added support, cut the decking to length, and attach (Figure 5).
- Locate and drill holes for the eyebolts in the main beam, measuring from the outside end. Attach the bolts.
- After routing edges and soaking the wood in preservative, erect the swing post and brace it plumb.
- Clamp on the main beam and level it at the proper height above the decking. Now you can mark and trim the posts to their proper length (Figure 6).
- Check the main beam and swing post for plumb and level, then bolt them together. Trim the end of the post, then pour the concrete footing, keeping the top of the footing 3 inches below grade.

- With a router, round over the edges of all decking and the tops and edges of all posts.
- Build the horizontal monkey bar ladder using a spade bit to drill the pipe holes. Don't let the bit's pilot come through the opposite side of the 2x6 (Figure 7). Let the 2x6s run long to be trimmed later.
- Dig holes for the posts supporting the horizontal ladder, treat them as you did the other posts, and brace them plumb. Clamp the ladder in position, make it plumb and level, and mark the ends of the posts for trimming.
- Trim the posts, bolt on the ladder, and pour the concrete footings. Bolt on the 2x4 rungs (following the dimensions given) and trim the ladder ends.

Figure 8: All nuts and bolt ends, and the heads of lag bolts, must be recessed for safety. Counterbore with a 1-inch spade bit.

**Cut-off Piece**

Figure 9: Begin the slide by cutting the rail at an angle and flipping the cut-off piece around. Round off the corner and bolt the piece on.

**Sheet Metal**

Figure 10: Kerf-cut plywood so it can bend at the bottom of the slide. With care, you can cut the kerfs by eye, just following the cut before.

Figure 11: Assemble slide with sheet metal sandwiched between plywood and rails. Bend the sheet over the ends and attach.

## Building the slide and panels

- Using 12-foot boards, make the angled cuts in the slide rails (see plan, page 93), and flip the short piece around to form the "dog leg" on the lower end (Figure 9). Drill bolt holes from the top edge, with a helper sighting along the drill bit from the side to make sure it's going in straight. Cut the curve, and bolt the two pieces together. Cut the lower ends to length.
- Cut the plywood slide bottom and saw $7/16$-inch-deep kerfs every $5/8$ inch starting 12 inches from the end and running for 12 inches (Figure 10). Round over the lower end.
- Wrap the sheet metal around the lower end and screw it underneath the plywood, folding over the cut metal edge for safety.

- With a caulking gun, lay a zigzag pattern of construction adhesive on the plywood. Then, starting with the lower end, screw the plywood onto the rails, sandwiching the sheet metal tightly (Figure 11). Wrap the top end of the sheet metal around the plywood end, and screw it down.
- Clamp the slide in place, level the lower end, and dig holes for the 2x6 slide posts. Mark the rails and posts, cut and round the edges, then screw and bolt everything in place. Check for level and plumb, then tamp dirt around the posts.
- Cut and screw the guardrails at the top of the slide.
- Cut out the plywood panels, round their edges, and screw them onto the structure.

**Figure 12:** Handrails that kids can grip are assembled from ¾-inch galvanized pipe and screwed to the wooden structure.

**Figure 13:** Pull swing chain through ¾-inch garden hose with a wire. The hose protects children's fingers and keeps the chain from rusting.

S-hook

**Figure 14:** Crimp the S-hooks that attach the swings to their chains, and the chains to the main beam. Be sure to check the crimping periodically.

**Figure 15:** Tires for the climber need a drainage hole in the bottom. Use only bias-ply tires.

## Adding safety features and climber

- Construct and attach the pipe handholds (Figure 12).
- Cut garden hose 1 inch extra long, and pull the swing chain through the hose (Figure 13). Attach the swings to the main beam, crimping the S-hooks tightly (Figure 14).
- In four used bias-ply (not steel-belted) tires, drill 1-inch drainage holes and ⅜-inch mounting holes (Figure 15). Bolt them on. Cut and bolt the safety blocks between the tires. The climber is finished.
- Round over any remaining corners and sand. Spread the cushioning material. The ground cover must extend 6 feet beyond the structure in all directions and 6 feet beyond the maximum extend of the swing.

# Multipurpose Yard Shed

## What You Need

| | |
|---|---|
| Circular saw | Shovel |
| Electric drill | Posthole digger |
| Jigsaw | Bull float |
| Hammer | Hand float |
| Chalk line | Finishing trowel |
| 4-foot carpenter's level | Pencil |
| Carpenter's square | Tape measure |
| Roof brackets | Hand saw |
| 8-foot stepladder | Screwdriver |
| Safety glasses | Staple gun |
| Hearing protectors | Paint roller and tray |
| Paintbrush | |

Wouldn't it be terrific to have a place to store the mowers, blowers, trimmers, tillers, ladders, sporting gear, and other trappings of our busy do-it-ourselves lives? There is such a place: a yard shed. Building a shed is cheaper than expanding the garage, more convenient than hauling stuff out of the basement, and safer than leaving your tools and treasures outside. Best of all, a yard shed puts everything right where you need it — in the yard.

The great feature of this shed is its spacious open eaves. They double the useful space with only a small increase in construction cost and labor. The eaves provide a protected space for storing such hard-to-house items as firewood, canoe, utility trailer, lawn furniture, or rabbit pen. They also can shelter activities like refinishing furniture, washing the dog, or just resting your weary bones. Of course, if you don't need or don't have room for the eaves, you can easily eliminate one or both of them. Simply shorten the roof rafters and eliminate the support posts, beam, and footings. With both eaves, this shed requires a space at least 16 x 27 feet; with one eave, 16 x 21 feet; and with no eaves, 16 x 15 feet. The enclosed space is 12 x 12 feet.

This shed is a lot more substantial than the barn-shaped pre-fab units available through home centers and other dealers. The few frills require just a little extra paint and cutting with the jigsaw — not much time or money. If you prefer a simpler look, you can modify the design.

## Before you begin

Check with your local building inspector to determine property line setback requirements (5 to 15 feet is common). Get information on the maximum size and height of outbuildings and find out if there are any special neighborhood regulations that might affect your project. Earthquakes, termites, and frost depth are regional factors that may require you to modify this design.

This is an intermediate to advanced-level project that will test all your DIY knowledge and perseverance. You're basically building a small house — starting with the concrete floor, working your way up through the wall and roof framing, and capping it off with shingles. You should be prepared to spend a good chunk of your summer spare time wearing a tool belt. Even an ambitious, well-seasoned DIYer will spend a solid weekend laying out and excavating the site, another weekend pouring the slab, and at least 100 hours building the framework, installing siding and shingles, building the doors, and adding the trim.

Some tasks, such as lifting the walls into place, installing the roof rafters, and hefting plywood onto the roof, require a helper — don't try to be a hero by doing it alone. You'll be working at heights, too, so use roof brackets and good ladder sense.

Other tasks might require the help of a professional. For example, pouring concrete is hard, heavy work, and goof-ups in concrete are, well, set in concrete.

All of the lumber in this project remains exposed, so pick straight boards. Use treated or cedar lumber wherever these instructions recommend it, and paint or seal the nontreated materials to protect them. Use galvanized nails and screws, too. Use ⅝-inch plywood rather than the normal ½-inch so that the tips of the ¾-inch roofing nails won't be visible from below. Paint the underside of the plywood before installation, so you don't have to do it later. To save money, substitute treated pine for the cedar, eliminate windows, and leave off an eave or two.

**CONCRETE PAD AND FOOTING DETAIL**

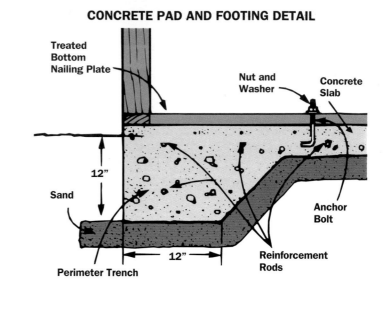

**EAVE POST FOOTING DETAIL**     **POST AND EAVE BEAM DETAIL**

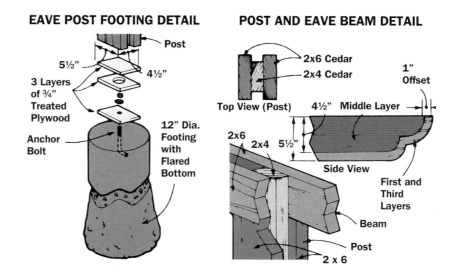

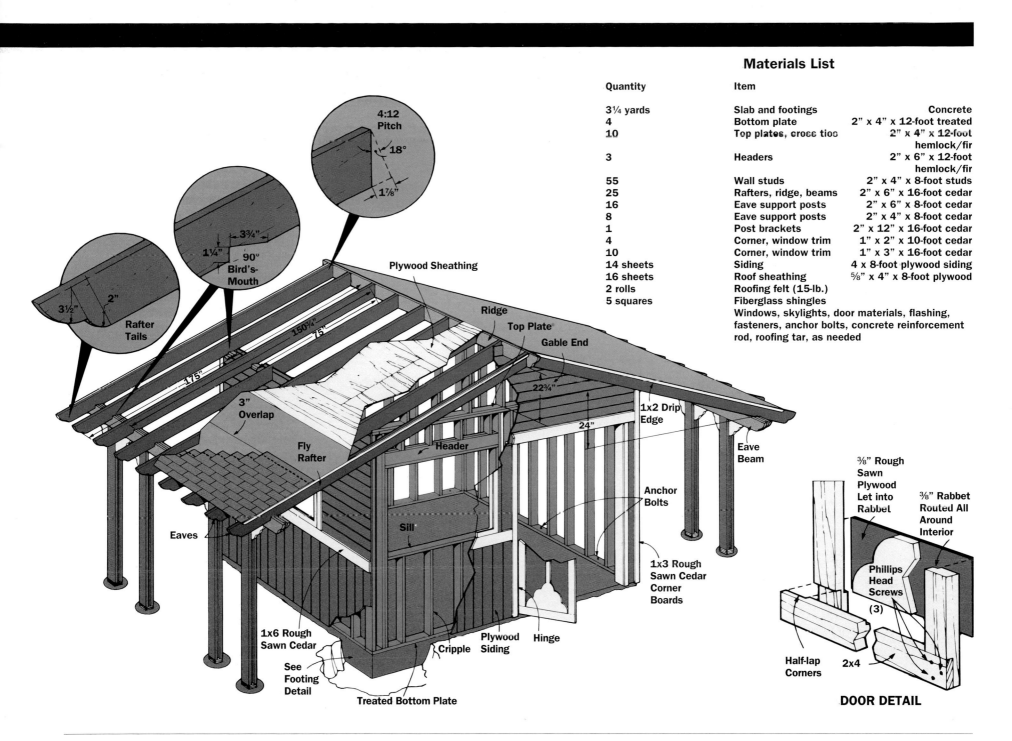

## Materials List

| Quantity | Item | |
|---|---|---|
| 3¼ yards | Slab and footings | Concrete |
| 4 | Bottom plate | 2" x 4" x 12-foot treated |
| 10 | Top plates, cross ties | 2" x 4" x 12-foot hemlock/fir |
| 3 | Headers | 2" x 6" x 12-foot hemlock/fir |
| 55 | Wall studs | 2" x 4" x 8-foot studs |
| 25 | Rafters, ridge, beams | 2" x 6" x 16-foot cedar |
| 16 | Eave support posts | 2" x 6" x 8-foot cedar |
| 8 | Eave support posts | 2" x 4" x 8-foot cedar |
| 1 | Post brackets | 2" x 12" x 16-foot cedar |
| 4 | Corner, window trim | 1" x 2" x 10-foot cedar |
| 10 | Corner, window trim | 1" x 3" x 16-foot cedar |
| 14 sheets | Siding | 4 x 8-foot plywood siding |
| 16 sheets | Roof sheathing | ⅝" x 4" x 8-foot plywood |
| 2 rolls | Roofing felt (15-lb.) | |
| 5 squares | Fiberglass shingles | |

Windows, skylights, door materials, flashing, fasteners, anchor bolts, concrete reinforcement rod, roofing tar, as needed

4:12 Pitch

18°

1⅞"

3¾"

1¼"

90°

Bird's-Mouth

2"

3½"

**Rafter Tails**

150¾"

175"

75"

**Plywood Sheathing**

**Ridge**

**Top Plate**

**Gable End**

22¾"

3" Overlap

24"

1x2 Drip Edge

**Fly Rafter**

**Header**

**Eave Beam**

**Anchor Bolts**

**Eaves**

**Sill**

1x3 Rough Sawn Cedar Corner Boards

1x6 Rough Sawn Cedar

**Cripple**

**Plywood Siding**

**Hinge**

See Footing Detail

**Treated Bottom Plate**

⅜" Rough Sawn Plywood Let into Rabbet

⅜" Rabbet Routed All Around Interior

**Phillips Head Screws**

(3)

**Half-lap Corners**

2x4

**DOOR DETAIL**

## Planning Your Shed

Determine what activities and equipment your shed will contain before you start building. This will help you find the best placement of doors, windows, benches, etc. Make a sketch before you build, showing the position of large items such as workbenches, riding and push mowers, snow blowers, and cabinets. Then plan and build storage cabinets and shelves to fit around them.

Plan to use every square inch of your shed. The rafter space can store light, infrequently used items; the cavities between the studs can hold lumber; even the backs of your double doors can provide a convenient place to hang shovels and brooms. Take advantage of the great, low-maintenance workshop and closet organizers on the market today.

**Figure 1:** Position the concrete form (above), then level and nail it to stakes driven firmly into the ground (inset, right). Cross braces keep the form square and straight.

**Figure 2:** Dig out and level the area for the concrete slab and dig holes for the eave post footings. Strings and batter boards locate the footings.

## Preparing the site

- The best location for your shed is one that's flat and out of the path of any water runoff. You can level a hilly site, but the excavation will be expensive and labor-intensive.
- Build a 12 x 12-foot concrete form from 2x4 lumber, then square and brace it. Move the entire form around until you're certain you have space for the eave areas, then level and stake the form securely (Figure 1).

- Dig the perimeter trench as shown in the plan. Level the rest of the area to a depth 4 inches below the top of the form.
- Stretch strings between batter boards to determine the location of the eave post footings (Figure 2). Dig these footings to the appropriate frost depth for your area using a post-hole digger and shovel, then tamp the bottom of each hole firmly with the end of a 2x4.

Figure 3: Level the concrete as you pour it into the form. Crisscrossed rebar in the slab and footing strengthen the concrete.

Figure 4: Float the concrete to even out high and low spots and further smooth the surface. Remove small ridges that may remain with a hand trowel.

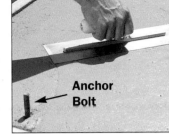

Figure 5: Trowel the concrete as it hardens. Anchor bolts, installed while the concrete is wet, secure walls to the slab.

A project this large is not the place to begin your concrete career. Your shed will be only as useful and long lasting as the slab it rests on. If you are not experienced with concrete, hire a reputable professional — one familiar with the soil and weather conditions that will affect your slab.

If you decide to hire a pro to pour the concrete slab, take care of the "grunt work" yourself so you pay the contractor for the skilled work only. You can level and stake the forms, excavate, and supply muscle power during the concrete pour. But let the pros order the concrete, place the steel reinforcing bars and anchor bolts, orchestrate the actual pour, and do the leveling and finishing of the concrete.

If you have a perfect yard shed location but can't get a concrete truck to it, use a wheelbarrow. It's a lot of hard work, and it will cost you more in waiting time for the truck, but you should not let location alone nix your project. It can be overcome.

## Pouring the concrete slab

- Install reinforcement rods, also called rebar, before pouring the concrete to strengthen your slab.
- Pour the concrete into the form. Roughly even it with the top using a long, straight 2x4, called a "screed" (Figure 3).
- Do further leveling and smoothing with a bull float, a hand float, and finally a finishing trowel (Figures 4 and 5). A smooth surface is the easiest to keep clean, but a broom finish or textured surface is less slippery.

- Install three anchor bolts per wall 1¾ inches from the slab edge while the concrete is wet — one a foot in from each corner, the other centered along the wall. Don't put one in the door opening.
- Concrete needs to cure and harden slowly. Cover it with plastic, keep it moist, and wait at least two or three days before removing the forms or beginning carpentry work.

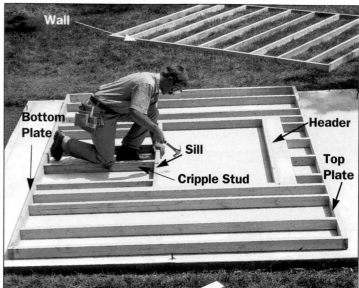

**Figure 7:** Nail walls together with 16d nails. Make certain the rough openings for windows and doors are the right size for the windows and doors you plan to use.

**Figure 6:** Mark the nailing plates in pairs to indicate the location of studs, doors, and windows. The bottom plate must be made of treated lumber.

## Framing the walls

• Cut four pairs of nailing plates (Figure 6) to length. Each pair consists of a bottom plate, which must be pressure-treated lumber, and a top plate, which doesn't have to be treated. Position each bottom plate on the edges of the slab, and drill holes in it to fit over the anchor bolts.

• Gang together the top and bottom plates of each wall and mark the locations of the studs, windows, and doors on each pair. Locate the studs 16 inches from center to center.

• The concrete slab provides a clean, flat surface for nailing your walls together (Figure 7). Separate the pairs of nailing plates, lay studs between the layout marks, and secure the studs to the plates with two 16d nails at each end.

• Install the headers, trimmers, sills, and cripple studs for the windows and doors as shown in the plan.

**Figure 8:** Nail on top plates to tie the corners together. Cross braces (reused from the concrete form) hold walls plumb and straight until you install the siding.

## Erecting the walls

- Build all four walls; then, with the help of an assistant, erect the walls around the edge of the slab, position the holes in the bottom plates over the anchor bolts, and secure them with washers and nuts. Sandwich a thin strip of foam sill sealer or butyl caulk between the bottom plate and the concrete slab to provide a weather-tight seal. A termite guard may be required in some areas.
- Nail the corner studs together, making sure the edges are aligned and even.

- Use a level to plumb each wall, then brace the walls by nailing a 2x4 diagonally across the inside of each wall (Figure 8). Since the siding, which gives the walls their rigidity, isn't installed until after the roof is complete, make sure you brace all four walls.
- Add the second top plate to the walls, overlapping the corners to tie them firmly together.
- Install two permanent cross ties, parallel to the roof rafters, to prevent the walls from bulging out (see plan).

For your rafters to fit, there are three important dimensions shown in the plan details on page 103 and at right you must follow:

• The distance between the framework of your 2x4 walls and the outside of your eave beam must measure 6 feet.

• The top of your ridge board must lie 28¼ inches above the top of the shed walls.

• The top of your eave beam must be 24 inches below the top of the shed walls. To measure accurately, run a straight 2x6-inch board with a level attached from the top of the shed wall over to a temporary post resting on each concrete post pad. Then measure down 29½ inches from the top of the beam (the 24-inch drop plus the 5½-inch depth of the beam) to get the correct post height. You can alter these dimensions to fit your design, but if you change one, you'll have to change the others.

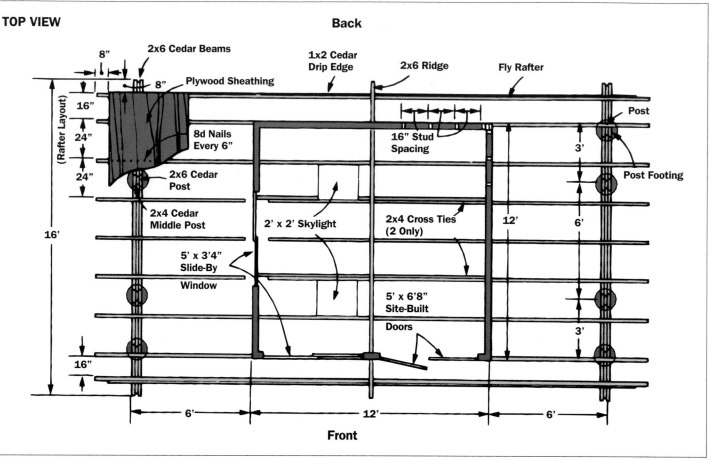

Plan view of roof frame including rafters.

## Framing the roof

• Install the ridge board and the three-member eave posts and beams (Figure 9). The center members of the beams and posts are inset 1 inch to avoid a boxy look.
• Plumb and brace the posts in both directions until the rafters are installed (Figure 10).
• Make layout marks for the rafters 2 feet apart, center to center, along the ridge, walls, and beams. Fly rafters (plan detail) are located 16 inches outside the walls.

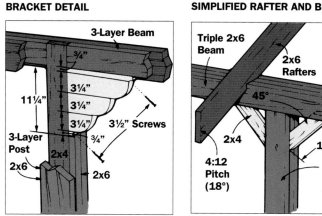

**Figure 9:** Install the ridge board on top of the support post. Decorative end cuts are quick and easy to make with a jigsaw.

**Figure 10:** Install eave beams and posts, then plumb and brace them. The narrower center member provides extra strength without looking boxy.

**Figure 11:** Cut rafters. One angled peak cut, two bird's-mouth cuts, and one decorative tail cut are required per rafter. Use the first rafter as a pattern for the rest.

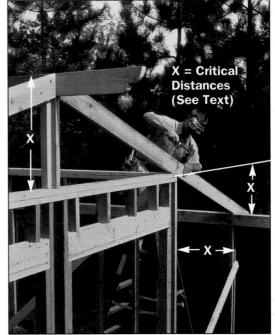

**Figure 12:** Nail rafters in place, installing the gable-end ones first. Space rafters every 2 feet and toenail them to beam and wall with 16d nails.

• Cut your rafters. Select the straightest 2x6 and cut it to the dimensions shown in the plan. There are four cuts per rafter: the angled peak cut, the two triangular "bird's-mouth" cuts (where the rafter rests on the wall and beam) and the curved tail cut. Saw the bird's-mouth by cutting up to the line with a circular saw and finishing the cut with a jigsaw or hand saw. (Figure 11).

• After cutting the first rafter, set it in place on both sides of both gable ends to check for a snug fit. Use this first rafter as a template to cut the others. (Don't cut the wall-top bird's-mouth in the four fly rafters.)

• Secure the two rafters at each gable end first, using 16d nails, then install the remaining roof rafters in opposing pairs (Figure 12).

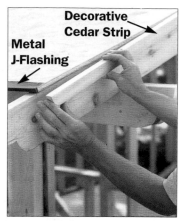

**Figure 14:** Protect the edges of plywood from moisture and humidity with 1x2 cedar on the gable ends and metal J-flashing at eaves.

**Figure 13:** Install plywood roof sheathing, trimming excess plywood after nailing. Stagger end joints and nail securely with 8d nails.

## Sheathing the roof

- To establish a straight line for laying the roof plywood, snap a chalk line near the eave end of the rafters. Eight inches of the rafter ends are left exposed on this shed, but you could also cover the rafters all the way to the ends.
- Stagger the end joints of your plywood (Figure 13) as you install the sheets, and nail the plywood firmly to each rafter with 8d nails, spaced 6 inches apart.

- Use a chalk line to mark any overhanging plywood and use a circular saw to trim it after it's nailed down.
- Cover the exposed edges with flashing and cedar strips (Figure 14) before shingling.

Tarpaper

**Figure 15:** Nail shingles over tarpaper. Stagger the shingles and fasten them according to manufacturer's directions on the wrapper.

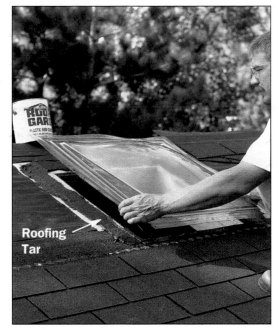

Roofing Tar

**Figure 16:** Install skylights, embedding them in roofing tar. Skylights located near the peak of the roof let in the most light.

Ridge Cap

Chalk Line

**Figure 17:** Install ridge cap. Individual shingle tabs with cut-off corners overlap one another to waterproof the ridge and give a finished appearance.

## Shingling the roof

- As always, use caution when working on a roof. Staple 15-pound roofing felt (tarpaper) over the entire roof right away to protect your project. Overlap horizontal seams at least 3 inches and end-to-end seams by 6 inches (Figure 15).
- Take care to lay the tarpaper parallel to the ridge so it can be used as a guide for laying the shingles. The best shingling instructions come on most shingle wrappers — follow them. Tread lightly on your installed shingles. In cold weather they're brittle; in warm weather they're hot and gooey.

- Skylights are optional, but brighten the interior (Figure 16). Inexpensive plastic skylights are available at most home centers. It will take about an extra hour to install each skylight and shingle around it. Skylights let in plenty of heat, too, so consider installing vents at gable ends for cooling.
- Install the ridge cap (Figure 17). Trim the upper corners of the individual tabs, then overlap the pieces as you nail them along the ridge. Snap a chalk line beforehand to keep the ridge cap straight.

**Figure 18:** Mark siding to fit around rafter tails while sheets are temporarily tacked in position. Use a jigsaw to carefully cut out the notches.

**Figure 19:** Install lower siding. Use Z-shaped flashing for weather tightness where siding changes directions. Blocking at seams adds extra support.

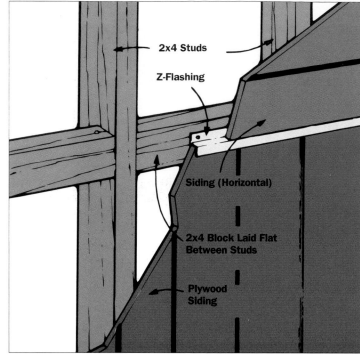

**Figure 20:** Siding Detail

## Installing the siding

• This project uses 4x8-foot sheets of plywood siding. It doubles as both structural sheathing and siding, eliminating the need to use plywood underneath. Also, the large sheets make it easier to notch and then slide the siding around the rafters, so you don't have to cut separate blocks to fit between the rafters.

• Mark and cut the upper sheets of siding that fit around the rafter tails first (Figure 18). Next, tuck in the Z-flashing and install the lower vertical siding (Figures 19 and 20).

• Before installing siding on the gables, fill in the space between the rafters and wall tops with cripple studs (see plan).

**Figure 21:** Install the windows and the cedar window trim. Horizontal 1x6 boards cover the siding seam and Z-flashing.

**Figure 22:** Fasten brackets in place to stabilize posts and beams. Paint, stain, or seal all exterior surfaces, and your shed is done.

## Windows, doors, and trim

- Install the windows, cedar corner boards, and horizontal 1x6s (Figure 21). The curved brackets (Figure 22) are both decorative and structural — they brace the eave posts and beams. You can change the bracket design, but be sure you leave some form of solid triangle between post and beam.
- Construct the doors and install them (see plan detail, page 103). A standard door sweep will help seal the gap between door bottom and concrete slab from wind and water.

- The window-opening measurements in this shed are for a particular type of sliding window, but you can use any make or style you like. You can build the doors yourself (see plan) to accommodate the largest likely resident of the shed, or install manufactured steel doors, or even an overhead garage door. If you increase the width of a door or window opening, you must increase the size of the support header above it. Consult your building inspector about the size.

# In the Yard

B ecause every yard is unique, some projects, like the paths, walls, patios, decks, and fences described here, must be tailored to each home owner's needs and tastes. Although the design is up to you, the basic techniques can be found in this chapter.

# Timber Retaining Wall

Timber walls are relatively inexpensive — about half the cost of masonry block walls. And, since each 8-foot-long timber creates 4 square feet of wall, timber walls can be built more quickly than masonry. To top it off, timber walls can be designed with great flexibility. They blend well with the earth around them, becoming part of the landscape, not an intruder upon it. Even the best constructed timber walls rarely last more than 25 years; moisture, fungus, decay, and weather extremes slowly but surely take their toll. Nevertheless, wood timbers have their own advantages that make them a good choice, and often the best choice, for a retaining wall.

Selecting high-quality timbers is the key to sturdy, long-lived walls. You're burying wood in dirt — not the greatest combination — so you must use pressure-treated timbers. These timbers are sold according to the weight of preservative retained by each cubic foot of timber, most commonly .25, .40, or .60 pounds. The higher the number, the greater the concentration of preservatives and the greater the timber's longevity. The most widely available timbers are treated to a .40-pound concentration and should be stamped or labeled as such.

Common timber dimensions are 4x4, 4x6, 5x6, and 6x6. The height and width of timbers will vary ¼ to ½ inch. The wall shown here uses 5x6s, with the 6-inch face stacked vertically. Use 6x6s for taller, longer walls; 4x6s for smaller projects.

These big timbers are heavy, and cutting them takes good technique. Some tips for handling the timbers are on page 119, and a guide to saws can be found on page 125.

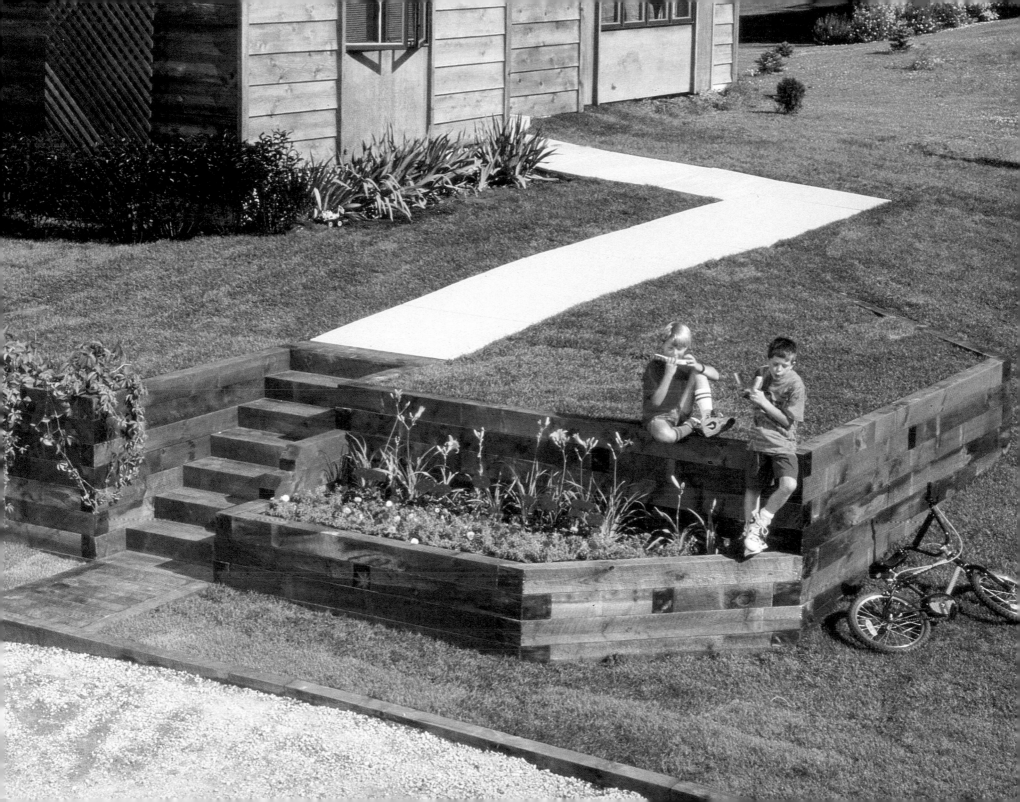

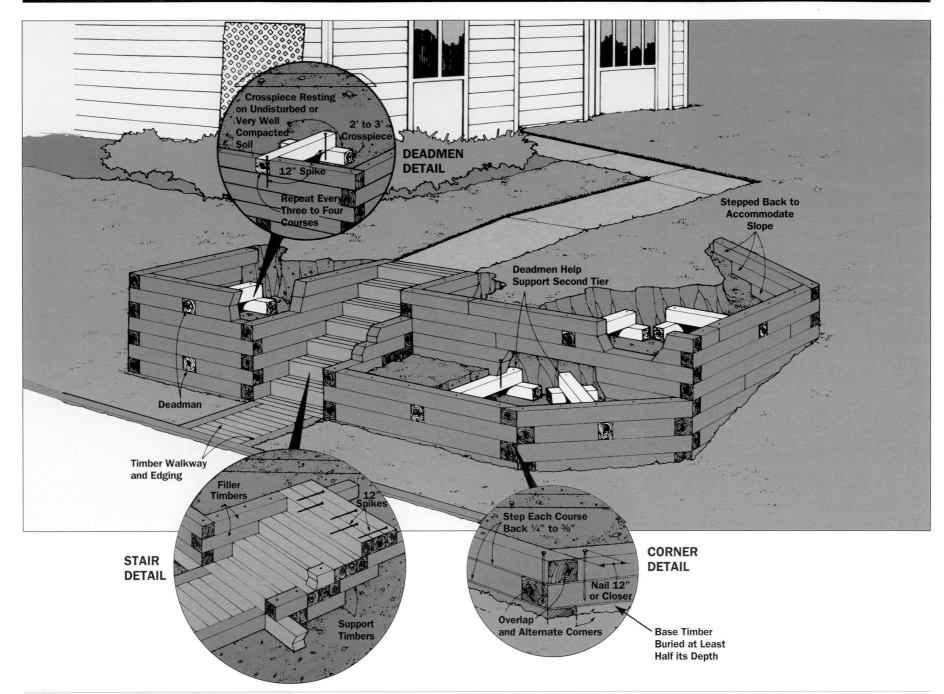

Crosspiece Resting on Undisturbed or Very Well Compacted Soil

2' to 3' Crosspiece

DEADMEN DETAIL

12" Spike

Repeat Every Three to Four Courses

Stepped Back to Accommodate Slope

Deadmen Help Support Second Tier

Deadman

Timber Walkway and Edging

Filler Timbers

12" Spikes

STAIR DETAIL

Support Timbers

Step Each Course Back ¼" to ⅜"

CORNER DETAIL

Nail 12" or Closer

Overlap and Alternate Corners

Base Timber Buried at Least Half its Depth

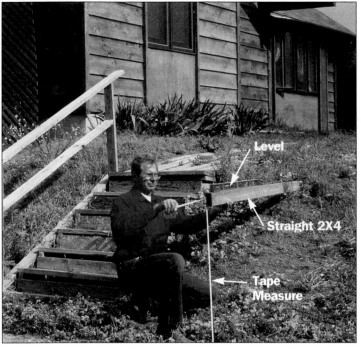

**Figure 1:** Determine the height of your retaining wall using a level, straight 2x4, and tape measure. To determine the number of courses, divide the height of the hill by the height of one timber.

## Planning your wall

- When it comes time to design your wall, you'll find that estimating outdoor spaces by eye is difficult — that "small" hill turns out to be 5 feet high; that "little" embankment, when measured, is actually 20 feet long.
- Start by using a tape measure, a level, and a straight 2x4 to size up the area involved (Figure 1), then make a graph paper sketch of the land. Play around with different designs.

- You'll want a wall that's strong and good-looking and that makes economical use of material and labor. You should break up long sections (more than 16 feet long) with angles, jogs, and corners; these add strength and visual interest.
- Match the wall to the hill. You may be in love with a design you've seen in a magazine or neighbor's yard, but unless you plan realistically, you may wind up hauling in, or digging out, literally tons of dirt.

## Deadmen

The basic procedure for laying timbers for the wall is repeated over and over. But this pattern is broken by a very crucial part of each wall, the indispensable deadman. You hardly see it when you're finished, but if you leave it out, you'll doom your structure. A deadman is an anchor, buried in the soil, that ties the retaining wall into the earth to prevent the wall from leaning or bulging. Deadmen should be installed in any wall two or more courses high or longer than 6 feet. As dirt settles, frozen soil expands, and water builds up, pressure increases against the back of a retaining wall. But since these forces also exert downward pressure, they lock the deadmen (and the wall) into place.

**Figure 2:** Excavate a level trench, making sure the first timber will be buried at least halfway for stability. String lines mark the rough outline of the retaining wall.

**Figure 3:** Install the first course of timbers, making certain they're level and resting on firmly packed earth. Use a hand sledge to help fine-tune timber height.

## Laying the first course

- Take the time and effort to get the first row of timbers installed solid, level, and in the right configuration. Do this and you'll greatly simplify the rest of your project.
- Pound in stakes and connect them with strings to indicate the front of your wall. Use a round-nose spade to dig a trench using the string as a guide (Figure 2).
- Start at the lowest spot, so you can step up timbers as necessary. You need to bury at least the bottom half of the lowest timber (see corner detail in plan) so that the pressure of the earth behind the completed retaining wall won't push the entire wall out. In clay soil (which is often hard to

work with and doesn't drain very well), you may have to dig your trench 4 inches deeper than usual, then fill it with gravel for easier leveling and better drainage (see Figure 13, page 124).
- Use a straight, 8-foot-long 2x4 and 4-foot level to create the level space for the first row of timbers; it's a lot easier than wrestling the actual timbers in and out of the trench for leveling. When the trench is within an inch of level, switch to a flat-nosed shovel to fine-tune a flat-bottomed trench. Repeatedly drop a sledgehammer head-first in the bottom of the trench to tamp the dirt or gravel.

¼" to ⅜"
**Step Back
Per Course**

**Alternate
and Overlap
Timber Ends**

**Long
Shaft
Drill Bit**

**Figure 4:** Step each course back ¼ to ⅜ inch. Alternate and overlap timbers at corners. Position all the timbers in a course, then spike them together.

**Figure 5:** Predrill spike holes at corners to prevent splitting. Use a 12-inch long spade bit that's slightly thinner than the spike itself.

## Laying remaining courses

- Place the timber in the trench and check it for level along its length with a 4-foot level and along its width with an 8-inch torpedo level. If the timber isn't quite level, use a sledgehammer to tamp down the high end (Figure 3). You can stand on the timber and wiggle it back and forth to help settle it securely in the trench.
- Continue leveling and laying as many first row timbers as the terrain allows. Pack dirt along both sides to hold the leveled timbers in place. As you work into a slope, step up your timbers, one end resting on the course below, the other set into the dirt.

- As you build higher, step each row back ¼ to ⅜ inch (Figure 4). Overlap alternating rows at the corners and drive in spikes to lock them firmly together.
- Prevent timbers from splitting at corners and ends by predrilling holes for the spikes with a 12-inch long, ¼-inch diameter bit (Figure 5). You can use either a small hand sledge or full-size sledgehammer for driving spikes. Once you perfect your swing, a big sledge requires fewer strokes and a lot less effort.
- When two timbers meet end to end, make sure a timber in the row above overlaps each end by at least 2 feet. This further helps lock the wall together. Secure every full-length timber with four spikes, one about 8 inches from each end and two more spaced evenly along its length.

2' Cross Piece

Deadman Leg

Undisturbed Soil

**Figure 6:** Position deadman anchors in all wall sections longer than 6 feet and taller than two courses. Build them from scrap timbers.

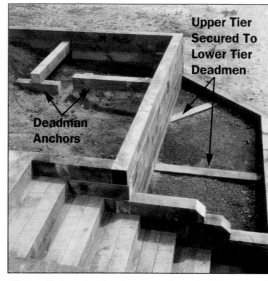

Upper Tier Secured To Lower Tier Deadmen

Deadman Anchors

**Figure 7:** Locate deadman anchors in the second or third course from the bottom and second course from the top. When terracing a hill, lower deadmen support the upper wall.

Sledge-hammer

Timbers Stepped Uphill

**Figure 8:** Step up hills by using progressively longer courses of timbers. Make sure timbers remain level as they reach from timber onto soil.

## Installing the deadmen braces

- Install deadmen in the second or third course from the bottom and in the second course from the top. A rule of thumb is to install one deadman for every 16 square feet of wall face. For walls exceeding 4 feet high, hire an engineer to determine the placement of deadmen.
- There's less chance of deadmen settling later on if they're laid on undisturbed soil (Figure 6). This means the length of the main leg will vary depending on the slope of the hill. Do some rough calculations using a level and 2x4 to determine how long the deadman leg should be. If you're terracing, make certain the deadmen in the second to top row are long enough to help support the bottom row of the next terrace back (Figure 7).
- Prebuild the T-shaped deadman by drilling and then spiking together the leg and a 2-foot crosspiece.

- Use ugly and short chunks of timber as deadmen.
- Position the free end on the wall (Figure 6). Level the cross piece by trial and error. When the deadman is level, drill and spike the free end to the timber wall.
- Pile up and pack dirt around the cross piece firmly with your foot. Pros rough-lay and position an entire course of timbers and deadmen before spiking them together. This allows them to make slight adjustments.
- Along steep embankments or among mature trees, where it may be impossible to install timber deadmen, use auger-type metal anchors, available at larger landscaping stores and home centers. These are "cork-screwed" into the embankment, then bolted to the back of the retaining wall. They don't hold as well, and any large rocks they meet will stop them dead, but sometimes they're the only alternative.

**Figure 9:** Spike together three timbers, keeping the top surface flat. Level support timbers (in background) for the next step unit to rest on.

**Figure 10:** Secure triple-step unit in place by spiking it to the support timbers. Upper step overlaps the lower step approximately 2 to 3 inches.

**Figure 11:** Add support timbers, triple-step units and filler timbers while tying the stairs into the main retaining walls on each side.

## Building stairs

- Stairs involve a lot of cutting, spiking, and head scratching. Plan on making each step one timber high so steps can interlock with the timber walls on each side (see plan detail).
- This wall uses triple-timber steps, which, once positioned and overlapped, create a 12-inch deep tread — a comfortable, natural step. You can decrease the depth of the treads for steep hills (as long as they measure at least 9 inches deep) or increase it and even add a landing halfway up to accommodate gentler hills.
- Cut your stair timbers 4 feet wide to make optimal use of 8-foot timbers (and to minimize cutting).

- Behind your base course, level in two stair timbers and two support timbers (Figure 9).
- Spike together two more 4-foot stair timbers, then a third, keeping the top surface flat (Figure 9).
- Spike this prebuilt unit in place so the front overlaps the lower step 2 or 3 inches and the back rests on the support timbers (Figure 10).
- Continue tying the step timbers into the walls on each side as you build higher. Use filler timbers to plug gaps between the wall and steps (Figure 11).

Figure 12: Install landscape fabric on the back side of the retaining wall to prevent soil from washing through cracks and gaps.

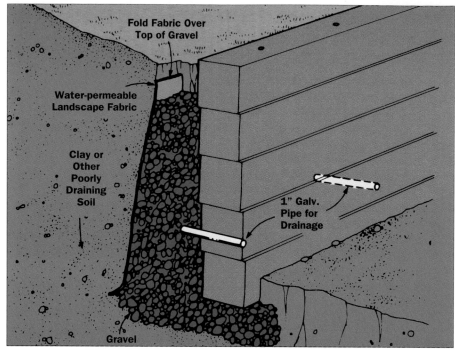

Figure 13: Use water-permeable landscape fabric and gravel behind your wall if you have poorly draining soil such as clay.

## Finishing up

- The top of your wall may be either level or stepped, depending on the contour of your yard. Just build it tall enough so soil won't wash over the top during heavy rains.
- Once your wall is finished, fill in with dirt behind it. But first, line the back side of the wall with landscaping fabric to prevent dirt from oozing through gaps between the timbers (Figure 12). If you need a truckload of dirt delivered, have it dumped on the uphill side of the wall if possible (but not so close that the truck threatens the wall).
- Pack dirt behind the wall firmly with your feet, in layers, 12 inches at a time. This minimizes future settling that might

affect your plantings. In soils with a lot of clay, pile gravel directly against the retaining wall and separate it from the dirt with landscaping fabric (Figure 13).
- Add weep pipes for water drainage. Drive lengths of galvanized steel pipe though pre-drilled holes in the second timber course. Make the pipe long enough so that it extends through the timber and several inches into the gravel behind it.

The 16-inch circular saw is very accurate, but expensive to buy and not always available for rental. This mighty tool can make square and angled cuts in a single pass through timbers as large as 6x6. When available, it can be rented for about $30 a day. You must use a sharp blade and a heavy-duty extension cord or the saw won't cut properly.

The chain saw is what most pros use. It's fast, great for angles, and can trim timbers even after they're installed. If you are handy with a chain saw, it is amazingly accurate. But if you've never used one before, a chain saw can be dangerous. When using a chain saw, mark the cut line on the top and on one side of the timber, then keep the saw bar aligned with both lines simultaneously.

A retaining wall takes lots of cutting. The one shown here required 90 square and 35 angled cuts. You'll want to use one of the saws described at left. Because neither end of a timber is necessarily perfectly square, check before measuring and cutting. Always support the timber off the ground so the cut-off end will drop free and not pinch the saw blade or bar.

After cutting timbers, soak the freshly cut end in a 5-gallon pail of wood preservative. This isn't as effective as pressure treating, but does add some protection.

A final word — because they've been treated with chemicals, never burn your scraps. Bury them behind your wall or dispose of them in a landfill.

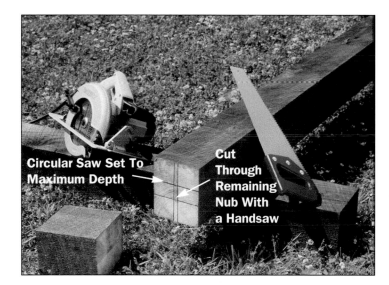

Circular Saw Set To Maximum Depth

Cut Through Remaining Nub With a Handsaw

The circular saw and handsaw are slow and labor-intensive, but most homeowners own these tools. Mark all four sides of the timber with a pencil and square, making sure the ends of these four lines meet. Set your saw to its deepest cutting depth, then cut along the mark on each side. Finish cutting through the remaining middle nub with a handsaw. For 45-degree cuts, mark the timber, cut through two sides with the saw base tilted at 45 degrees and the remaining two sides with the blade set square.

# Backyard Paths and Steps

The rugged beauty of a flagstone-and-timber path makes an attractive addition to any backyard landscape, and has the strength and durability of two of the oldest building materials around.

Make sure of one thing, though: this is labor-intensive work. If you don't like to dig or lift heavy objects (or you can't), then this project isn't for you. But if you don't mind some perspiration, you can save two-thirds of the cost of having a walk like this installed professionally.

Don't plan to complete the project in one weekend. Set aside a couple of weekends or three or four days. As with all projects that are long on labor, planning will reward you with a lighter workload and better result.

The design shown here cannot take into consideration every possible curve, angle, and slope in your yard. These instructions cover the steps common to all path and step projects. Here's your chance to be creative as well as practical, and to come up with something truly unique. Don't hesitate to try several layouts; virtually anything is possible.

You might want to recruit some helpers when it's time to position the 6x6-inch landscape timbers and the larger pieces of flagstone, which can weigh more than 100 pounds apiece. You'll also need to figure out how and where to dispose of the extra dirt and sod you're left with. This may be the time to build a raised-bed garden using some extra timbers and the soil removed from the walk. If you can't spread the dirt around your yard, you may want to rent a large trash container.

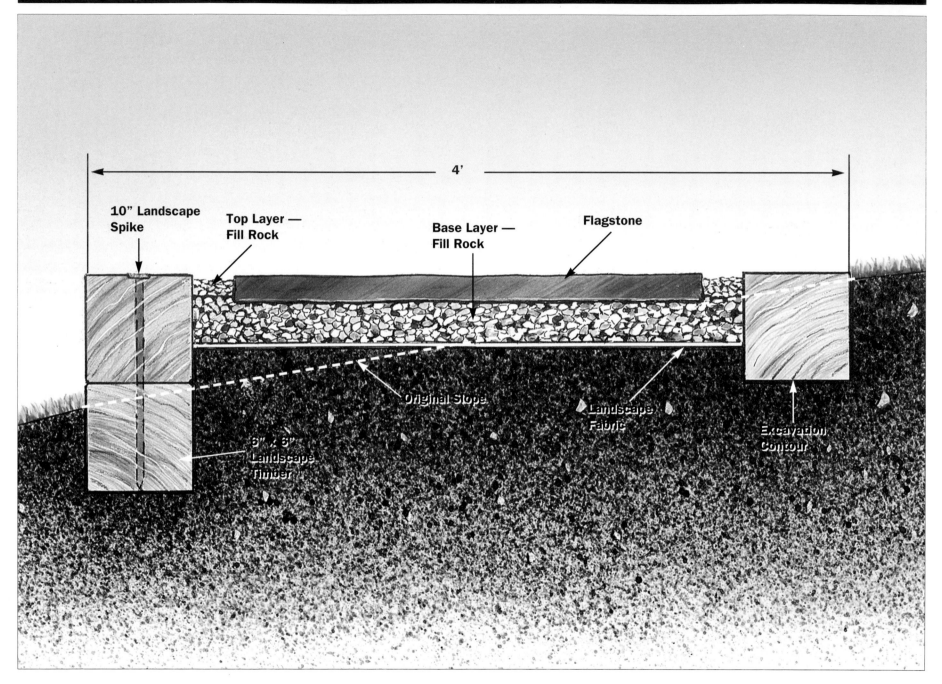

10" Landscape Spike

Top Layer —
Fill Rock

Base Layer —
Fill Rock

Flagstone

4'

6" x 6"
Landscape
Timber

Original Slope

Landscape
Fabric

Excavation
Contour

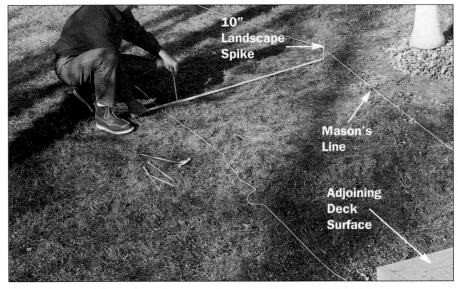

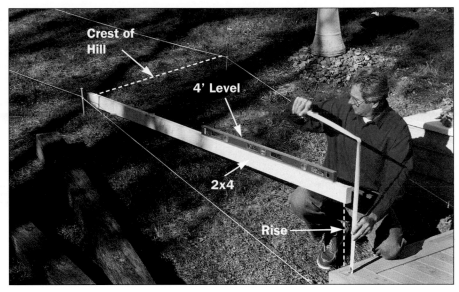

**Figure 1:** Lay out the path and steps using mason's line and 10-inch landscape spikes. This is the time to fine-tune your plan — before you start digging.

**Figure 2:** Position a 2x4 that's long enough to span from the crest of the hill to the front edge of what will be the bottom step, in this case the same height as an adjoining deck surface. Place a 4-foot level on the 2x4 and level the board. Measure the distance from the bottom of the 2x4 to the step. This is called the "rise."

## Materials to use

The quantities will depend on the size of your project, but here are the materials you'll need:
• 6x6-inch pressure-treated landscape timbers.
• 10-inch landscape spikes to secure the timbers to the ground and fasten one timber to another.
• 6-inch pole barn spikes to fasten timbers together at corners, or to hold together angled timbers on steps and landings (see page 131).
• Flagstone for path stepping pads.
• Wallstone for stair treads.
• Fill rock, used as the base for setting the flagstone and for filling the gaps between these pieces.
• Landscape fabric. This fabric comes in 3- and 4-foot widths and is laid on the dirt before putting down the base layer of fill rock. It keeps weeds from growing between the stones but lets water run through. Sold in 25-foot-long rolls, it is available where you buy the stone or at home centers.

## Laying out a plan

• Before you even think about picking up a shovel or ordering any materials, you need to outline where you want the path to go. It doesn't matter which end of the proposed path area you start at, just measure from one end to the other, including any curves, to get your total linear footage. Once you know the path's total length and you've decided how wide you want it, you can lay it out.
• Outline your path and step area with mason's line and spikes to estimate your materials (Figure 1). This also allows you to fine-tune your design before you do any digging.

The path and steps should be wide enough for two people to walk comfortably side by side. A 3-foot-wide walking area, measured from the inside of one timber to the inside of the other, works well. This means that the total width of the path will be about 4 feet, including the timber edges.

Having suggested one rule, it should be said there aren't any hard-and-fast dimensional requirements or building codes that apply to this project. Throughout these pages, however, you'll find rule-of-thumb dimensions that work well. It's also a good idea to check with your building inspector for any specific rules or regulations regarding landscape renovations.

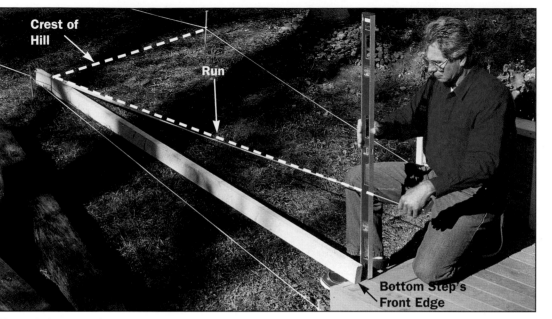

**Crest of Hill**

**Run**

**Bottom Step's Front Edge**

**Figure 3:** Measure from the crest of the hill to the front edge of where the bottom step will be located. This distance is the "run" of the steps, or the length of the step area. You need to know both the rise and run to calculate the number of steps.

## Calculating the steps

- Your next move is to calculate how many steps you need to build (if any). To do this you need to know the "rise" (the total height of all the steps) and the "run" (the length of the step area). The rise is measured from the crest of the hill (where the hill begins to slope in the direction of the steps) to the tread of what will be the lowest step. In this project, the lowest step comes directly off a deck, so the height of the lowest step is the height of the deck.
- To find the rise, position a long 2x4 at the crest of the hill and place a 4-foot level on a very straight 2x4. Some duct tape will hold the level in place, if necessary.
- Adjust the 2x4 until it is level. Then measure the vertical distance from the step's tread surface, which in this case is the same height as the deck, to the bottom edge of the 2x4 (Figure 2 on page 129).
- To find the run, measure from the crest of the hill to what will be the front edge of the bottom step, or in this case the edge of the deck (Figure 3).

- Calculate the number of steps, using the measurements from this project: Divide the rise (28 inches, in this case) by the thickness of the timber (6 inches) to get the approximate number of steps (4.67). Generally, you round any fraction down to the nearest whole number. For this project, that means constructing four steps. However, if you find you're very close to having the higher number of steps — say, 4.97 — round up instead. Just remember, the greater the number of steps, the shallower the tread depth, or stepping area.
- To determine how deep each tread will be, divide the run (here, 108 inches) by the number of steps (four). This gives you a tread depth of 27 inches. (Had you rounded the number of steps up to five, the tread depth would have been about 21 inches.)

**Figure 4:** Overlap the front and side timbers approximately 12 inches over the timbers directly beneath them. This stabilizes the bottom timber. Put a ½-inch layer of fill rock in the trench to give the side timbers a firm base and to make leveling easier.

**Figure 5:** Dig trenches 10 to 12 inches wide and 5½ to 6½ inches deep for the edge timbers. Remove 3½ to 5½ inches of dirt from the center path area for 1½ to 2 inches of fill rock and flagstone or wallstone tread.

**Figure 6:** Check the side timbers for level by placing a 4-foot level across the step. Raise low timbers by adding fill rock under them.

**Figure 7:** Secure the 45-degree mitered corners with 6-inch pole barn spikes — two in the front, two from the side. To secure overlapping timbers, drill a ⅜-inch-diameter hole through the overlapped areas, then drive a 10-inch landscape spike into the timbers.

## Digging and shaping

• If your path begins at the top step, the steps must be constructed first because the path's origin and the top step's tread are one and the same. If the path leads up to the steps, the path is constructed first. Just remember, build from the bottom up.

• The cutaway plan on page 128 and Figure 5 shows what the ground should look like after digging. A garden spade (a flat-nosed shovel) works best for this type of digging. It cuts cleanly and easily removes layers of soil.

• The trench area for the timbers should be 10 to 12 inches wide. This makes leveling the timbers much easier. The trench should be about 5½ inches deep if you want the timber to be slightly above ground or 6½ inches deep if you want the timbers slightly below ground.

**Figure 8**: Cut the landscape fabric to fit the step area. Lay the fabric directly on the dirt. Cut the fabric on a scrap piece of lumber to avoid scarring the landscape timber.

**Figure 9:** Spread an even, 1½- to 2-inch-thick layer of fill rock over the fabric. This is the same rock that's used to fill the gaps between the flagstone and timbers.

**Figure 10:** Place the step tread stones (wallstones) onto the layer of fill rock. Check the height of the tread surface against the height of the side timbers. The tread should be level with the timbers.

## Constructing the steps

- You'll notice that you don't have to remove all of the dirt from the middle of the path area. Remove only enough dirt for the timber trenches and the depth of the fill rock and flagstone. This significantly reduces the amount of dirt you need to haul around.
- The excavated, or tread, area for the path need only be deep enough for the layer of base fill rock (1½ to 2 inches) and the thickness of the flagstone or wallstone (about 2 inches or 4 inches, respectively).
- The stone tread surface should be as level as possible with the top of the timbers. Adjust the height of the tread by adding or removing some of the fill rock under it.

- Start with the bottom step and work uphill. Each step overlaps the one beneath it by about 12 inches to help stabilize the lower step (Figure 4 on page 131).
- Assembling the components is easy. After you cut the ends of the front timber member at 45 degrees, place it at the tread depth that you calculated — this tread is 27 inches.
- Before positioning the side timbers, place about ½ inch of fill rock in the trench (Figure 5). The fill rock provides a firm, stable surface for setting the timbers.
- Position the side timbers. Check for level across the side timbers (Figure 6) and if level, secure the mitered corners with four 6-inch pole barn spikes (Figure 7).

**Figure 11:** Set the tread into the fill rock by moving it in a back-and-forth, twisting motion. Recheck the tread height. If it's too high, twist it farther into the fill rock. If the tread's too low, add more fill rock under it.

**Figure 12:** Fill the gaps between the treads and the timbers with another layer of fill rock; ¾-inch rock is easiest to spread and comfortable to walk on.

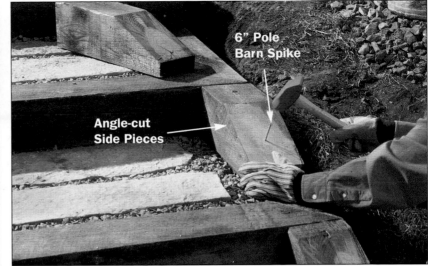

**Figure 13:** Angle-cut end pieces give the timber edges a contoured look. Cut the pieces with a chain saw and secure with 6-inch pole barn spikes. Coat the cut ends with a liquid wood preservative.

- Recheck the side timbers to make sure they're still level. Secure the double row of timbers together with a 10-inch landscape spike, driven with a sledgehammer. Drill a ⅜-inch pilot hole to make driving easier.
- Once the timbers are level, cut the landscape fabric to fit and lay it on the dirt in the step tread area (Figure 8). Cover the fabric with a layer of base fill rock (Figure 9), then lay the wallstone treads on the fill rock (Figure 10).
- Check the height of the tread against the height of the timbers. If the tread is more than ½ inch above the timber, you can twist, or "set," it into the fill rock using a back-and-forth motion (Figure 11).

- If the tread is ½ inch or more below the timber height, add more fill rock under the tread. Now, set the tread into the fill rock. Remember, the more level the treads, the easier and safer the path will be to walk on.
- Once the treads are in place, fill the gaps between the treads and timbers with the fill rock (Figure 12).
- To retain soil at the ends of the steps, or simply to define their ends, consider installing smaller (about 12-inch-long), tapered timber side sections (Figure 13). These pieces are secured with 6-inch pole barn spikes. These side pieces are angle cut with a chain saw. Don't forget to treat the freshly cut end with a liquid wood preservative.

## Flagstone and Fill Rock

Flagstone is a flat, random-sized slab of stone up to 2" thick. Pieces of this quarried stone that are thicker than 2" are called "wallstone." These thicker pieces are used in stone wall construction, as steps, and as stair treads. Flagstone and wallstone are sold by weight, usually by the ton. A ton of 1½"-thick flagstone covers about 100 square feet. A ton of wallstone, depending on its thickness, covers about 35 square feet.

Fill rock, or landscape rock, is available in a variety of colors and sizes. The most commonly used size is ¾". It's easy to spread, allows for easy setting of the flagstone and wallstone, and is more comfortable to walk on than larger, 1¼" stone. Landscape rock is usually sold by the cubic yard, or portion thereof, and prices vary depending on the type of rock. A cubic yard covers approximately 108 square feet at 3" thick.

When buying flagstone and fill rock, don't buy too much. The dealers won't take back any excess.

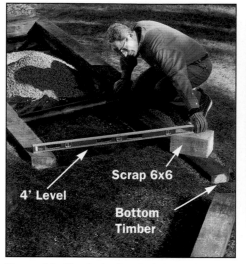

**Figure 14:** Check the level of the path's edge timbers. To make leveling easier, check each row of a double row of timbers. Use a piece of 6x6 under the 4-foot level.

**Figure 15:** Place the flagstones on the fill rock. Don't be afraid to move them around or to use large pieces. Have some fun with the pattern, but try not to leave more than 2 to 4 inches between pieces.

**Figure 16:** Fill in the space between the flagstones and timbers with a layer of fill rock. Use a metal garden rake to spread ¾-inch rock.

## Side-to-side slopes

- If your path is on land that slopes from one side of the path to the other, you may need a double row of timbers, one on top of the other, on the low side to maintain a level walking surface. The cutaway plan illustrates how it fits together. The additional row of timbers may be needed on either the steps or path, depending on the slope of the hill and the location of the steps and path on the hill.
- Secure these double rows to each other with a 10-inch landscape spike, driven by the maul. Drill a ⅜-inch-diameter hole through both timbers to make driving the spike easier.

## Building the path

- The path begins where the steps end, and the construction is similar. The only difference is that each path section is much longer. You need to dig the trenches for the timbers, position them, and then check for level (Figure 14).
- Level each layer of timbers in a double row. Figure 14 shows the best way to do this is by placing a scrap piece of timber on the bottom timber, then checking for level. Moving a scrap piece is easier than wrestling with an 8-foot timber if you need to adjust the lower one.
- Place the flagstone on the layer of fill rock as you did the step treads (Figure 15). Since these pieces are random shapes and sizes, you'll do a lot of mixing and moving of pieces before you're ready to spread the final layer of fill rock (Figure 16).

# Cutting Angles

**Figure A:** Mark the correct angle for miter cuts using a Speed square. Its degree markings allow you to make 22½ and 45-degree cuts.

- Mark timbers at either a 45-degree angle for the step corners or at 22½ degrees for a gradual curve in the path. Use a Speed square — a square that has degree angle markings. Figures A and B show marking the correct angle and the starting cut line. Figure C demonstrates the correct technique for cutting the timber with a chain saw. Be sure to wear heavy-duty gloves and hearing and eye protection when using a chain saw.
- After you've cut a treated timber, be sure to coat the cut end with a brush-on liquid wood preservative. Check with your local paint store to find out what products are available in your area. Some states restrict certain types of wood-treating products.

**Figure B:** Mark a perpendicular line across the timber to connect the two angle lines. This timber is being cut at 22½ degrees for use at one of the path corners.

**Figure C:** Cut the timber with a chain saw. Turn the timber so that the chain saw bar is vertical when cutting. Coat the cut end with a liquid wood preservative.

# Building a Patio

## What You Need

| | |
|---|---|
| Garden hose | Class 5 crushed |
| 2x4s | limestone |
| Shovel | Coarse sand |
| Hammer | Levels |
| Spray paint | Tape measure |
| Wood stakes | Flat-plate vibrator |
| String | Masonry saw |
| Pavers | Landscape timbers |
| Edging | Pipes |
| 12" spikes | |

Patios require careful planning from the first shovelful of dirt thrown to the last paver laid. But you'll get what you work for: a beautiful, usable, outdoor space that will last a lifetime. This patio is "dry-laid," meaning there's no wet concrete used, just precast concrete pavers laid on a bed of sand. This one is a large ambitious project with curves, paths, and steps; you'll need a lot of time and muscle power.

Every patio is different — the one you build may be larger, smaller, square, or round, but everything you need to know about building a dry-laid patio is right here. One of the beauties of the patio shown on these pages is its use of pavers. Each individual paver is lightweight, versatile, and easy to handle. Assembled, pavers create a durable, beautiful surface that has the permanence of concrete without requiring special tools and know-how of you, the builder.

A patio covered with pavers withstands abuse by flexing, rather than cracking, under stress. This is ideal for regions that go through freeze-and-thaw cycles; the individual pavers absorb heaving and movement without cracking. A dry-laid patio has another advantage over a slab — it's much easier to repair small sections. As long as the underlying gravel and sand base is properly prepared, pavers can be used almost anywhere.

This project is strictly a low-tech enterprise, but some modern tools are recommended, principally the use of a flat-plate vibrator to compact the patio and a masonry saw to cut the pavers. Skilled workers built patios for years without these tools, but you'll wind up saving time, muscle, and materials if you use them.

## Designing your patio

A well-designed patio must take into account the terrain, the landscape, and the needs and pocketbook of your family. Not all yards are candidates for a patio. In uneven terrain, a raised deck — which can span hill and dale — might be the best option.

Any patio needs to be tied in with existing trees, planting beds, and decks. Measure first and then create a small scale drawing of the house and existing landscape on paper. You can use a straight, 16-foot 2x4 with a 4-foot level on it and a tape measure to get a rough idea of how much your yard slopes (note that on your drawing, too). Then lay tracing paper on top of your scale drawing and doodle a half-dozen patio designs. Here are a few additional helpful tips:

## Slope

Patios must have a slight slope (1 inch for every 4 to 8 feet) for proper drainage. If you don't provide enough slope, rainwater will settle into low spots, eventually softening and washing out the sand and subbase materials beneath. A flat or poorly sloped patio could even direct water into your basement. Too much slope and you'll feel you're on a listing ship. Bear in mind you can build up low spots with an extra-thick layer of subbase.

## Size

Ask yourself how you'll be using your patio. Do you need space for a grill? Lounge chairs? A wading pool? Planters? Hopscotch? Sketch these on your tracing paper as you doodle. Experts recommend a minimum of 25 square feet of patio per house occupant. Also, a patio at least 16 feet long in one direction is often the most functional. Plan for at least a 6 x 6-foot area out of any traffic path for a dining table and chairs.

## Pattern

The simple rectangular pavers used here can be laid in a variety of patterns. Other paver shapes are available: squares, zigzags, keyholes, and even some that look like fancy floor tile. Shop around at home improvement and landscaping centers for more information on the paver shapes available locally.

In small areas, use simple pavers and patterns. In large areas, you can break up the expanse with a variety of patterns or dividing bands. Curves add interest and grace to the patio — but also loads of extra work cutting and fitting.

When you have considered all these factors and drawn the outline on a sheet of paper, you are ready to lay out your patio on the ground.

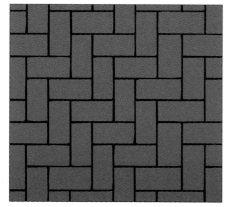
Herringbone pattern

Herringbone pattern at 45°

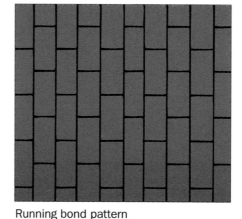
Running bond pattern

Basketweave pattern

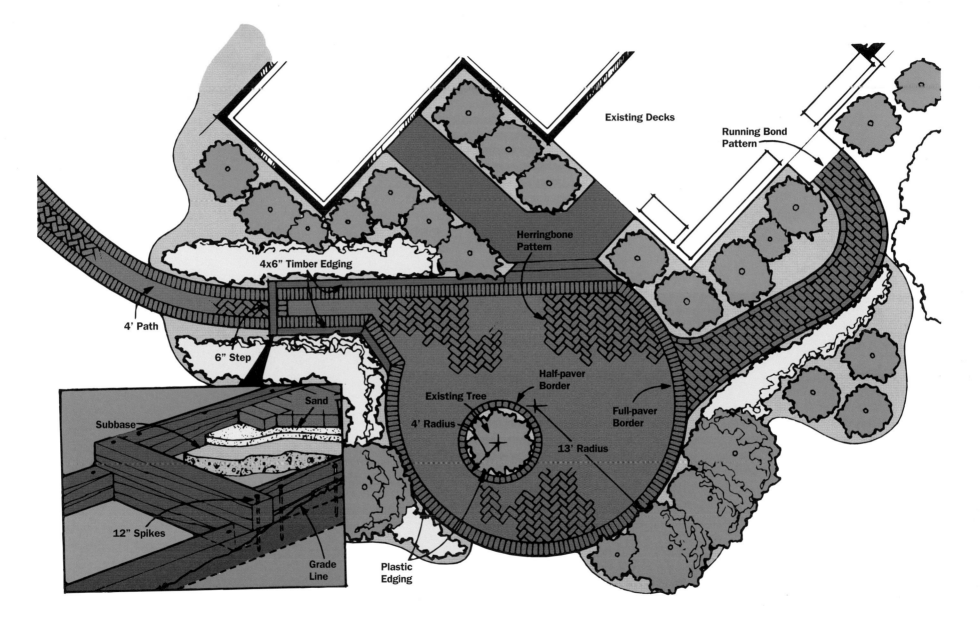

**Existing Decks**

**Running Bond Pattern**

**Herringbone Pattern**

**4x6" Timber Edging**

**4' Path**

**6" Step**

**Sand**

**Subbase**

**Half-paver Border**

**Existing Tree**

**4' Radius**

**13' Radius**

**Full-paver Border**

**12" Spikes**

**Grade Line**

**Plastic Edging**

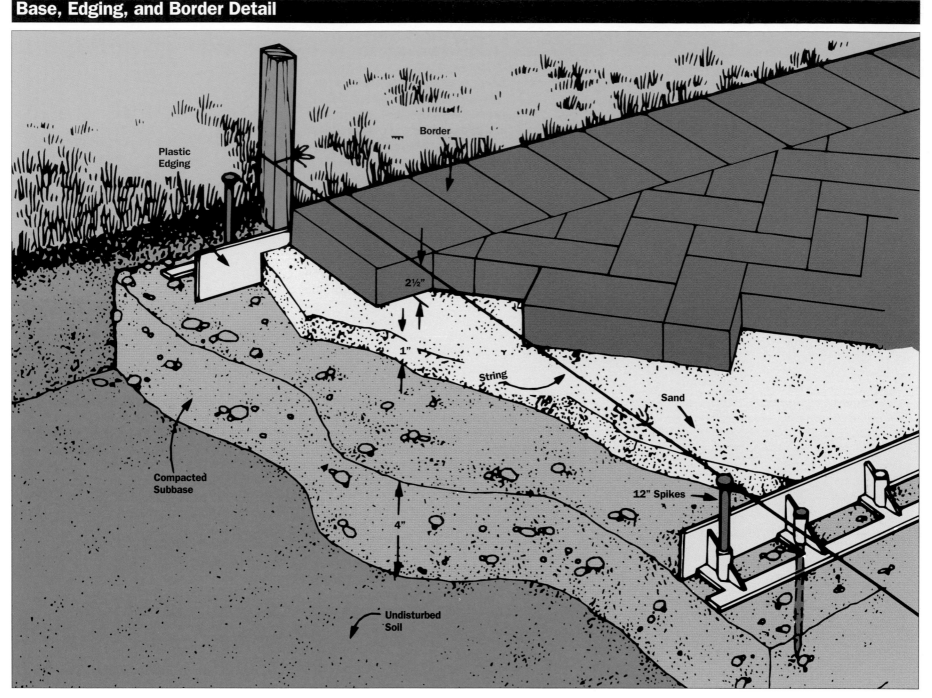

Plastic Edging

Border

2½"

1"

String

Sand

Compacted Subbase

12" Spikes

4"

Undisturbed Soil

Figure 1: Outline the patio perimeter using a garden hose for curved areas and long 2x4s for straight sections.

Figure 2: Remove sod in an area extending 8 inches beyond the boundaries of the patio. Spray paint indicates the excavation line.

## Pavers, materials, and tools

- Plan to use "class 5" crushed limestone for the subbase. Class 5, a grade of material commonly used for road beds, is widely available. It consists of ¾-inch rock and smaller particles, which nest together firmly when compacted.
- When ordering (look under "Sand and Gravel" in the phone book), tell the quarry or trucking company you'll be using the material for a patio subbase. If they don't have class 5 limestone, they should be able to offer crushed gravel or another suitable substitute.
- You'll need to rent a flat-plate vibrator and a masonry saw. With proper planning, you shouldn't need to rent either tool for more than two days.
- All the materials and rental charges for a project like this one can really add up. But even with the rental of labor-saving equipment, you'll save one-half to two-thirds the cost by doing it yourself.

## Laying out the patio

- With your graph paper plan in hand, lay down garden hose (Figure 1) and 2x4s to form an outline of your patio. Use your level and a straight 2x4 to double-check the lay of the land for proper slope. Before you go further, think through the details: Where will you lay the last paver? Will the last row be whole pavers, or will they have to be cut? Now is the time to make adjustments in the size or shape that will ease construction and make your patio look its best.
- Once you're certain of the patio boundaries, spray-paint a line 8 inches outside the outline of your patio to act as a line for excavating. Strip away the sod at this point, so grass doesn't get in the way of the guide strings you'll soon be setting up (Figure 2).

Compacted earth, once dug up and tossed, tends to double its previous volume. Move it as few times as possible — preferably once. If you're going to use the dirt to fill in a low area, shovel the sod and dirt right into the wheelbarrow and dump it in its final resting spot. If it's going to be hauled away, park the trailer, truck, or trash bin as close as you can.

Be equally wise with the materials you haul in. Do all your excavating, then have your subbase dumped directly on the patio site. Have your leveling sand and pavers delivered close to the patio. The patio shown here took 2,500 pavers — that's a lot of hauling by hand! Consider access to your backyard. Can you back a truck close to the patio site? Will a heavy truck damage tree roots or your soft asphalt driveway on a hot day? If a truck can't get close, be prepared to do a lot of hauling by wheelbarrow.

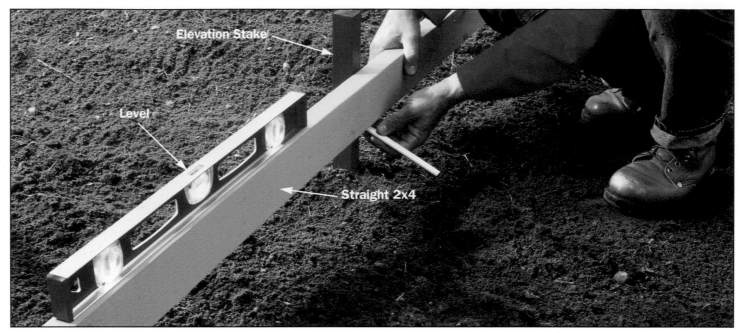

**Figure 3:** Use a level, a 2x4, and stakes to determine the slope of the patio. A slope of 1 inch per 4 to 8 feet away from house is ideal. Run stakes and a grid of string to mark the top of the finished patio, then excavate 7½ inches below the strings.

## Excavating the site and building the base

- Use the bottom of a door or a set of stairs abutting the patio area as the starting point for establishing the final height and slope of your patio. Your entire surface should slope away from the house at a rate of 1 inch every 4 to 8 feet. This slope can be crowned slightly so water will run off in more than one direction.
- Place one end of a 2x4 at the bottom of the stairway or an inch below the door threshold, then level across to stakes driven at the patio perimeter and make a mark (Figure 3).
- Make another mark the appropriate distance down the stake to indicate the slope. In this case, after making a level mark on the stake with a level and 12-foot 2x4, you can make another mark 2 inches down to obtain a slope of 2 inches in 12 feet (1 inch for every 6 feet).
- Make a gridwork of stakes and guide strings to indicate the finished height and slope of your patio, then excavate 7½ inches below these lines. This will provide room for a 4-inch subbase, the 1-inch sand base, and the 2½-inch pavers themselves (4 + 1 + 2½ = 7½ inches). If the area is hilly, you'll need to go back and forth between excavating, leveling, and setting strings to get things right.

Figure 4: Spread class 5 subbase to a depth of 4 inches over the entire patio area and 8 inches beyond. Measure from the guide strings to obtain a uniform height.

Figure 5: Tamp the subbase using a rented flat-plate vibrator. Work in a circular motion and compact the area twice.

• Soil conditions vary greatly across the country. If after digging 7½ inches below your strings, you still find pockets of loose dirt or black soil, remove it or it will eventually settle, creating a wavy patio. The extra depth of crushed limestone subbase that is needed to fill these pockets will promote better drainage and more stability.

• Next, spread the subbase material up to a height 3½ inches below your guide strings (Figure 4). The subbase should be at least 4 inches deep in all places and extend 8 inches beyond the edge of the patio to provide room for the edging.

• If you need to build up an area to accommodate your patio, remove sod and loose soil, then build up the area with subbase material. Building a 10- to 12-inch subbase is common; even 20 inches is not unusual. Compact the subbase with a flat-plate vibrator (Figure 5). Go over the area twice.

**Figure 6:** Install the edging on the tamped subbase using 12-inch spikes. Inset: Cut the webbing on the edging's back side to make it flex for curves.

**Figure 7:** Install landscape timbers for edging in areas where you need to change levels or step down. Be certain to overlap corners.

## Adding the edging

- Edging is a must for maintaining the integrity of your patio. Without solid edging, the sand base and pavers will drift apart as rain, frost, and foot traffic pound away.
- You can use landscape timbers or a proprietary product made especially for the task. The proprietary edging shown in Figure 6 remains straight and rigid until it's cut. Then it can be bent to form curves. Secure the edging to the compacted subbase with 12-inch spikes.

- If you use landscape timbers for combination edging and steps in a sloped area of the yard (Figure 7 and detail on page 139), crisscross corners and use double timbers on the front of steps (even though the lower one will be buried). This lower timber prevents the subbase and sand from washing out. The tops of the timbers should be raised to the height of the finished patio surface. (See "Cutting Timbers" on page 125 for more on cutting and installing timbers.)

**Figure 8:** Spread and level a 1-inch bed of sand over the compacted subbase. Pipes provide a guide for the 2x4 screed.

## Spreading sand

- Sand provides the final base for your pavers. If this surface is uneven, the pavers on top will be, too.
- Ideally, the sand should be 1 inch thick, but if it's necessary to make it thicker or thinner in spots to make the surface dead-level, that's okay. What you want is a firm, flat surface for laying pavers. Sand also locks the pavers in place. When you vibrate the pavers, they'll settle slightly into the sand.
- If your patio is less than 10 feet wide, use a screed board with a 2-inch notch on the ends to ride along the edging to level the sand. On larger expanses, level long lengths of iron pipe in the sand 2 inches below your guide strings, then run your screed along the top of the pipes. (When you're done with the pipe, remove it, then fill in the groove that it leaves behind with extra sand.)

- In many cases you'll use a combination — a notched screed board riding along the edging on one end, with the other end of the screed running along iron pipe (Figure 8).
- Whichever screeding method you use, roughly dump and level the sand over the compacted subbase, then fill in low spaces and rake away excess sand as you drag your 2x4.
- Shuffle the screed lightly from side to side as you work. You don't want to compact the sand, just create a firm, solid bed.
- Screed only as much sand as you can cover with pavers in one day. Screeded sand left any longer is guaranteed to be ruffled by wind, rain, kids, or a stray cat thinking he's found the world's biggest litter box.

**Figure 9:** Install the pavers starting along the longest, straightest edge. Border pavers provide a crisp finished edge, especially along curved portions of the patio.

**Figure 10:** Continue laying pavers using a layout string to keep them in line as you work. Put a gap between pavers or tap them tighter to stay in line.

## Laying pavers

- You should now be standing before an expanse of sand that's flat as a pancake but slightly sloped.
- Take down the guide strings you used to determine height and slope and put up new stakes and strings to mark the lines for the pattern of your pavers (Figure 10).
- Start along your house or other long straight edge and lay down the border pavers (Figure 9). A border isn't essential, but it adds a crisp, finished look, especially along curves.
- Lay the rest of your pavers in your selected pattern. Just lay the pavers in place — don't bang on them or twist them.
- Measure to your string every few rows as you work to ensure you're staying on track (Figure 10). You can leave a slight gap between pavers or tap them tighter together with a rubber mallet.

- If you've taken the time to set things up right, laying the pavers goes amazingly quickly. Many pavers have little nubs on the sides to serve as spacers. Don't walk or kneel on the edge of the patio until after you've vibrated it; otherwise these pavers can sink unevenly.
- You can let your pavers run "wild" near the curved edges (Figure 11 on the facing page), then mark and cut them to mate with the border pavers.

**Figure 11:** Mark pavers that run "wild" into the border area. Then remove the pavers, cut them to size, and place them back in position along with the border pavers.

**Figure 12:** Use half pavers for bordering tight circles. Smaller pavers cut down on the size of the pie-shaped gaps between each piece.

**Figure 13:** Cut pavers with a masonry saw. The saw has a built-in sliding carriage for moving pavers past the blade. Recirculating water keeps the blade cool and lubricated.

- Using a paver as a guide, mark the inner pavers, remove them, and cut them on a masonry saw, then reinstall the cut inner piece and the border piece. On tight radius circles follow the same procedure, but use half pavers for the border to avoid large, pie-shaped voids between them (Figure 12).
- As intimidating as the masonry cutting saw appears, it's actually safe and easy to use. A constant stream of recirculating water keeps the blade cool and lubricated, and a sliding tray carries the paver past the blade. A cut takes about 10 seconds. Be sure to wear heavy work gloves and hearing and eye protection (Figure 13).

- When all your pavers are cut and in place, vibrate the entire patio, starting at the outer edge and working inward in a circular motion. The vibrator will lock the pavers into the sand and help even up the surface (Figure 14 on page 148).
- Don't let the vibrator sit in one place too long, or pavers could settle unevenly or crack. Some pros place plywood down and vibrate on top of that to help distribute the weight of the machine.
- If a paver sinks deeper than its neighbors, use a pair of screwdrivers to pry it up, sprinkle a little extra sand in the void, and replace the paver.

**Figure 14:** Tamp the patio with a flat-plate vibrator after all the pavers are installed. Tamp the entire outside edge first, then circle in.

**Figure 15:** Sweep coarse, dry sand between the cracks of the pavers to lock them together and fill voids. Repeat with more dry sand in a few days.

**Figure 16:** Landscape around the completed patio with flowers, shrubs, and grass. Grass will root through the open spaces in flexible edging and help anchor the edging in place.

## Sweeping and upkeep

- Spread coarse sand across the surface of your patio. After the sand dries, sweep it around the patio to fill the spaces between the pavers (Figure 15). Make sure the sand is dry — wet sand will bridge, rather than fill, the gaps.
- It may take two sweepings a few days apart to completely fill the gaps. The sand helps lock the pavers together, and also keeps dirt from entering and providing a foothold for weeds.
- You may choose to roll two coats of a water sealer over the completed patio. This doesn't protect the pavers — they don't need protecting — but it does enrich the color.

- Landscape around your patio with grass, sod, or planting beds to give it a finished look (Figure 16). Bring in dirt to even out the space between the new patio and existing yard. Keep dirt at least ½ inch below any plastic edging to allow rainwater and runoff to easily drain away from the patio.

**Figure A:** Smooth and level the sand using a notched screed board riding along the edging for a guide. Include a slight tilt for good drainage.

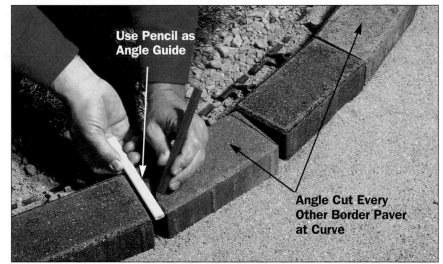

**Figure B:** Install the border, marking and cutting every other paver at an angle at curved areas.

A pathway can be part of a larger project or a project in itself. A walkway made from pavers is an attractive way to link your driveway to your front door, existing deck to new patio, or back door to garden area. Here are a few tips:

- Keep the pattern simple; a border running parallel to the path with a simple staggered pattern within is often the most attractive.
- Put a slight tilt in the path for drainage. One-half inch across a 3-foot-wide path is adequate.
- Take extra care to keep the edgings an equal distance apart; it will make screeding, cutting, and paver laying much easier.
- The technique of laying the path pavers is similar to that for a full patio. The illustrations on this page will guide you.

**Figure C:** Lay the pavers using a string for a guideline. Cut and install pieces that butt up to the border later.

# Deck Building Tips

Building a deck is a big project, but the work that goes into it can be made a little easier when you take advantage of some of the techniques the pros use.

Squared-up post ends, snug-fitting notches and smoothly ripped boards make a deck — or any project — look better and last longer. These details say "quality" to everyone who sees them. This has nothing to do with using expensive tools. You can achieve quality and ease of working using only ordinary hand tools and basic power tools.

A skilled carpenter learns by watching and doing, by asking questions, listening to advice, and accumulating experience. Sure, the pros work hard and concentrate on what they're doing. You can, too. But a skilled carpenter also knows what to give the most time and attention. Over time, the professional learns how to achieve high quality while using the least time and effort.

The experience you accumulate is up to you. The next few pages are your chance to watch how the pros do it. With a little practice, you'll find yourself building more quickly and efficiently, and with higher quality results.

Your deck may not be as elaborate as the one on the facing page, with its built-in planters, tiled area and privacy screen. But it can be built just as well. And to be sure your dream project doesn't turn into a nightmare, have your plans approved by the local building inspector.

# Tip 1: Cut a Post to Length

**Figure 1:** Draw a line around the post using a framing square for accuracy. The line ends must meet exactly.

**Figure 2:** Cut one side with a power saw, rotate the post one quarter turn, and continue the cut. Repeat on all four sides, taking to cut in the same kerf.

• Start this project with freshly sharpened saw blades.

• Square, accurate cuts can be difficult when a post or beam is too thick to saw in one pass. The 6x6 in these photos should sit squarely on a redwood block atop a concrete pier. To assure a square end, start by drawing a pencil line completely around the post using a framing square (Figure 1).

• If the line on the final side fails to meet the line on the first side, rework the lines until they meet. Post material rarely has smooth sides, but the long blade of the framing square helps bridge uneven areas.

• Before you cut, check the angle of your saw blade with your square to be sure it is exactly 90 degrees (Figure 2). Otherwise, the cuts won't align, and the post bottom won't be flat.

• On thick beams, use a handsaw to cut through the final nub of wood in the center (Figure 3).

**Figure 3:** Complete the cut with a hand saw, since the power saw blade won't reach the center of a 6x6 post.

## Tip 2: Notch a Post for a Beam

**Beam Notch**

**Close Kerfs at Knot**

**Figure 1:** Outline the size of the beam on the post, then set your saw blade depth to the beam thickness, in this case 1½ inches.

**Figure 2:** Begin sawing just inside one mark. Cut a series of kerfs ½ inch to ¾ inch apart. Make many close cuts through hard knots.

**Figure 3:** Break out the chips with a chisel or hammer. Chisel the remaining rough areas flat. They don't have to be perfectly smooth.

- Many DIYers shy away from notching, thinking that this type of joint is too complex and difficult. Not so, when you use this technique.
- Plan to notch the post in advance so you can lay it on sawhorses while you cut, rather than trying to cut the notch after you've put the post up. You can use the beam, in this case a 2x8, as a pattern to measure both the width and depth of the notch (Figure 1). Try for a close fit; you can always widen the notch slightly if necessary.
- When sawing the kerfs, pay particular attention to knots (Figure 2). They don't chip out easily, so cut extra kerfs through each knot.
- Use a sharp chisel to chip out the wood between the kerfs (Figure 3).
- Notching a post for a beam makes a stronger joint then bolting the beam without the notch. The notch carries the weight of the deck rather than the weight being carried by the shanks of the bolts (Figure 4).
- One caution: These photos show a 6x6 post being notched. If you cut a 1½-inch-deep notch into a 4x4 post, you'll significantly weaken the post, so avoid doing this where strength is critical.

**Figure 4:** Check the fit. Widen the notch with more saw cuts if needed. The bolts hold the beam in place, but they do not carry weight.

## Tip 3: Saw a Deck Board Lengthwise

**Figure 1:** Mark the proper width at both ends of the deck board, AND in the middle if the board is warped. A chalk line marks the cut.

**Figure 2:** Hook the chalk line at one end, stretch it tightly, lift the center straight up and let it snap down to leave a perfectly straight line.

- Usually the last board laid on a deck will have to be ripped — cut length-wise — to fit the space. This is easy to do on a table saw or radial arm saw, but even if you don't own one of them, you can still make the cut quickly and accurately with a hand-held circular saw. (In fact, you can easily make long tapered cuts with your circular saw that are very difficult to make on a table saw.)
- Measure and mark the width of the board to be cut (Figure 1).
- Carefully snap a chalk line to establish a perfectly straight line (Figure 2). If your board is warped somewhat, measure the cut at the center as well as the end and snap the string twice, once in each direction for the center.
- Some pros can cut accurately freehand, but you and the pros will get better results if you run your saw along a straight guide board tacked to the deck board (Figure 3).

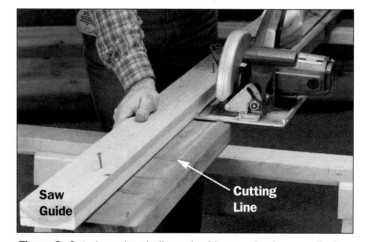

**Figure 3:** Cut along the chalk mark with your circular saw. Tack a saw guide to the deck board for a straighter cut.

## Tip 4: Toenailing a Post

**Figure 1:** Blunt the nail by tapping its sharp point with a hammer, so the wood won't split when nailing close to the edge.

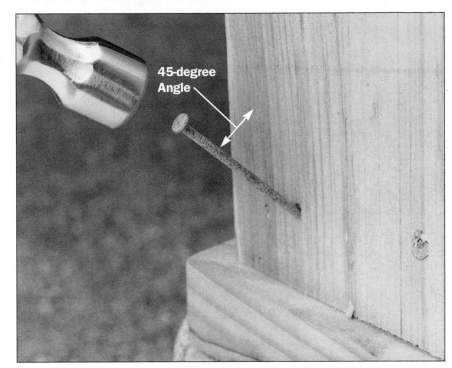

45-degree Angle

**Figure 2:** Start the nail one third its length form the post end, at a 45-degree angle. Use a nail set to finish so you avoid hammer marks.

- Toenailing gets easier with practice. Blunt the nail and position it as shown in Figure 1. It's always hard to hold your board, or post in this case, on the mark and still strike the nail solidly. And the first nail tends to drive the post off the mark.
- You'll avoid the problem if you hold the post off line slightly, toward the side of the first nail.

- Sometimes, you can simply let a second nail from the opposite side drive the post back.
- Holding the post with your foot from the opposite side is another time-honored method, but practice first or you may find your shoe nailed, too!

# Tip 5: Guiding Your Saw with a Framing Square

Framing Square

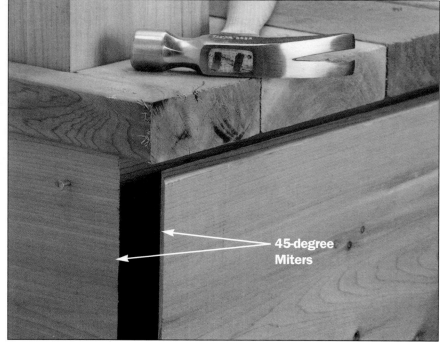

45-degree Miters

**Figure 1:** Hold the long blade of a framing square tightly against the board edge. Run your saw base along the square's short blade.

**Figure 2:** Miter cuts need to be accurate. Make the most difficult angle cuts first. This technique requires a little practice.

- Although your circular saw is not a precise tool for making finish cuts, sooner or later you'll have to use it to make them. Use your framing square as a guide to help out (Figure 1).
- In these steps, the preservative-treated framing material is covered with ⅞-inch cedar trim boards. A miter joint will look much better than a butt joint, which shows the end grain. Since this technique requires practice, leave enough board for a second try (Figure 2).

- Another option is to buy an adjustable guide that's specially designed for 90-degree and angle cutting. Look for these guides at home centers or hardware stores.

## Tip 6: Crafting a Post Top

**Figure 1:** Sketch out your design and cut it into the post. Be sure to use a square for accuracy. Practice angle cuts on a scrap piece.

**Figure 2:** As you rotate the post, saw toward the previous cuts to avoid splintering the edges. Observe safe saw practices.

- Post tops are purely decorative frills, so let your imagination run and have fun. Cut angles, kerfs, or notches as shown here, or make it even fancier.
- Practice on scrap pieces until you find a pleasing design, then transfer the design to a post. Use your framing square first to draw the lines and then as a cutting guide (Figure 1). It's a lot easier to cut the designs before you install the posts, so you'll have to measure the post height carefully in advance.

- Use a sharp blade in your saw to get the cleanest cuts with the least splintering. Eventually you may want to apply a water repellent or finish to the posts to retard splitting and cracking.
- Cut toward previous cuts to reduce splintering (Figure 2).

# Tip 7: Constructing a Jig to Cut Balusters

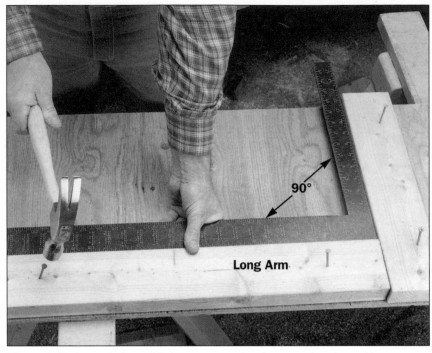

**Figure 1:** Tack two 2x4s at 90 degrees to each other onto the plywood base. Make the long arm at least as long as the balusters.

**Figure 2:** Nail a saw guide at a 90-degree angle to the long arm. Use two washers to space the guide slightly above 2x4s.

- Power miter saws, radial arm saws, or table saws simplify operations — where you need 30 or 40 balusters for your deck guardrail, for example. You only have to measure one, clamp a stop block in place and cut away.
- To do the job right, you really can't measure and cut each baluster freehand. It takes too long. And if you botch just a couple of pieces, your deck guardrail won't assemble easily.

- There is a way to accomplish this task, however, even if your only tool is a hand-held circular saw. You can quickly make up a temporary jig that will serve well. Use a scrap piece of plywood for a base, and make sure all pieces are square to one another. Follow the steps above and on the next page. It's simple — and very rewarding.

**Butt Ends**

**Balusters**

**Figure 3:** Slip lengths of baluster stock under the guide, hold them tightly against the 2x4 stops, and cut them off. To prevent excess splintering and to save time, cut several at once. You can make this jig in only five minutes using scrap material, and it will guarantee better results.

# Building Wooden Fences

## What You Need

| | |
|---|---|
| Hammer | Power auger (optional) |
| Circular saw | Wheelbarrow |
| Jigsaw | ¾" pipe |
| Coping saw | String line |
| Posthole digger | Felt-tip marker |
| Carpenter's level | Tape measure |
| Shovel | |

Building a fence is an easy job you can do yourself. Even if you've never tackled anything larger than a doghouse, a fence is a great project.

These pages will show you how to build a typical wood fence easily and successfully. There are plenty of types of fences you could build other than the one shown here, from the simplest prefab panel fence to an elaborate historical design. But no matter which one you choose, the techniques described here will help make building your fence easier.

The skills needed to build a fence vary depending on the terrain (level is easier) and the length of your fence (long is harder). The critical part of fence building is accurately laying out and setting the posts.

There is nothing difficult about the construction itself, although fence building is hard physical work. Fence posts are heavy and digging holes is a chore. If anybody owes you some labor, this is the time to call in the debt.

Materials costs depend on the lumber you use. This fence was made from clear cedar; if made from a knotty grade, it would have cost less.

This fence design is easy to build, even though it looks fancy. The fence boards are simply nailed up side by side, but they're livened up by having a scalloped top — a curve sweeping between posts. You can buy posts with decorative tops from your fence-lumber dealer. A good choice of wood is clear cedar with a natural clear finish to show off the wood, but any sound wood will work, properly protected by paint or other coating.

# Dealing with Slopes

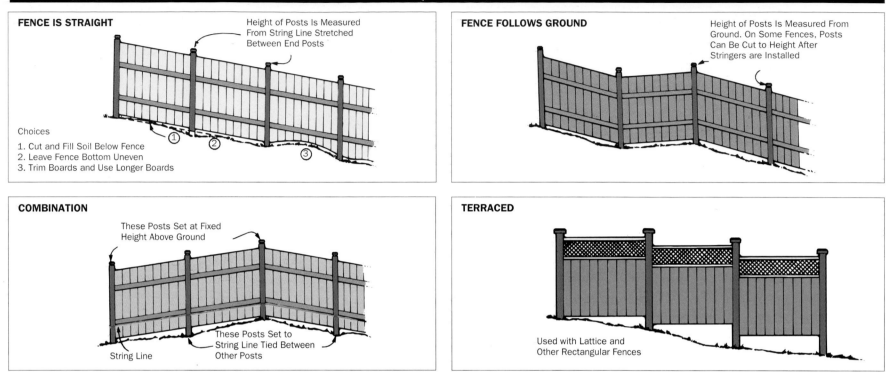

**FENCE IS STRAIGHT**

Height of Posts Is Measured From String Line Stretched Between End Posts

Choices

1. Cut and Fill Soil Below Fence
2. Leave Fence Bottom Uneven
3. Trim Boards and Use Longer Boards

**FENCE FOLLOWS GROUND**

Height of Posts Is Measured From Ground. On Some Fences, Posts Can Be Cut to Height After Stringers are Installed

**COMBINATION**

These Posts Set at Fixed Height Above Ground

These Posts Set to String Line Tied Between Other Posts

String Line

**TERRACED**

Used with Lattice and Other Rectangular Fences

There is no cut-and-dried, mathematically precise way to get a fence to look right on irregular terrain (and that's what most people have). It's a matter of trusting your eye and making adjustments.

You have two choices: Let the fence follow the ground, or have it go straight. For a straight fence, set the corner posts, string your line, and set the height of the remaining posts a fixed distance above that line. The advantage of this method is that the fence looks good; the disadvantage is that you may have large gaps and humps under it (top left illustration).

To have a fence follow the ground, each post is set to a fixed height above the ground. The advantage of this is that there is a constant, even gap at the bottom of the fence; the disadvantage is that following minor humps and hollows can make your fence look jagged (top right).

A good-looking fence is usually a compromise between these two extremes. It follows a smooth curve or has just a few changes in slope (bottom left). You can accomplish this by adjusting the height of intermediate posts where there is a change in slope. Put a nail in these posts at the lower stringer height and wrap your string line around it to use as a reference. Soften an abrupt change in slope by adjusting the height of a couple of posts on either side of the break in slope. As long as the posts are just set in tamped dirt, you can adjust them until the line of the fence is just right.

For small humps and hollows, cut or fill the soil, cut some of the fence boards to fit, or use a few longer fence boards. If you have complicated slopes, it will be easier to install a fence style that allows you to trim off the tops of the posts after they're set (bottom right).

## Planning your fence

- Ask your utility companies to mark on the ground the locations of their cables and pipes. Stay at least 18 inches away from the marks.
- Check with your local building officials to see if the building code regulates fences. Often the code will require that the better side of the fence face out, toward the street or neighbors. There may also be restrictions on fence height or how close you can approach property lines (called "setback").

## Mapping out your fence

- Once you know the legal requirements, put up stakes and strings to mark the location of your fence posts. The strings should be at least 6 inches inside your property lines. Draw the fence on a sheet of graph paper, showing the length of each section.
- Calculate how far apart the posts will be for each section of fence. The posts should be 8 feet apart or less, measured from the center of one post to the center of the next. Here's how to figure the correct distance: Take the total length of the section in inches and divide it by 96. Take that number and round it up to the next highest whole number. Divide the total length of the fence section by that number for the center-to-center distance.
- If you want a gate, decide on its location. It should be on as level a spot as possible, with the hinge on the downhill side. The opening for the gate should measure a whole multiple of the fence board width, plus ¾ inch.
- Mark the post and gate locations and the distance between post centers on your fence map.

## Ordering materials

- Using your fence map as a guide, order your lumber, concrete, and fasteners. A fence dealer will have the best selection of lumber.
- All the lumber for this fence is rough cut, rather than planed smooth. Surprisingly, "dog-eared" fence boards (the kind with the corners cut off) are sometimes cheaper than plain boards, so you can buy them and cut the ends off when you cut the scalloped tops. For common grade fence material, allow 10 percent extra for waste. For clear grades, 5 percent.
- If you're mixing the concrete yourself, figure about two 80-pound bags per post. Otherwise, figure roughly 1 yard of concrete for 40 posts.
- Choose aluminum, stainless steel, or hot-dipped (not electroplated) galvanized nails to minimize rust staining. You can recognize hot-dipped nails by their rough texture.

Besides looking handsome, a fence does all the practical things you want it to — like keeping your kids in and the nosy next-door neighbor out.

### Keep in Mind . . .

Tell your neighbors you plan to build a fence. A surprise fence can turn out to be the first volley in a neighborhood war.

Locate your property lines and any underground utility lines (gas, electric, phone, and cable). You may be able to locate the stakes or "monuments" used to mark the corners of your lot (a metal detector helps), but if not, your city or county government can sometimes help. They'll have plat maps or other documents that give a legal description of your property. Your entire fence, including the footings around the posts, must lie inside your property lines. Hire a surveyor if necessary.

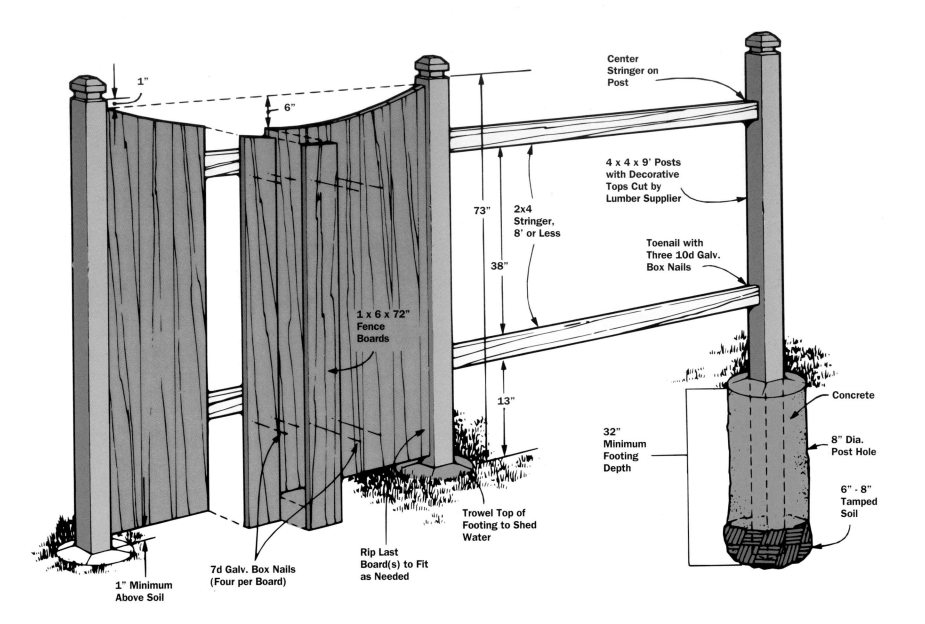

1"

6"

Center
Stringer on
Post

4 x 4 x 9' Posts
with Decorative
Tops Cut by
Lumber Supplier

73"

2x4
Stringer,
8' or Less

Toenail with
Three 10d Galv.
Box Nails

38"

1 x 6 x 72"
Fence
Boards

13"

Concrete

32"
Minimum
Footing
Depth

8" Dia.
Post Hole

6" - 8"
Tamped
Soil

Trowel Top of
Footing to Shed
Water

1" Minimum
Above Soil

7d Galv. Box Nails
(Four per Board)

Rip Last
Board(s) to Fit
as Needed

**Figure 1:** Begin by digging holes for the precut corner and end posts. Strings and stakes mark the fence location, just inside your property lines.

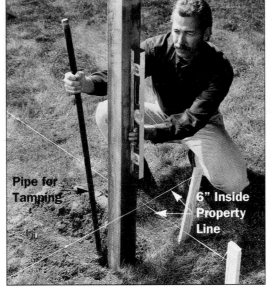

**Figure 2:** Tamp 6 to 8 inches of dirt around the corner posts, doing an inch or two at a time. Make sure the post is plumb and the right height.

**Figure 3:** Set a string line between the corner and end posts at the height of the lower 2x4 stringer. Mark the other post locations with a felt-tip pen.

## Setting the corner posts

- The first step in building your fence is to set the posts on the ends and corners of the fence. It's important that the posts be deep enough: 32 inches deep is the minimum for a 6-foot-tall fence.
- Dig the postholes with a clamshell-type posthole digger (Figure 1), making sure that the holes are flat and solid on the bottom.
- Remember that a fence like this one, with precut decorative post tops, must have the posts set to the right height. Adjust the posts so they're the right height above the ground, either by tamping extra dirt at the bottom of the hole or by deepening the hole. Posts without pre-cut decoration can be set extra high and trimmed after the stringers are nailed on. When a post is the right height, tamp 6 to 8 inches of dirt around the base to keep the post plumb (straight up and down) in both directions (Figure 2). Tamping dirt is a simple activity, but it takes a little practice to get it right. Do an inch or two at a time, tamping evenly around the post and using your level to test for plumb. Start gently and then tamp harder as you go around. If you try to tamp hard right away, it'll push the post to the side. A length of capped ¾-inch pipe makes a great tamping tool.
- Tie a mason's string line between your corner posts and end posts, at the height of the bottom of the lower stringer (Figure 3). This string will be used to locate all the other posts, so pull it tight and check its position twice.
- Measure from your string to the ground to see how the slope changes. See "Dealing with Slopes" (page 162) to determine how you'll need to adjust the string line, and perhaps your corner and end posts, to get your fence to follow the contours of your lawn.
- Using a felt-tip marker, mark the string where the remaining posts will be located.

Corner Post →

String Line Temporarily Moved Away

**Figure 4:** Dig the remaining postholes and set the posts in tamped dirt. You can ease the job by using a power auger, locating two thirds of the hole inside the string line.

**Figure 5:** Check the posts to be sure they're plumb and square, and that the tops form an even line. Because the posts are set in dirt, you can adjust them if necessary.

**Figure 6:** Fill the holes with concrete, after making a final check that the posts are plumb, square to the line, and in a straight line along the length of the fence.

## Setting intermediate posts

- Dig the rest of the postholes by hand or use a rented power auger if your soil isn't too rocky. Either way, be sure to locate each hole so two thirds of it is inside the line, and one third is outside (Figure 4).
- Mark the bottom of the lower stringer on your remaining posts. Set the posts in their holes, lining up the mark with the string line. Add well-tamped dirt to raise a post, or dig the hole deeper, as needed.
- Tamp 6 to 8 inches of dirt around each post to hold it in place. Make sure that each post is: (1) plumb in both directions, (2) at the right height in relation to the string line, (3) square to the string line, and (4) just barely touching it (Figure 5). Don't let the posts push the string outward. If any of your posts are bowed, arrange the bow so it's parallel to the fence.
- If rocks are a problem, try prying with a pick and pry bar. If that doesn't work, you have several options. If the rock is a foot or more deep, just cut off the end of the post (interme-

diate posts only). You can also move the post to one side — in the direction of the fence only — without it being very noticeable. As a last resort, you can shift the bottom of the post in or out an inch or two perpendicular to the fence line. If you keep the tops of the post in line, the fence will still look straight, even if the bottom edge sticks out in one spot. Tree roots are less of a problem. Cut the smaller ones and move the post around the larger roots.

- Stand back now, and look at the posts. Do they look straight up and down? Stand on a ladder and look down the tops. Are they in a line? Are they the right height? When you look from the side, do the tops of the posts make a straight line or a pleasantly smooth curve? Since the posts are just tamped in place, you can adjust them as much as you want.
- After the posts get your final approval, fill the holes with concrete (Figure 6). Mound the concrete up and trowel the top of it smooth so it sheds water (Figure 7 on page 167). Let it cure and harden overnight.

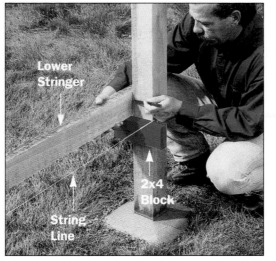

**Figure 7:** Trowel the tops of the concrete footings to shed water. After a year, you can caulk the gap between the wood and concrete.

**Figure 8:** Temporarily tack 2x4 blocks to hold the lower stringer while you mark it for cutting the ends. Blocks also hold the stringer in position so you can nail it on without a helper.

**Figure 9:** Spacer boards ensure that the upper and lower stringers are parallel and hold the upper stringer both for marking the end cuts and for nailing. Toenail the stringers into the posts with galvanized nails.

## Nailing on the stringers

- You'll save a lot of walking if you start by laying out the stringers in pairs along your fence. (Use a wheelbarrow to carry the boards.)
- To install a stringer, hold it up to the posts at the right height and mark each end for cutting. Trim off the ends, then toenail the stringer to the posts at each end, keeping the ends at just the right height. The trick to doing this quickly, easily, and accurately is to use a couple of 2x4 blocks (Figure 8) and a pair of 38-inch spacer boards made of 1x6 (Figure 9). Tack these onto the posts to locate the stringers and hold them for nailing. The 2x4 blocks hold the lower stringer, first for marking and then for toenailing. The 1x6 spacers locate the upper stringer a precise distance above the lower stringer, then hold it for toenailing. If you've ever done it, you know that sometimes the board shifts as you nail it. The blocks and spacer boards will keep your stringers in the right spot.

- Toenail the stringers with three 10d galvanized nails at each end, centering the stringer on the post (Figure 9). The lower stringer should have two nails on the side and one on the top edge. The upper stringer should get two nails on each edge and one on the side. When you nail on the side, do it on the side where the fence boards will be attached in order to hide the nails. If you have warped stringers, use them on the bottom, not the top.

**Figure 10:** Mount the fence boards using a jig to make sure the tops of all boards are at the right height. Keep the boards plumb as you nail them.

**Figure 11:** Fill the gap left at the end of a section of fence boards by ripping the last board or boards. Fill a very small gap by spacing out several boards.

**Figure 12:** Trace the curve for the top of the fence boards using a thin strip of ¼-inch hardboard bent between three nails.

## Nailing on the fence boards

- Spread your fence boards out along the fence as you did the stringers, and start nailing them up. Once again, a jig will make this part of the project go quickly and accurately, guaranteeing that the tops of all the fence boards are the right height above the upper stringer (Figure 10).
- Start at one post and nail the boards to the upper stringer only with two 7d galvanized box nails. The jig ensures that each board will be at the right height.
- Nail all the boards between two posts this way. If the gap left at the second post is uniform, top to bottom, go back and nail the boards to the bottom stringer.
- If the gap at the end is 3 inches wide or more, rip the last board to fit (Figure 11). If the gap is 1 to 3 inches wide, rip the last two boards. If the gap is less than an inch, remove a few boards and increase the distance between them slightly.

- After all the boards are nailed on, mark the curved cuts that give the fence its scalloped look. For each post-to-post section, tack on three nails, two on the posts just at the tops of the boards, and the other in the middle of the fence section, 6 inches down from the other nails. A strip of quarter-inch hardboard or plywood, bent between these nails, will form a smooth curve for the cutting line (Figure 12).
- Cut out the curve with a jigsaw (Figure 13), finishing the end of the cut with a coping saw if necessary, and smooth the cut edge of the boards with a rasp.

**Figure 13:** Cut the curves with a jigsaw, finishing the ends with a coping saw if necessary. Smooth the cut ends of the boards with a rasp.

**Figure 14:** Assemble the gate on the ground, using only one nail at each end of the board so the gate stays flexible.

**Figure 15:** Twist the gate so the stringers line up with those on either side. Then finish nailing the boards and add a diagonal 2x4 brace pointing toward the bottom hinge.

## Building the gate

- The trick to building a gate is to initially tack it together on the ground, using only two nails for each board (Figure 14).
- Fit the gate into the opening, twisting it so the stringers line up on either side, then finish nailing (Figure 15).
- Lay a 2x4 across the stringers for a diagonal brace, trace the ends, and cut it to fit. Toenail the brace in place, being sure that it points from the latch side down to the hinge side. (Reversing this brace causes many a sagging gate.)
- Cut the scalloped top on the gate as you did for the fence, then mount the hardware.

## Final touches

- Left to weather naturally, cedar will turn gray. Although this is acceptable to many people and doesn't affect the longevity of the wood much, you may choose to treat your fence with a clear water-repellent sealer to keep it golden brown.
- Any sealer that's designed for cedar decks will work, although you'll have to reapply the finish every few years to keep it looking fresh.
- After your fence has been up for a year, you should apply a moistureproof caulk between the concrete footings and the posts to keep water out.

# Some Other Popular Fences

There are a million styles of fences, and half the fun of building one yourself is designing it. You'll probably see a wide variety of fences right in your own neighborhood. The building method we've shown for the scallop-top fence is typical for most fences. But here are three other popular styles:

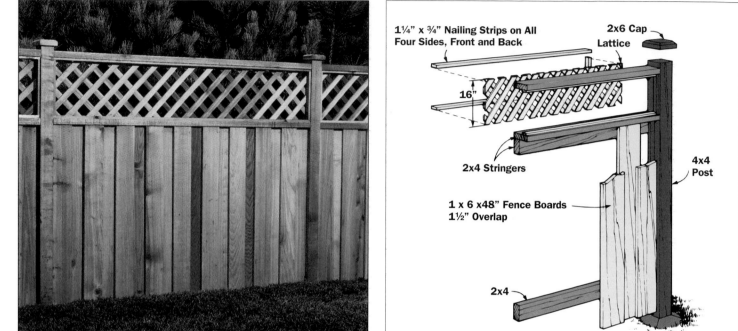

1¼" x ¾" Nailing Strips on All Four Sides, Front and Back

2x6 Cap

Lattice

16"

2x4 Stringers

1 x 6 x48" Fence Boards
1½" Overlap

4x4 Post

2x4

**Overlapped Board Fence with Lattice:** This is one of the more complicated fences to build, though it's also one where doing it yourself will save the most money. It gives good privacy, is very strong (because of the overlapping boards), hard to climb, and sophisticated looking. It must follow slopes in steps. A table saw or radial arm saw is almost a necessity to rip the thin nailing strips for this fence.

In the fence built in this example, the posts run long and are topped with a beveled cap that was cut on a table saw. The details of the construction are shown in the plan above. You can adapt this design to make a fence that's entirely lattice, or one that's entirely overlapping board.

**Alternate Board Fence:** This fence looks equally good from both sides, is very easy to build, allows good ventilation, and follows ground contours well. Building this style, you can set the posts without worrying about height, and trim them after the top stringer is nailed on. This makes post-setting go much faster. The 1x6 fence boards should be spaced about 3 ½ inches apart on each side (use a jig), although the spacing of the last few can be varied to fit.

**Picket Fence:** This is one of the easiest fences to build. It provides more of a visual boundary than it does privacy or protection. Fence dealers carry a wide variety of decorative pre-cut pickets and matching posts. Posts should be buried a minimum of 24 inches deep, and typically they are 7 feet long. You can use just tamped dirt for the fill on intermediate posts, but concrete is better and should definitely be used on corner, end, and gate posts. Space standard 1x4 pickets about 2 ½ inches apart, with the stringers 27 inches apart in a 4-foot fence. Use four nails per picket.

# Two-day Projects

Not all outdoor enhancements involve major construction and carpentry. Here are four items that can be built in a couple of days, give or take a little, and are guaranteed to brighten up your yard or garden.

# Deck Lounger

Have you ever wanted to own one of those teak deck loungers that hark back to the era of luxurious ocean-crossing passenger ships? Or perhaps you've thought of building one, but were put off by the apparent complexity of its curved parts?

This Danish-style classic deck chair may be the answer. It's very simple to build, abounds in comfort, and transports or stores easily because of its take-apart design.

This project is not inexpensive, however, because it's best built using woods that can withstand outdoor use. You must use a hardwood for the chair to have adequate strength. This project shows white oak for its outdoor resilient properties and pleasing look. You may also use teak.

After you've lived with this chair for a while, the cost will seem perfectly acceptable. You'll see how beautifully the design, the construction, and the wood itself bring you comfort and enhance your outdoor setting.

## Cutting

- At a full-service lumberyard, have the following pieces cut from ¾-inch white oak: two 8-inch x 42½-inch back pieces; two 6½-inch x 36½-inch seat pieces; two 2-inch x 24½-inch crossbars; thirteen 2-inch x 28-inch seat slats.

## Assembling

- Carefully lay out and mark the arcs for one of the 42-inch curved back pieces. See the detail illustrations for an easy method of marking the arcs.
- Cut out the curved section and use it as a template to mark and cut the remaining seat and back curves. Although the lengths of the back and seat pieces are different (42 and 36 inches, respectively) the radius of the arcs is the same. The inner radius is 40 inches and the outer radius is 42 inches.
- Mark a full 1-inch radius on all four ends of the seat and back sections, then cut with a jigsaw and sand them smooth.
- Cut the four 1-inch wide slat supports with a 40-inch inner radius out of the leftover oak from the second step. You need two of each length. See the plans for exact sizes.
- Attach the slat supports to the seat and back section curves using both a waterproof construction adhesive and No. 10 x 1¼-inch pan head Phillips stainless steel sheet metal screws.
- Mount six seat slats to the seat section curves with a 1½-inch overhang on each side and a 1-inch space between each slat.
- Apply the construction adhesive to each slat, and screw in place using No. 10 x 1½-inch pan head Phillips stainless steel sheet metal screws.
- Mount the remaining seven back slats to the back section curves with a ¾-inch overhang on each side. Use the construction adhesive and screws for each slat as you did when attaching the slat supports.
- Using a tape measure, locate and mark the position of the front and back crossbars on the two front legs. Attach the two crossbars to the front and back edges of the front legs' curves flush with the outside surface. Screw and glue in place.
- Sand all edges using 150-grit sandpaper. Finish with a clear water-repellent

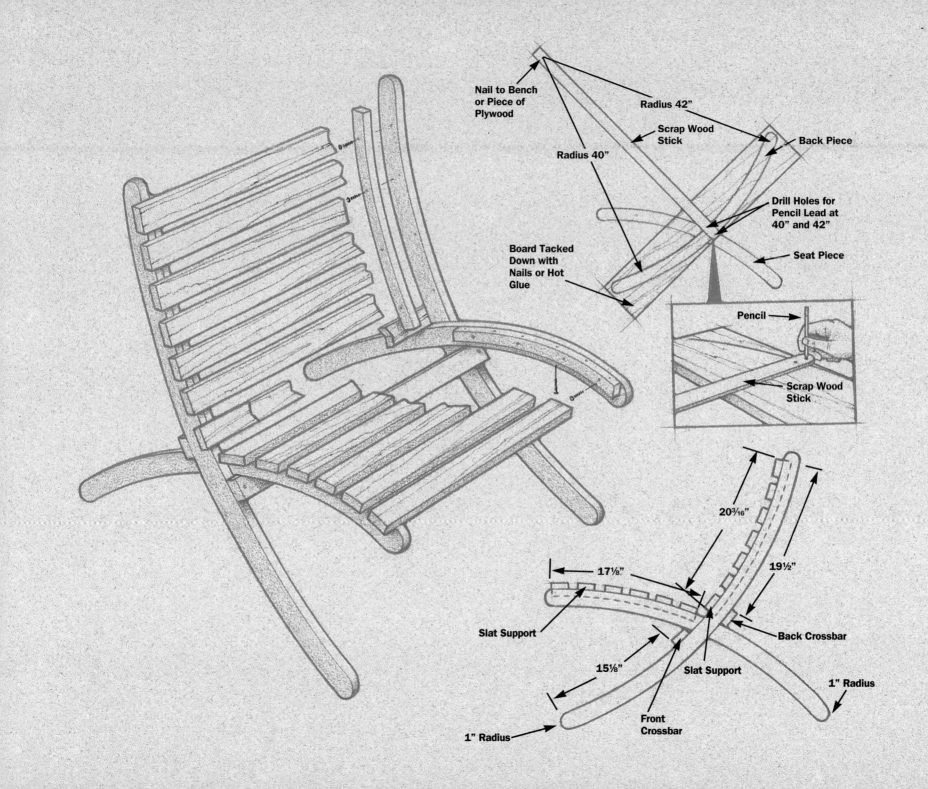

Nail to Bench or Piece of Plywood

Radius 42"

Radius 40"

Scrap Wood Stick

Back Piece

Drill Holes for Pencil Lead at 40" and 42"

Board Tacked Down with Nails or Hot Glue

Seat Piece

Pencil

Scrap Wood Stick

20³/₁₆"

17⅛"

19½"

Slat Support

Back Crossbar

15⅛"

Slat Support

1" Radius

1" Radius

Front Crossbar

# Flower Box

## What You Need

- 2 6-foot lengths of 1" x 6" boards
- 4 No. 6 x 1½" galvanized screws
- 18 No. 6 x 2½" galvanized screws
- 4 No. 6 x 3" galvanized screws
- 1 plastic flower tray, 8" wide x 36" long x 6" deep

Here's a window flower box so easy to build that you can make several of them in just a few hours. And with its drop-in-place beveled mounting rail, the box is instantly removable for transplanting plants or storing at the end of the growing season.

You can start by purchasing a flower box tray insert made of fiberglass-reinforced plastic that is both lightweight and rugged. These trays are available at most lawn and garden supply outlets or home centers.

The flower box is made of 1x6 pressure-treated wood. You can paint it a bright color to coordinate with the flowers as well as the house, or leave it natural.

The size of your flower box will depend on where you plan to mount it and the size of the tray you purchase. The dimensions of the box shown here fit a standard 36-inch-long tray, but trays are available in other sizes as well.

The only power tools you'll need are a jigsaw and a drill.

## Cutting

- Cut the following from treated 1x6s: three 34¾-inch pieces for the face, back, and rails; two 10-inch pieces for the ends.
- Using a jigsaw set at a 45-degree angle, bevel a 34¾-inch piece into one 2¼-inch top mounting rail and one 3¼-inch bottom mounting rail.
- Slightly round the front edges of each end and cut the curved detail, if desired, into the bottom of the face board using a jigsaw.

## Assembling

- Attach both ends of the box to the front face, using three No. 6 x 2½-inch galvanized screws at each end. Countersink each screw head slightly. Assemble all the pieces on a flat surface to make sure the board edges align.
- Secure the top mounting rail to the back piece, flush to the top edge, using No. 6 x 1½-inch galvanized screws.
- Mount the back assembly flush to the top, inside both end pieces, with the rail to the outside of the box. Use No. 6 x 2½-inch galvanized screws. Countersink each screw head.
- Putty over the screw heads. Sand the box and, if you choose to paint it, apply primer and a coat of exterior enamel.
- Drill three ½-inch-diameter holes in the tray bottom for drainage. Cover the bottom with a layer of coarse gravel or small loose rock, then fill with potting soil and flowers.
- Attach the bottom mounting rail to the wall location as shown, using four No. 6 x 3-inch galvanized screws. Drop the top rail piece onto the bottom rail piece to mount the box on the wall.

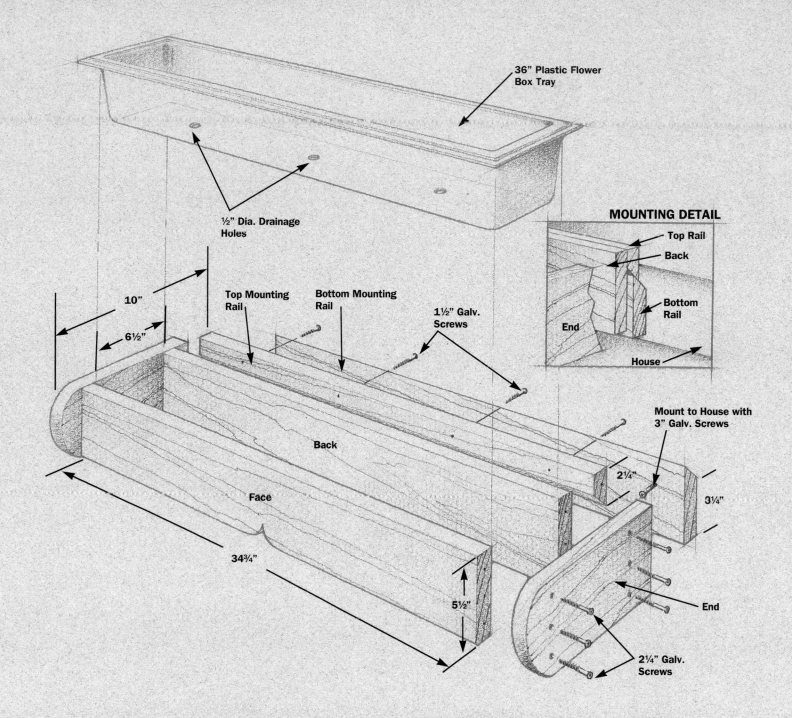

36" Plastic Flower Box Tray

½" Dia. Drainage Holes

10"

6½"

Top Mounting Rail

Bottom Mounting Rail

1½" Galv. Screws

Back

Face

34¾"

5½"

Mount to House with 3" Galv. Screws

2¼"

3¼"

End

2¼" Galv. Screws

**MOUNTING DETAIL**

Top Rail

Back

Bottom Rail

End

House

# Sandbox with Cover

## What You Need

- **8 8-foot x 3½" x 4½" landscape timbers**
- **3 8-foot 1" x 2" boards**
- **1 roll chicken wire to cover 64 square feet**
- **12 60d pole barn nails**
- **½ cubic yard fine sand**
- **⅜" staples**
- **2½" drywall screws**

This frontier-style sandbox will amuse your children for hours. Built to the dimensions shown, it will hold a half-dozen five-year-olds at one time.

The cross-lap joints at each corner of the box come straight from log-cabin building techniques. The joints are simple to cut with a circular saw and wood chisel, and provide the flush surface needed for stacking the box-framed landscaping timbers.

Covers made with chicken wire keep pets out when the sandbox is not in use. These covers are lightweight, yet durable enough so that the kids can walk on them without damage to cover or child.

Built as shown, the sandbox takes ½ cubic yard of fine (also called washed or mason's) sand. It's sold by home centers, landscapers, or masonry suppliers. If you need to have the sand delivered, you'll find that many of these places have a minimum delivery policy of one cubic yard.

Do not place plastic in the sandbox bottom. Keeping it bottomless allows rain to drain through and the sand to dry rapidly.

## Cutting

- Mark the location of the joints on the timbers, as shown in Figure A.
- Set your circular saw's blade to a cutting depth of 2¼ inches. Carefully cut into the timbers every ¼ inch between the marks (Figure B).
- With a wood chisel, break out the remaining scraps and clean the notch. Extreme precision is not necessary — a little slop is okay — and you'll find that the cutting goes fast and easy (Figure C).

## Assembling

- Stack the interlocking timbers on a fairly level area, adjusting until they're square. If the ground isn't perfectly level, just shim the timbers with wood scraps. Then fasten the corners together with 60d pole barn nails.
- Build the two covers from 2x2s using 2½-inch drywall screws. If you want even lighter covers, adjust the dimensions so you have three covers. Attach the chicken wire with ⅜-inch staples.

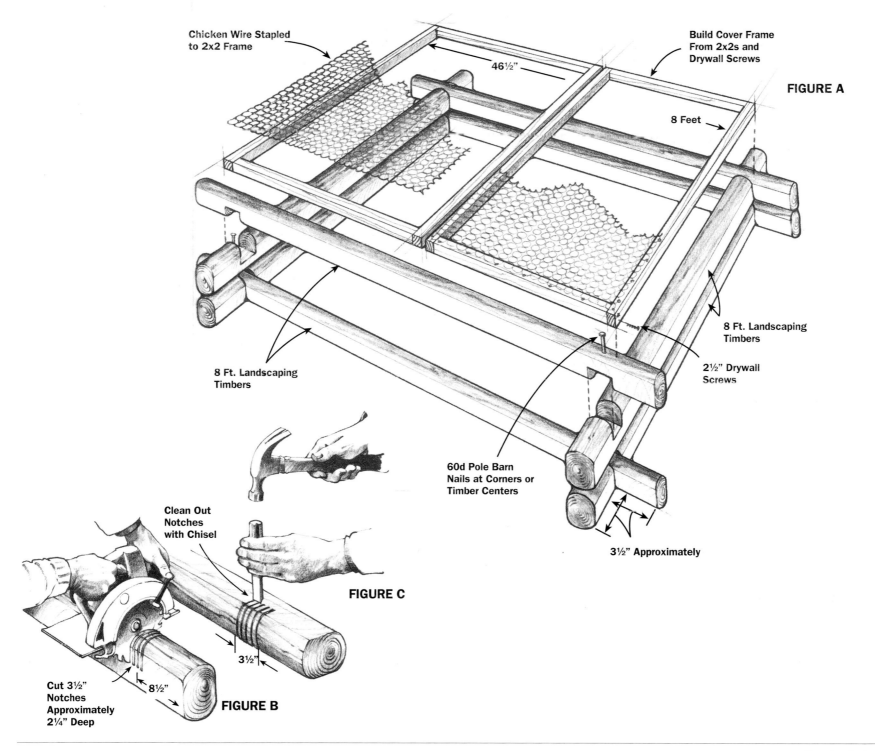

Chicken Wire Stapled to 2x2 Frame

Build Cover Frame From 2x2s and Drywall Screws

**FIGURE A**

46½"

8 Feet

8 Ft. Landscaping Timbers

8 Ft. Landscaping Timbers

2½" Drywall Screws

60d Pole Barn Nails at Corners or Timber Centers

3½" Approximately

Clean Out Notches with Chisel

**FIGURE C**

Cut 3½" Notches Approximately 2¼" Deep

8½"

3½"

**FIGURE B**

# BBQ Grill Table

## What You Need

- 36 linear feet 1" x 3" clear cedar
- Two ¼" x 1¼" nuts, carriage bolts, washers, and lock washers
- Two ⅜" x 2" carriage bolts with washers, lock washers, and wing nuts
- 2 one-hole, ½" heavy-duty snap-on straps for conduit
- ⅜" dowel rod
- 6d galvanized casing nails
- Waterproof cement
- Wood preservative
- 1⅝" galvanized drywall screws

Most barbecue grills seem to have been designed for people with at least three hands. This simple-to-build table provides a place to park the food, tools, and condiments while you cook.

The table folds up for easy storage. The dimensions provided here are for a 22-inch kettle grill, but can be easily adapted to your grill's shape and size. The table top measures 3 feet in length by 18 inches wide and rests securely on two retractable legs. Electrical conduit clips are bent to conform to the shape of the grill rim and then bolted to the table. Building the table takes about three hours.

Clear cedar in 1x3 size was used because of its resistance to warping and rot. A water-repellent finish should be applied as the final step. Materials costs will vary, depending on the quality of wood you choose.

## Cutting

- Cut the following pieces from 1x3-inch stock: two 3-foot pieces for the table sides; two 16-inch pieces for the table ends; thirteen 18-inch pieces for the table top; one 14⅜-inch leg brace.

## Assembling

- Assemble the table frame according to the diagram. Predrill holes near the end of the stock and assemble with 1⅝-inch galvanized deck screws.
- Nail 12 of the table top pieces to the frame with 6d galvanized casing nails, with a ¼-inch overhang on the front and ends. Start at the leg end of the table and use a piece of scrap to maintain a uniform ¼-inch spacing.
- Trace the grill's curve onto the thirteenth table top piece and then cut out the curve with a saber saw or coping saw. Sand the curve smooth. (If your grill has straight sides rather than curved, skip this step.)
- Using pliers, shape two conduit snap-on straps around the lip of the grill. Bend the metal so the straps separate the wood from the hot grill.
- When the clips are shaped right, drill two ¼-inch holes in the top piece and attach the conduit clips to the last curved top piece with the 1¼-inch carriage bolts and washers. (Don't attach this thirteenth piece to the table yet.)
- Cut two leg stops 4¼ inches long, with a 15-degree angle on one end. Flip the table upside down and screw the leg stops to the inside of the front frame. The angled end faces the grill, with the long side at the top.
- Cut two legs 28⅛ inches long, with a 15-degree angle at one end. At the other end, draw a semicircle with a 1¼-inch radius, and cut it out.
- In the rounded end of each leg, center a ⅜-inch hole 1 inch from the end.
- From the front of the frame, measure back 6 inches and drill a ⅜-inch hole centered on the 1x3 board (refer to the diagram) on both sides of the frame.
- Attach legs with a 2-inch carriage bolt, washer, lock washer, and wing nut.
- Position the 14⅜-inch leg brace and attach with drywall screws.
- Nail the thirteenth table top piece in place.
- Drill four ⅜-inch holes in the front side piece, spaced about 1 inch apart. Insert and glue four 2¼-inch pieces of ⅜-inch dowel rod.
- With a sanding block or pad sander, lightly chamfer the edges of the table top pieces. Then apply a wood preservative.

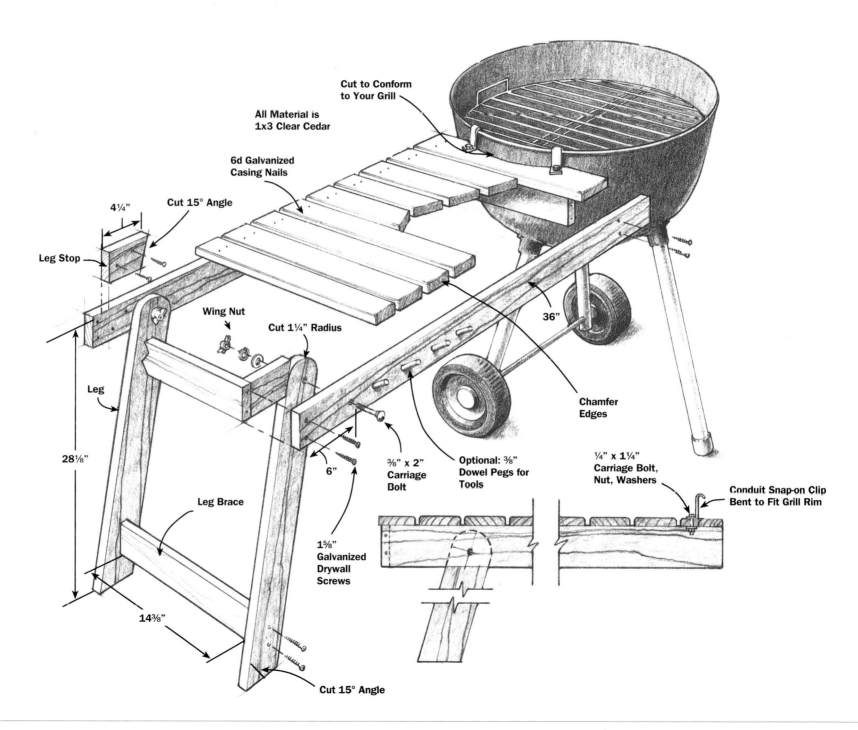

Cut to Conform to Your Grill

All Material is 1x3 Clear Cedar

6d Galvanized Casing Nails

Cut 15° Angle

4¼"

Leg Stop

Wing Nut

Cut 1¼" Radius

36"

Chamfer Edges

Leg

28⅛"

Leg Brace

6"

⅜" x 2" Carriage Bolt

1⅝" Galvanized Drywall Screws

Optional: ⅜" Dowel Pegs for Tools

¼" x 1¼" Carriage Bolt, Nut, Washers

Conduit Snap-on Clip Bent to Fit Grill Rim

14⅜"

Cut 15° Angle

# Buying Lumber

Is going to the lumberyard the least favorite part of your building project? Do you find yourself saying, "With all these stacks of lumber, where do I begin?" "Am I going to end up taking home a pile of stuff I don't want?"

If you understand a few simple basics about buying lumber, it will demystify the language of a jargon-filled industry.

## What's a 1x6? A 2x12?

When you go to a home center or lumberyard, you'll find two main categories of lumber: boards (which are generally "thin") and dimension lumber (which is generally "thick"). Boards are lumber that is five-quarter ($\frac{5}{4}$) and thinner. This translates as any piece of lumber that is $1\frac{1}{8}$ inches thick or less. Dimension lumber is any wood $1\frac{1}{2}$ inches thick or more.

The illustrated chart on page 184 will help you understand basic dimensions on your next trip to the lumberyard. Five-quarter lumber is not listed; it is a somewhat specialized size, often irregular in width.

Don't expect the dimensions to be exact. Thickness and width can vary as much as $\frac{1}{2}$ inch from the standard sizes because of differences in moisture content and variations in sawing at the lumber mills.

As a general rule, most board lumber is kept under roof to protect it from the weather. The better grades of dimension lumber, especially redwood and cedar, are often stored inside as well because they're expensive. Lesser grades of dimension lumber, however, are often stacked outside.

# Lumber rundown

The woods listed here are softwoods, sometimes referred to as evergreen varieties. However, you may also apply some of these general buying guidelines to hardwood varieties such as oak, birch, maple, walnut, and cherry. Your lumberyard, depending on the region where you live, may have a wider selection, but the general rules for choosing lumber are the same.

*Pine* lumber is white to amber in color and comes from a variety of trees: sugar pine, Ponderosa pine, white pine, southern yellow pine, and many more. Other softwoods, such as spruce and hemlock, closely resemble pine, and most lumberyards lump all these together and simply call them pine.

*Douglas fir* is strong and rigid and is used mostly for heavy structural loads. Many find its amber to pink color and attractive grain pattern appealing, so it's also used for doors, interior trim, and other items that will receive a natural finish.

*Western cedar* is light brown to white in color and an ideal lumber for exterior use because of its high resistance to decay. There are cedar log homes more than 200 years old still in use. However, cedar lacks the structural strength of pine and Douglas fir.

*Redwood* is also very resistant to decay, and the clear grades are attractive. Lumber that's cut from the center of the tree, called "heartwood," is brownish red and much more resistant to decay. Sapwood, which is that lumber milled from the outer part of the log, is less decay-resistant and can be identified by its lighter color. Redwood is best used for surface treatments, and its limited supply makes it more costly than the other softwoods.

*Treated lumber* characteristics are discussed on page 186.

## Which Lumber to Use and Why

| TYPE OF SOFTWOOD | BOARD LUMBER USES | DIMENSION LUMBER USES | PROS | CONS |
|---|---|---|---|---|
| PINE | Shelves<br>Furniture<br>Molding and trim<br>Paneling | Joists<br>Studs<br>Rafters<br>Trusses | Easy to nail<br>Easy to cut<br>Paints well | Rots easily<br>Hard to stain |
| DOUGLAS FIR | Porch flooring<br>Furniture<br>Shelves<br>Molding and trim | Framing<br>Joists<br>Studs<br>Rafters<br>Trusses | Rot resistant<br>High strength<br>Attractive grain<br>Paints well<br>Stains well | Hard to nail |
| WESTERN CEDAR | Exterior trim<br>Siding<br>Fencing<br>Patio furniture<br>Outdoor crafts | Decks<br>Fencing<br>Patio furniture<br>Planters | Rot resistant<br>Paints well<br>Stains well | Splits easily<br>Low strength |
| REDWOOD | Patio furniture<br>Exterior trim<br>Siding<br>Planters | Decks<br>Fencing<br>Patio furniture | Very rot<br>  resistant (heart)<br>Nails easily<br>Attractive grain | Splits easily<br>Low strength<br>High cost |
| TREATED PINE (page 186) | Exterior only<br>Deck railings<br>Fencing<br>Patio furniture<br>Garden edging | Exterior only<br>Joists<br>Decks<br>Planters<br>Fencing | Very rot<br>  resistant<br>Ground contact<br>Nails easily<br>Stains well<br>Paints well | Green or brown<br>  color<br>Tends to warp |

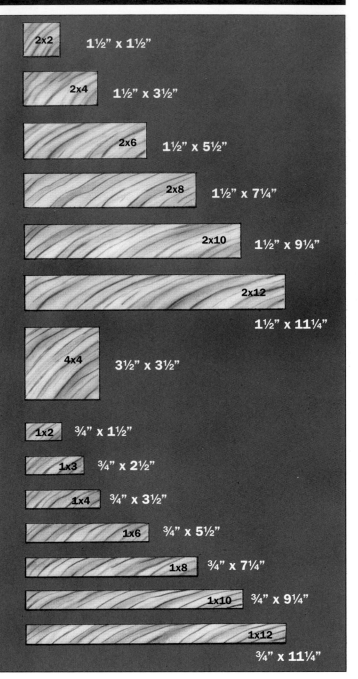

## Lumber Size: Nominal vs. Actual

2x2 — 1½" x 1½"

2x4 — 1½" x 3½"

2x6 — 1½" x 5½"

2x8 — 1½" x 7¼"

2x10 — 1½" x 9¼"

2x12 — 1½" x 11¼"

4x4 — 3½" x 3½"

1x2 — ¾" x 1½"

1x3 — ¾" x 2½"

1x4 — ¾" x 3½"

1x6 — ¾" x 5½"

1x8 — ¾" x 7¼"

1x10 — ¾" x 9¼"

1x12 — ¾" x 11¼"

## Lumber size

Most softwood lumber is sawed rough at the mill, and planed to finished dimensions. Because of planing and normal shrinkage, the actual size of the lumber you buy is smaller than the nominal size by which it is sold. The nominal size, for example, of a common piece of lumber is 2x2, but its actual size when you buy it at the lumber yard is 1½" x 1½". As the chart to the left shows, this same principle applies to all common lumber sizes.

## Lumber grading

Lumber is graded on the basis of its appearance. The samples shown on the facing page illustrate this grading system for pine board lumber. For all softwood board lumber, the higher the number, the poorer the grade of wood. The best grade is referred to as clear, a specific grade division of No. 1, meaning free from defects.

Dimension lumber has its own grading rules and jargon. When selecting framing lumber such as 2x4s, you'll find the grade stamped on each piece such as construction, standard, utility, and stud.

Construction grade lumber is stronger, has fewer defects than standard grade, and has a better appearance. Utility and stud grades usually come in shorter lengths, and some are precut to 8 feet or shorter for wall framing.

Wide dimension lumber such as 2x6s or 2x8s will be described in terms such as select structural, No. 1, No. 2, or No. 3 stamped on each piece. Select structural is the best. No. 1, No. 2, and No. 3 are lesser grades — No. 3 being the poorest. When you're building a project where strength is important, choose the highest grade available.

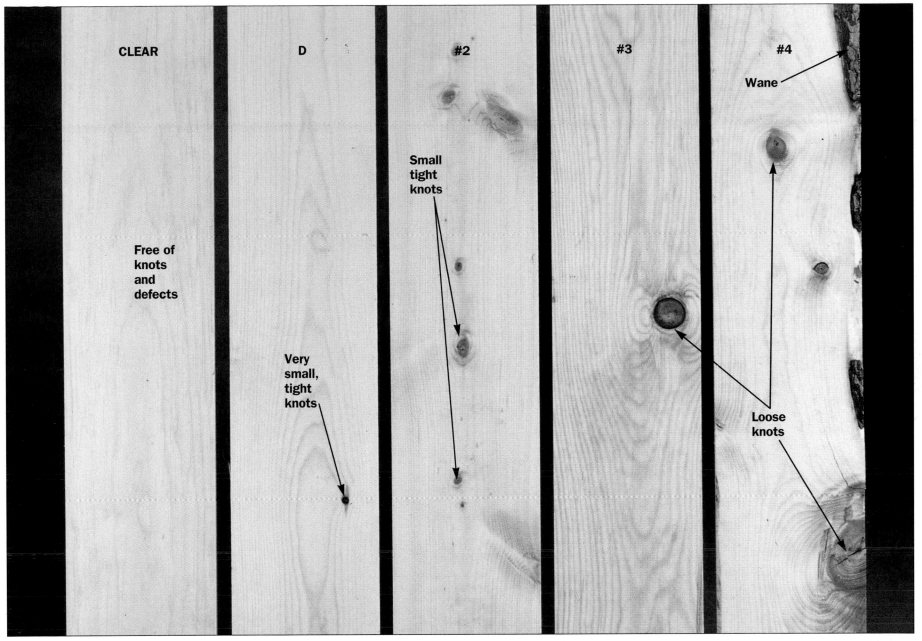

CLEAR

D

#2

#3

#4

Wane

Free of
knots
and
defects

Very
small,
tight
knots

Small
tight
knots

Loose
knots

Grading standards for softwood board lumber are illustrated in these examples. Pine is shown here, but other types of board lumber are graded the same way. A piece of lumber with an excellent appearance will be free from most defects and also structurally stronger than poor-appearance lumber. Some lumberyards may classify "Clear" and "D" as variations of grade No. 1. With practice, woodworkers learn to buy less costly grades and cut good pieces out of them.

## Pressure-treated lumber

Years ago wood was plentiful, and people used whatever grew nearby or whatever the local sawmill had on hand. Today, wood isn't as cheap or plentiful, so we've had to choose or develop lumber best suited for each use. A good example of this is the development of pressure-treated pine, which is included in the chart on page 183. As redwood and cedar became scarce, a substitute was needed for ground-contact wood, so researchers came up with a chemical treatment for pine to reduce fungal growth under moist conditions, making it even more decay- and insect-resistant than cedar. Working with pressure-treated wood, however, can give you itchy eyes and red rashes. The effects don't show up unless you work with it for hours, so be sure to cut pressure-treated lumber in a well-ventilated area (outside is best) and wear a protective mask, eye protection, and gloves.

## Defects: what to look out for

Perfect lumber doesn't exist, and you'll have to make compromises. But even so, when you're selecting, keep a sharp eye out for defects. The illustrated examples on these pages will help you know what to look for. A word about lumber care: Treat your lumber like a new car, especially board lumber. Keep the wood out of direct sunlight; the lumber at the top of the pile will dry out and may develop surface cracks and cup. Keep your lumber straight by storing it in a dry shaded place, off the ground, and either vertically or horizontally, but not leaning or resting at an angle.

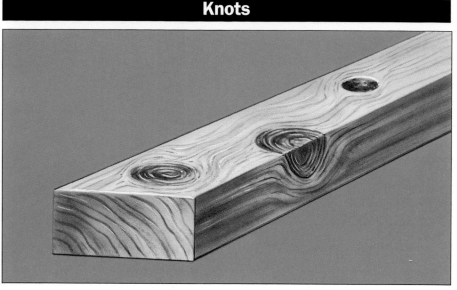

### Knots

Knots are not always undesirable; in some paneling and specialty boards, they're coveted for their character. Avoid loose knots near the edges because they'll weaken the overall strength of the piece. No matter what you do, knots will show through paint.

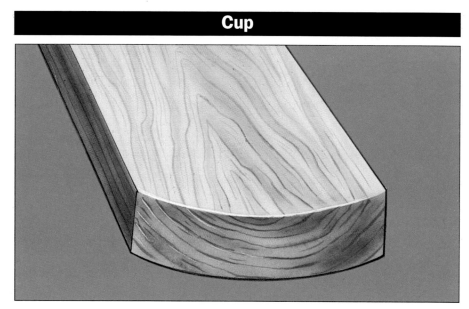

### Cup

Cupped wood is slightly rounded from edge to edge along the face of the piece. This is usually most severe in board lumber. It's caused by the way the board was sawn from the log and the shrinking that occurs during the drying process.

## Splits

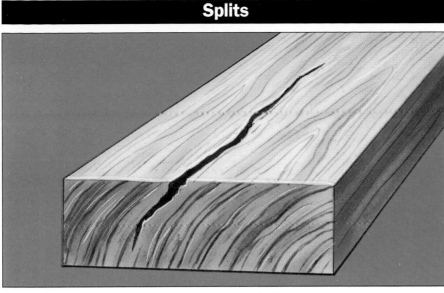

Splits are cracks that weaken structural lumber. Splits are common near the ends of lumber, and minor ones aren't a problem; you may have to buy a longer board than you need, then cut off the split end.

## Wane

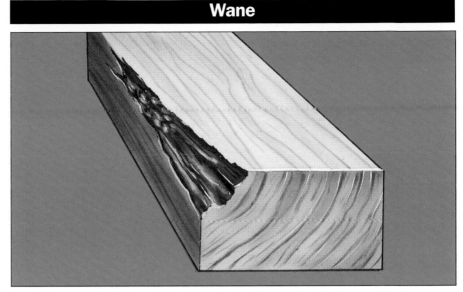

Bark or missing wood on the edge of a piece of lumber is called wane. Missing wood on the edges of lumber may be okay if all the edges aren't critical for your project. In most cases, however, the missing wood will give you trouble.

## Shake

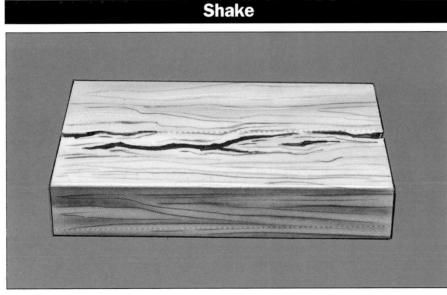

Shakes are cracks that may run the full length and thickness of the piece. Check the entire surface carefully and choose another piece if you find shake; it's a serious structural flaw. A board with shake can be cut into two narrow pieces.

## Crooks and Bows

Crook (above, left) is a deviation from straightness on the edge of lumber, and bow (above, right) is deviation on the wide face of the lumber. Boards for shelving should be free of crooks and bows.

# Index

This book was produced by Redefinition, Inc.,
for The Reader's Digest Association, Inc.,
in cooperation with *The Family Handyman* magazine.


If you have any questions or comments, feel free to write us at:

The Family Handyman
7900 International Drive
Suite 950
Minneapolis, MN 55425

# More Top-Rated How-To Information From Reader's Digest® and The Family Handyman®

### THE FAMILY HANDYMAN WOODWORKING ROOM BY ROOM

Furniture, Cabinetry, Built-Ins and Other Projects for the Home

The easiest, most complete guide of over 20 different projects, ranging from straightforward items beginners can easily master to more sophisticated pieces for experienced woodworkers looking for new challenges; includes such projects as a country pine bench, traditional bookcase and Victorian hall stand.

192 pages
10 $^{11}/_{16}$ x 8 $^{3}/_{8}$
over 500 color photographs
ISBN #0-89577-686-3
$19.95

### THE FAMILY HANDYMAN WEEKEND IMPROVEMENTS

Over 30 Do-It-Yourself Projects for the Home

Now all the how-to information homeowners need to complete short-term projects can be found in this one clear and comprehensive volume. From basic fix-ups to full-fledged facelifts, this book covers every room in the house and features great techniques for keeping the yard and the exterior of the house looking fit as well.

192 pages
10 $^{11}/_{16}$ x 8 $^{3}/_{8}$
over 500 color photographs
ISBN #0-89577-685-5
$19.95

### THE FAMILY HANDYMAN EASY REPAIR

Over 100 Simple Solutions to the Most Common Household Problems

Designed to help save hundreds, even thousands, of dollars in costly repairs, here is that one book that should be in every household library. It offers simple, step by step, quick and easy solutions to the most common and costly household problems faced at home, from unclogging a sink to repairing broken shingles to fixing damaged electrical plugs.

192 pages
10 $^{11}/_{16}$ x 8 $^{3}/_{8}$
725 color photographs
ISBN #0-89577-624-3
$19.95

# Measuring the Metric Way

Use these guides and tables to convert between English and metric measuring systems.

## Fasteners

**Nails** are sold by penny size or penny weight (expressed by the letter d). Length is designated by the penny size. Some common lengths are:

| | |
|---|---|
| 2d | (25 mm/1 in.) |
| 6d | (51 mm/2 in.) |
| 10d | (76 mm/3 in.) |
| 20d | (102 mm/4 in.) |
| 40d | (127 mm/5 in.) |
| 60d | (152 mm/6 in.) |

Below are metric and imperial equivalents of some common **bolts**:

| | |
|---|---|
| 10 mm | ³/₈ in. |
| 12 mm | ¹/₂ in. |
| 16 mm | ⁵/₈ in. |
| 20 mm | ³/₄ in. |
| 25 mm | 1 in. |
| 50 mm | 2 in. |
| 65 mm | 2¹/₂ in. |
| 70 mm | 2³/₄ in. |

## Calculating Concrete Requirements

Multiply length by width to get the slab area in square meters. Then read across, under whichever of three thicknesses you prefer, to see how many cubic meters of concrete you will need.

| Area in square meters (m²) | Thickness in millimeters | | |
|---|---|---|---|
| (length x width) | 100 | 130 | 150 |
| | volume in cubic meters (m³) | | |
| 5 | 0.50 | 0.65 | 0.75 |
| 10 | 1.00 | 1.30 | 1.50 |
| 20 | 2.00 | 2.60 | 3.00 |
| 30 | 3.00 | 3.90 | 4.50 |
| 40 | 4.00 | 5.20 | 6.00 |
| 50 | 5.00 | 6.50 | 7.50 |

If a greater volume of concrete is required, multiply by the appropriate number. To lay a 100-millimeter-thick patio in an area 6 meters wide and 10 meters long, for example, estimate as follows: 6 meters x 10 meters = 60 meters square = area. Using the chart above, simply double the concrete quantity for a 30-meter-square, 100-millimeter-thick slab (2 x 3 m³ = 6 m³) or add the quantities for 10 m² and 50 m² (1 m³ + 5 m³ = 6 m³).